Journeys through
American
Literature

Journeys through American Literature

by

Myra Shulman

Ann Arbor

THE UNIVERSITY OF MICHIGAN PRESS

To Serena, Gabriel, and Juliette

Acknowledgments

This revised edition is the result of the suggestions of many teachers and students who were especially eager to read modern American literature, so I am grateful for their comments. Also, I want to thank my editors Kelly Sippell and Christina Milton for their support and understanding. Others who contributed to this text include Vera and Marc Ovadia, Elsa and David Smithgall, Margot and Ken Sarch, Eve Mezvinsky, David Shulman, Deana Shulman, and K.W. Gooch, all of whom offered ideas, help, and love.

Grateful acknowledgment is given to the following for use of copyrighted material:

Angelou, Maya. "Is Love." From *I Shall Not Be Moved* by Maya Angelou. Copyright © 1990 by Maya Angelou. Reprinted by permission of Random House Inc., and Virago Press.

Bontemps, Arna. "The Day-Breakers" and "Nocturne of the Wharves" by Arna Bontemps. Copyright © 1963 by Arna Bontemps. Reprinted by permission of Harold Ober Associates Incorporated.

Chopin, Kate. "Madame Célestin's Divorce." Reprinted by permission of Louisiana State University Press from *Complete Works of Kate Chopin,* edited by Per Seyersted. Copyright © 1969 by Louisiana State University Press.

Cisneros, Sandra. From *The House on Mango Street.* Copyright © 1984 by Sandra Cisneros. Published by Vintage Books, a division of Random House, Inc., and in hardcover by Alfred A. Knopf in 1994. Reprinted by permission of Susan Bergholz Literary Services, New York, and Bloomsbury Publishing, Plc. All rights reserved.

Cullen, Countee. "Heritage" (first three stanzas) by Countee Cullen. Copyrights held by the Amistad Research Center, administered by Thompson and Thompson, New York, New York.

Dickinson, Emily. "Because I Could Not Stop for Death," "Could I but Ride Indefinite," "I Heard a Fly Buzz When I Died," "There Is No Frigate Like a Book," and "Wild Nights! Wild Nights!" Reprinted by permission of the publishers and the Trustees of Amherst College from *The Poems of Emily Dickinson,* Thomas H. Johnson, ed., Cambridge, Mass.: The Belknap Press of Harvard University Press, Copyright © 1951, 1955, 1979, 1983 by the President and Fellows of Harvard College.

Frost, Robert. "Acquainted with the Night" from *The Poetry of Robert Frost* edited by Edward Connery Lathem, ©1956 by Robert Frost. Copyright 1928, © 1969 by Henry Holt and Company, Inc. Reprinted by permission of Henry Holt and Company, Inc., and Jonathan Cape, Ltd.

Gilb, Dagoberto. "Love in L.A." From *The Magic of Blood* by Dagoberto Gilb. Copyright ©1993 by the University of New Mexico Press. Reprinted by permission of the University of New Mexico Press.

Ginsberg, Allen. 29 lines from "A Supermarket in California" from *Collected Poems 1947–1980* by Allen Ginsberg. Copyright © 1955 by Allen Ginsberg. Copyright Renewed. Reprinted by permission of HarperCollins Publishers, Inc., and Penguin Books Ltd.

Giovanni, Nikki. "A Poem of Friendship" from *Cotton Candy on a Rainy Day* by Nikki Giovanni. Copyright © 1978 by Nikki Giovanni. Reprinted by permission of William Morrow & Company, Inc.

Hughes, Langston. "Afro-American Fragment," "Warning," and "The Negro Speaks of Rivers" from *Collected Poems* by Langston Hughes. Copyright © 1994 by the Estate of Langston Hughes. Reprinted by permission of Alfred A. Knopf, Inc., and Harold Ober Associates Incorporated.

Kingston, Maxine Hong. Excerpt from *The Woman Warrior* by Maxine Hong Kingston. Copyright © 1976, by Maxine Hong Kingston. Reprinted by permission of Alfred A. Knopf Inc., by the author, and by Macmillan Publishers Ltd.

Levertov, Denise. "Arrived" and "On the Eve." From *Evening Train.* Copyright ©1992 by Denise Levertov. Reprinted by permission of New Directions Publishing Corp. and Laurence Pollinger LTD.

McKay, Claude. "If We Must Die" and "Outcast." From *Selected Poems of Claude McKay.* Harcourt Brace & Company 1979.

Momaday, N. Scott. Excerpt from *The Way to Rainy Mountain* by N. Scott Momaday. Copyright © 1969 by the University of New Mexico Press. Reprinted by permission of the University of New Mexico Press. "Wreckage," from *In the Presence of the Sun* by N. Scott Momaday. Copyright © 1992 by N. Scott Momaday. Reprinted by permission of the author.

Pound, Ezra. "A Pact." Ezra Pound: *Personae.* Copyright © 1926 by Ezra Pound. Reprinted by permission of New Directions Publishing Corp. and Faber and Faber Limited.

Silko, Leslie Marmon. Excerpt from *Ceremony* by Leslie Marmon Silko. Copyright © 1977 by Leslie Silko. Used by permission of Viking Penguin, a division of Penguin Putnam, Inc.

Walker, Alice. "Beyond What" from *Revolutionary Petunias and Other Poems,* copyright © 1973 by Alice Walker, reprinted by permission of Harcourt Brace & Company and David Higham Associates.

Note on Illustrations

The photograph of Robert Frost is reprinted with permission of Bettmann/CORBIS Images © Bettmann/CORBIS. All the other illustrations are from the private collection of David Francis. Photographs were taken by Patrick Loughney. Reprinted with permission of David Francis.

Cover: River scene: handpainted lantern slide, c. 1860; "Departure of Peruvian captain from Saryacu"; Newton and Company, Fleet Street, London

Page
xxii.   Robert Frost: photograph, c. 1915

33.   Edgar Allan Poe: from a daguerreotype taken in 1849

33.   Virginia Poe (Mrs. Edgar Allan Poe): photograph of a painting, c. 1850

103.   African American family: from one-half of stereo view, c. 1895

118.   Walt Whitman: engraving

126.   Henry Wadsworth Longfellow: carte de visite, Woodburytype, c. 1880

133.   Percy Bysshe Shelley: engraving

179.   American Indian male: from one-half of stereo view, February 2, 1872; Sioux Brave, "He Looks Well Standing," from Whitney's Gallery, 174 Third Street, St. Paul, Minnesota

180.   American Indian female: from one-half of stereo view, c. 1872; Charles A. Zimmerman, Photographer, Third Street, St. Paul, Minnesota

187.   Canton, China: handpainted lantern slide, c. 1850; from a series on the ports of call of a Royal Mail steamer, Newton and Company, Fleet Street, London

Preface

Journeys through American Literature is an advanced-level, content-based textbook that contains selections from the masterpieces of American literature. It is intended for students of English as a second or foreign language who want to read literary works written in the English language, but it can also be used by American students who need a general introduction to American literature.

In this text, selections were limited to works written originally in English whose theme is a journey, either metaphorical or literal. Of course, the journey or quest is one of the most common metaphors in literature and has served as the framework for innumerable works, both ancient (*Gilgamesh* and the *Odyssey*) and modern (James Joyce's *Ulysses* and Charles Frazier's *Cold Mountain*). The readings were chosen on the basis of literary merit, reasonable length, and interesting, yet accessible, content. I have organized the book's chapters chronologically to give readers the experience of moving through the historical periods of American literature, from the early nineteenth century to the end of the twentieth century.

The selections are a balanced combination of fiction and nonfiction, poetry and prose. Altogether, they offer a wide variety of authors, content, styles, forms, and traditions. My choices include brief whole works (poems and short stories) as well as excerpts from longer works (novels, autobiographies, and long poems). In choosing to include excerpts, I am giving readers a glimpse of an author's style and content, with the hope that they will become enthusiastic enough to read the work in its entirety. Similarly, I hope students will be motivated to read other poems, short stories, and essays by those authors whose writing they especially enjoy and can identify with. Indeed, the intent of this text is to encourage readers to delve further into the great works of American literature.

An overview of each literary period and genre and biographical sketches of the authors introduce the readings and describe the literary period or tradition to which the author belongs. I have also outlined the major themes and general characteristics of an author's style to facilitate comprehension of the selection. Preceding the biographical sketches are quotations from that author and well-known writers or other figures. These quotations serve to broaden the context of the readings and stimulate discussion.

Prereading tasks (skimming, scanning, questioning) prepare students for the literary world they are about to enter and allow them to call on their existing knowledge of the theme and subject, thus enhancing comprehension. The postreading exercises were influenced by Louise Rosenblatt's reader-response theory, in which reading is seen as the interaction among reader, writer, and text, and the personal response is considered the central element in reading literature. Rosenblatt says: "The reading of any work of literature is, of necessity, an individual and unique occurrence involving the mind and emotions of some particular reader."[1] Accordingly, the reader's response comes first, before analyzing the text or the author's intent. Therefore, these exercises begin with discussion questions, followed by analysis of style and language, writing assignments, group work, and a chapter synthesis.

This book implements the theory that reading and writing are interrelated skills that should not be separated, so students are given opportunities to write before and after completing the readings. (Various writing strategies are presented in the appendixes.) Many of the writing assignments and group work activities ask readers to compare their responses to various selections, as this offers opportunities to develop not only critical analysis and judgment but also literary appreciation. My purpose is to help readers formulate and express their own preferences and opinions. Because the power of beautifully written poetry, short stories, and novels can evoke strong emotional responses in readers, students are generally eager to discuss or write about works of literature. These essays and classroom discussions allow students to sharpen their critical-thinking skills while they are improving their communicative competence. But more importantly, they lead to the discovery that there is not one correct interpretation; there are many interpretations.

Journeys through American Literature is unique because it combines the reading of literature, the analysis of literary styles and techniques, and the acquisition of language skills. It is a learner-centered text with an integrated-skills approach to teaching English as a second language (ESL). Students use their reading, writing, listening, and speaking skills as they undertake the tasks in each chapter, and the teacher should function more as a facilitator and equal participant than as a traditional teacher lecturing to the class. The text, while encouraging independence and self-reliance, also emphasizes group work. Most activities can be done with students working in teams or with partners in an atmosphere of collaborative learning. As the students work in groups and share their responses, a community among readers is developed, which is a positive factor in a cross-cultural ESL classroom.

The goals of *Journeys through American Literature* are the following:

1. to increase students' understanding and enjoyment of literature;
2. to provide examples of great works of American literature;
3. to encourage critical analysis of ideas, structure, and style in literary texts;
4. to strengthen logical thinking in written and oral expression;
5. to improve reading comprehension and vocabulary; and
6. to broaden cross-cultural perspectives.

One of the challenging tasks in reading these works is understanding the vocabulary. Literary works tend to contain a large number of unfamiliar words and creative structures, and readers may be slowed down by their inability to guess the meaning of a word or phrase from the context. Therefore, each selection is followed by an extensive glossary with definitions of difficult or unusual words, including archaic forms ("hath"), regionalisms, and slang. The definitions that are given are specific to the context. The glossaries are based on definitions from *Webster's New World Dictionary*, Second College Edition, copyright © 1986.

---

1. Louise Rosenblatt, *Literature as Exploration* (New York: Appleton-Century, 1938).

On Books and Reading

"If thou wouldst profit by thy reading, read humbly, simply, honestly, and not desiring to win a character for learning."
Thomas à Kempis, *Imitation of Christ*, c. 1420

"He hath never fed of the dainties that are bred of a book; he hath not eat paper, as it were; he hath not drunk ink: his intellect is not replenished; he is only an animal, only sensible in the duller parts."
Shakespeare, *Love's Labor's Lost*, c. 1595

"There's no book so bad that something good may not be found in it."
Cervantes, *Don Quixote*, 1615

"When I am reading a book, whether wise or silly, it seems to me to be alive and talking to me."
Jonathan Swift, *Thoughts on Various Subjects*, 1706

"No entertainment is so cheap as reading, nor any pleasure so lasting."
Lady Mary Wortley Montagu, letter, 1753

"I hate books, for they only teach people to talk about what they do not understand."
J. J. Rousseau, *Émile*, 1762

"I cannot live without books."
Thomas Jefferson, letter to John Adams, June 10, 1815

"Read the best books first, or you may not have a chance to read them at all."
H. D. Thoreau, *A Week on the Concord and Merrimack Rivers*, 1849

"There are books which take rank in your life with parents and lovers and passionate experiences."
Ralph Waldo Emerson, "Books," *Society and Solitude*, 1870

"If you cannot enjoy reading a book over and over again, there is no use reading it at all."
Oscar Wilde, *The Decay of Lying*, 1889

"All books are either dreams or swords, You can cut, or you can drug, with words."
Amy Lowell, *Sword Blades and Poppy Seed*, 1914

"The greatest gift is a passion for reading."
Elizabeth Hardwick, *The Writer's Chapbook*, 1989

"When I was about eight, I decided that the most wonderful thing, next to a human being, was a book."
Margaret Walker, *I Dream a World*, 1989

"A book is like a garden carried in the pocket."
Arab proverb

"Books and friends, few and good."
Spanish proverb

Contents

Works are arranged chronologically, and chapters may have contrastive pieces from different periods. Bold print indicates the main readings in the chapter; regular print indicates contrastive readings.

For the Student

Reading literature is a joyful and enriching experience, full of excitement and pleasure. Sharing this experience is the dominant goal of this textbook. For most readers, literature offers a chance to enter a new world—a world of elegant or unusual language, beautiful imagery, and meaningful thought. Whether expressed with brief intensity as a poem or in longer form as a novel, short story, or essay, literary works capture reality in an original way and enable readers to see the world from a new perspective. Thus, literature may be a form of education as well as entertainment and amusement, and reading is a journey of discovery, an exploration of the unknown.

The English word *literature* derives from the Latin word *littera*, meaning letter. This derivation reflects the fact that in Western cultures, unlike many of the world's traditions, literature was primarily written and recorded in unchanging forms. *Webster's New World Dictionary* defines *literature* as "all writings in prose or verse, especially those of an imaginative or critical character" and also "all of such writings considered as having permanent value, excellence of form, great emotional effect." Literature is a means of social expression, a mirror of life, and an interpretation of the human experience that helps us understand how to live. All cultures have literature, and the impulse to form words into expressive creations is universal.

Although literature has endless forms and subjects, it can be divided into two major categories: fiction and nonfiction. Fiction means literary works based on the imagination; fiction includes novels, short stories, poetry, and drama (plays). Nonfiction conventionally means literary works based on facts that can be verified; nonfiction includes personal essays, travel writing, history, biography, and autobiography. Newspaper articles and academic textbooks are also types of nonfiction but would not be considered literature.

Fiction can be further subdivided into poetry and prose. Prose is writing without rhyme or meter. It includes narrative writing of any kind, such as novels, short stories, plays, and satires. Poetry may be defined as an attempt to capture emotions and ideas in a concentrated written form that is often characterized by rhyme and meter (rhythm).

Writers and philosophers throughout history have attempted to explain how and why human beings create works of literature. Plato, in about 390 B.C., wrote that "all good poets, epic as well as lyric, compose their beautiful poems not by art, but because they are inspired and possessed . . . for not by art does the poet sing, but by power divine" (the *Ion*). Writing during the Romantic age, William Wordsworth, in his preface to the second edition of *Lyrical Ballads* (1800), said that "all good poetry is the spontaneous overflow of powerful feelings." In modern literature, the idea of divine inspiration is no longer taken for granted, but the true source of literary creation remains a mystery. In "The Making of a Poem" (1946), Stephen Spender writes: "Paul Valéry speaks of the 'une ligne donnée' of a poem. One line is given to the poet by God or nature, the rest he has to discover for himself."

In the first century B.C., Horace said in the *Ars Poetica* that art and literature should instruct and delight. In 1388 Chaucer's opinion was that the best story "gives the fullest measure of good morality and general pleasure." Henry James echoed his idea in 1884 when he stated that "literature should be either instructive or amusing" (*The Art of Fiction*). However, what is instructive, amusing, delightful, or beautiful to one person may not be to another. Reading is generally a solitary activity, and each individual's reaction to a work of literature is personal and unique. According to David Hume in "Of the Standard of Taste" (1757): "Beauty is no quality in things themselves: It exists merely in the mind which contemplates them; and each mind perceives a different beauty." While you read the various selections in this text, you will have the chance to discover what to you is beautiful, moving, and particularly meaningful. I hope that you will enjoy your journey of discovery and adventure.

How to Read Literature

Reading literature is different from reading other forms of writing such as articles in journals or newspapers. First of all, it involves reading for pure pleasure as well as reading for knowledge. Second, works of literature are open to interpretation; there is more than one way to understand a poem, essay, or short story. Finally, reading literature demands a special sensitivity to language since it is the beauty of an author's language that gives his or her ideas emotional force and lasting meaning. To read the selections in this book with maximum comprehension, I would suggest that you adopt the following sequence:

> Preview reading
> Casual reading
> Close reading

A. Preview reading
   1. Read the title, first line, or first sentence of the reading.
   2. Skim the reading to get an idea of its form and length.
   3. Answer the preview question, which relates to a central idea in the reading.
   4. Answer the scanning questions to get a brief idea of the content and style.

B. Casual reading
   1. Read the selection without worrying about difficult vocabulary or content.
   2. Underline words and sentences that seem meaningful or beautiful to you.
   3. Think about the author's theme or message.
   4. Write a few questions that you have about the reading.

C. Close reading
   1. Read the selection slowly and carefully.
   2. Look up unfamiliar words in the glossary following the reading.
   3. Underline main ideas, major points, and important words.
   4. Write brief notes in the margin on your responses to the author's ideas.

On Literature

"Thieves cannot destroy it, and it is improved by time; it is the only monument that is proof against death."
Martial, *Epigrams*, c. 95

"Literature is a kind of intellectual light which, like the light of the sun, may sometimes enable us to see what we do not like."
Samuel Johnson, *A Project for the Employment of Authors*, 1756

"Our high respect for a well-read man is praise enough of literature."
Ralph Waldo Emerson, *Letters and Social Aims*, 1875

"It takes a great deal of history to produce a little literature."
Henry James, *Hawthorne*, 1879

"The difference between literature and journalism is that journalism is unreadable, and literature is not read."
Oscar Wilde, *The Critic as Artist*, 1891

"Literature is my Utopia."
Helen Keller, *The Story of My Life*, 1902

"The final measure of the greatness of all peoples is the amount and standard of literature and art they have produced."
James Weldon Johnson, preface to *The Book of American Negro Poetry*, 1921

"The test of literature is, I suppose, whether we ourselves live more intensely for the reading of it."
Elizabeth Drew, *The Modern Novel*, 1926

"Literature is news that stays news."
Ezra Pound, *The ABC of Reading,* 1934

"Exciting literature after dinner is not the best digestive."
Charlotte Perkins Gilman, *The Living of Charlotte Perkins Gilman*, 1935

"Of course the illusion of art is to make one believe that great literature is very close to life, but exactly the opposite is true. Life is amorphous, literature is formal."
Françoise Sagan, *Writers at Work*, 1958

"Don't ask me to live in tranquil times. Literature doesn't grow there."
Rita Mae Brown, *Starting from Scratch*, 1988

"Only after the writer lets literature shape her can she perhaps shape literature."
Annie Dillard, *The Writing Life*, 1989

Robert Frost, c. 1915

Chapter 1

Prelude to the Journey: Understanding Literature

Chapter 1 is an explanatory chapter intended to encourage the enjoyment of reading literature as well as interest in reading critically. Therefore, I have presented two reading selections in this chapter, a poem and short story, with examples of exercises that appear in the following chapters, answers to the exercises, and an analysis of the major characteristics of each selection. These models should provide help in completing the exercises and activities in this book.

Before reading the poem and short story in this chapter, discuss the quotations and read the biographical sketches of the authors. Then do the preview activities in order to get an overview of the form, content, and style of each selection.

Robert Frost **"Acquainted with the Night"**

"Is not the night mournful, sad, and melancholy?"
Rabelais, *Gargantua*, I, 1535

"Come, gentle night, come, loving, black-brow'd night."
Shakespeare, *Romeo and Juliet*, III, c. 1596

"Of all exercises walking is the best."
Thomas Jefferson, letter to T. M. Randolph, Jr., 1786

"Walking is also an ambulation of mind."
Gretel Erlich, *Montana Spaces,* 1988

"Walking makes for a long life."
Hindu proverb

Robert Frost (1874–1963) is one of the great American poets of the twentieth century. He is considered a poet of New England, where he lived for most of his life. Frost's poetry is written in a simple, conversational style that often uses traditional rhyme and meter but re-creates the natural rhythms of spoken English.

Frost won the Pulitzer Prize for his poetry four times. During the 1960s in the John F. Kennedy administration, he served as an unofficial poet laureate and as a cultural ambassador to Russia. Frost has written many beautiful poems about the world of nature, country life, and moral values, including "The Road Not Taken," "Stopping by Woods on a Snowy Evening," "Mending Wall," "The Gift Outright," "Design," "Birches," and "Fire and Ice."

Preview

Skimming: Skimming involves looking over the reading to gain a general impression.
1. Read the title and first line of the poem.
2. Skim the poem to get an idea of its form and length.

Questioning: Questioning encourages you to think about a central idea in the reading and to draw on your personal experience. Answer the following question and discuss your answers.
Do you enjoy going for long walks at night?

Scanning: Scanning involves quickly looking over the reading to find specific information. Scan to answer the following question to get an idea of the poem's content and style.
What did the poet see against the sky?

Acquainted with the Night   1928
Robert Frost

I have been one acquainted with the night.
I have walked out in rain—and back in rain.
I have outwalked the furthest city light.

I have looked down the saddest city lane.
I have passed by the watchman on his beat
And dropped my eyes, unwilling to explain.

I have stood still and stopped the sound of feet
When far away an interrupted cry
Came over houses from another street,

But not to call me back or say good-bye;
And further still at an unearthly height,
One luminary clock against the sky

Proclaimed the time was neither wrong nor right.
I have been one acquainted with the night.

Glossary	"Acquainted with the Night"
acquainted	having personal knowledge
beat	regular route
luminary	shining with light
proclaimed	declared publicly, officially
unearthly	not earthly, supernatural
watchman	guard

Discussion

1. What feelings does the poet experience as he is walking in the night?
2. How does the setting reflect the poet's mood?
3. What implied conflict is found in the poem?
4. What is the theme of the poem?
5. Do you feel that you are "acquainted with the night"? Please explain.
6. Have you ever written poetry? Could you write a poem like this one?
7. Do you enjoy reading poetry? Who are your favorite poets?
8. How do you like "Acquainted with the Night"? Write a few sentences explaining your response to this poem, and share your reaction with the class.

Comprehension

1. What is the poet describing?
2. What has the poet seen during his walks?
3. Why does the poet drop his eyes when he sees the watchman?
4. What does the poet hear during his walks?
5. What does the clock tell him about the time when he is walking?
6. Why does the poet feel he has become "acquainted with the night"?

Style and Language

Understanding the style and tone of an author is essential to understanding what the author has written. Therefore, this activity helps you analyze the style, tone, and language of this poem. Circle the letter next to the correct answer(s). More than one answer may be correct. Be prepared to justify your choices by giving specific examples from the reading selection.

1. Style refers to the author's manner of writing. The style of "Acquainted with the Night" can be characterized as
   a. personal.
   b. impersonal.
   c. formal.
   d. informal.

2. Tone reveals the author's attitude toward his or her subject and audience and helps create the mood of the poem or story. The tone of "Acquainted with the Night" can be described as
   a. melancholy.
   b. angry.
   c. calm.
   d. humorous.
   What specific words and phrases create this tone?

3. Analysis of an author's language centers on sentence structure, word choice, and figures of speech. Frost's language contains
   a. short, conversational expressions.
   b. lengthy, formal statements.
   c. metaphors[1] and similes.[2]
   d. personifications.[3]
   Give examples from the poem of this language.

4. Choose the best paraphrase of the following lines: "One luminary clock against the sky / Proclaimed the time was neither wrong nor right."
   a. The poet was taking a long walk at an unusual hour.
   b. The clock showed the time without judging whether it was early or late.
   c. The clock showed that it was very late to be walking.
   d. The clock was making the poet feel confused.

5. The rhyme scheme is the pattern of similar sounds that are usually at the ends of lines in a poem. The rhyme scheme of "Acquainted with the Night" is
   a. aba bcb cdc ded aa.
   b. abb bcc cdd dee bb.

Writing Assignments

1. Write a two-sentence summary of Frost's poem "Acquainted with the Night."

2. Write a poem about taking a long walk at night. (For suggestions on how to write poetry, see Appendix F, "Writing a Poem.")

3. Read "On the Eve" by Denise Levertov (1923–), a contemporary poet who was born in England and emigrated to the United States in 1948. Then write an essay comparing and contrasting "On the Eve" with "Acquainted with the Night" by Robert Frost. In your essay, discuss the form (structure), content (subject), and style of these poems. Use the following thesis: Although "On the Eve" and "Acquainted with the Night" are both informal and conversational in style, they differ in their form and content.

---

1. figures of speech comparing unlike ideas or objects
2. figures of speech comparing unlike ideas or objects, using *like* or *as*
3. figures of speech describing nonhuman things as humans

On the Eve   1964
Denise Levertov

The moon was white
in the stillness. Daylight
changed without moving,
a hint of sundown
stained the sky. We walked
the short grass,
the dry ground of the hill,
beholding
the tinted west. We talked
of change in our lives. The moon
tuned its whiteness a tone higher.

Group Work

Working with a partner or in a small group, read the following poem by Denise Levertov. Then
compare the form (structure), content (subject), and style (manner of writing) of Levertov's "Arrived" with Frost's "Acquainted with the Night." What are their similarities? What are their differences? Write a brief summary of your discussion, and include a one-sentence statement of the main
idea of each poem.

Arrived   1964
Denise Levertov

Away from home,
the reality of home
evades me. Chairs,
sofa, table, a cup—
I can enumerate objects
one by one, but they're inventory,
not Gestalt.[1] This house
I've stayed in often before,
the open suitcase,
my friends who live here,
that's what's real.
And that face
so vivid to me these past three months
evades me too: the shape

---

1. integrated patterns

of his head, or
color of his eyes appear
at moments, but I can't
assemble feature with feature.
I seem to have landed
upon this *now*
as if on a mid-ocean island,
past and future two continents, both
lost in immense distance,
the mist and seasons
of months at sea—the voyage
from yesterday to today.

Analysis

"Acquainted with the Night," by Robert Frost, is a powerful poem describing the poet's contrasting emotions of both loneliness and contentment that he experiences during his walks late at night. It is personal and informal in style and subjective and balanced in tone.

In "Acquainted with the Night," Frost uses the traditional fourteen-line sonnet form but also writes in terza rima, the form the Italian poet Dante uses in *The Divine Comedy*. The rhyme scheme is aba, bcb, cdc, ded, aa, which links each tercet (three-line stanza) together and lends a musical quality to the verses. The rhythmic pattern is iambic pentameter, with five stressed syllables in every line.

The poet begins by explaining that he is familiar with the night because he often takes long walks, even if the weather is rainy. He hints that these walks may be the result of a conflict or problem with another person at home ("an interrupted cry . . . but not to call me back or say good-bye"). However, he does not clarify the reason for his walking: "And dropped my eyes, unwilling to explain." He expresses neither enjoyment nor dislike of these evening walks, merely discussing them in a matter-of-fact tone.

Frost focuses on physical sensations throughout the poem: the motion of walking in the first and last stanza, the sense of sight in the second stanza, the sense of hearing in the third stanza, and both sight and sound in the fourth stanza. Overall, the poem conveys a feeling of restless movement that embodies the long walks the poet is describing.

The poem contains several striking visual images that have the effect of creating a rather melancholy atmosphere. Frost establishes this atmosphere in the first stanza by referring to the night rain. He then mentions the "furthest city light," the "saddest city lane," the "watchman on his beat," and "one luminary clock." In addition, Frost uses figurative language to increase the emotional effect of his poem. Through personification, he humanizes "the saddest city lane" and "one luminary clock" that "proclaimed the time was neither wrong nor right."

"Acquainted with the Night" shows Frost's gift of evoking inner emotional states or experiences by focusing on external objects, sights, and sounds. The poem incorporates an occurrence of everyday life into beautiful and meaningful verse that has a profound effect on the reader.

Answers to Exercises

Discussion (Answers will vary.)

1. The poet feels emotions of sadness, loneliness, and melancholy, but he also seems to feel comfortable and contented in the night.
2. The setting is one of darkness and rain, which matches his feelings of loneliness and sadness. The poet is alone except for seeing the watchman. He hears a cry from someone far away who does not say good-bye or ask him to return home.
3. A conflict between the poet and another person can be inferred by the poet's hearing a cry "but not to call me back or say good-bye." Perhaps the poet walks away from his home at night because of arguments with someone.
4. Walking late at night comforts the poet in times of conflict or distress.

Comprehension

1. The poet is describing his walks in the night.
2. The poet sees the city lights, lanes, a watchman, and a clock.
3. The poet does not want to explain why he is out walking at night.
4. The poet hears a cry from far away.
5. The clock tells him the time is "neither wrong nor right."
6. He often goes on long walks at night, so he knows the night well.

Style and Language

1. a: personal. Frost uses "I" and reveals his inner thoughts and emotions throughout the poem.
   d: informal. Frost speaks in natural language and uses simple expressions.
2. a: melancholy. Frost describes walking late at night in rain and with sadness. Examples: "walked out in rain—and back in rain," "saddest city lane," "dropped my eyes," "not to call me back or say good-bye"
   c: calm. Frost describes his long walks with calmness and acceptance. Examples: "I have been one acquainted with the night," "the time was neither wrong nor right"
3. a: short, conversational expressions. Example: "I have been one acquainted with the night."
   d: personifications. Examples: "saddest city lane" (lane is described as a person), "clock . . . proclaimed the time" (clock is described as a person)
4. b: The clock showed the time without judging if it was early or late.
5. a: aba bcb cdc ded aa

Hamlin Garland   From *Main-Travelled Roads*

"If you have not lived in the country, you do not know what hardship means."
Chinese proverb

"Garland's stories, truthful to the hardships of the Midwest frontier, were of no very smiling aspect
of life, yet they justified themselves as honest portraiture."
Wallace Stegner, introduction to *Selected American Prose: The Realistic Movement,* 1962

Hamlin Garland (1860–1940) was born on a farm in Wisconsin and lived in Iowa and North and
South Dakota during the pioneer days. Tired of the drudgery of farm life, he moved to Boston when
he was 24. There he devoted himself to writing and teaching, becoming a successful novelist and
short story writer in the realistic movement (1841–1900). Garland, who invented the term *veritist,*
meaning realist, to describe his writing style, belonged to the midwestern school of "Chicago realists," which included Booth Tarkington, Theodore Dreiser, Sinclair Lewis, and Carl Sandburg.

Garland is also known as a regionalist, or local-color writer, because his writing centers on the
common people of the Midwest. His characters are examples of the proud, strong-willed, independent American pioneers who, in spite of their brutal struggles to survive, believed in their land and
their country. His books reveal him as a social critic of an economic system that caused hardship
and injustice during the days of the American frontier.

In 1917, Garland wrote in his autobiography: "Every genuinely American writer must deal
with the life he knows best and for which he cares the most."   Garland described himself as "a
farmer by birth and a novelist by occupation."   His famous *Main-Travelled Roads* contains stories
based on his years on a farm in the Midwest. William Dean Howells called these stories "historical
fiction," for they present a vivid picture of farm life and of the strong, determined men and women
who faced the harsh wilderness with courage. His other works include his autobiography, *A Son of
the Middle Border,* and *A Daughter of the Middle Border,* which won a Pulitzer Prize.

Preview

Skimming: Skimming involves quickly looking over the reading to gain a general impression.
1. Read the title and first sentence of the story.
2. Skim the story to get an idea of its form and length.

Questioning: Questioning encourages you to think about a central idea in the reading and to draw
on your personal experience. Answer the following questions and discuss your answers.
1. Have you ever lived on a farm?
2. How common are acts of human kindness?

Scanning: Scanning involves quickly looking over the reading to find specific information.
Scan to answer the following questions to get an idea of the story's content and style.
1. Who are the major characters in the story?
2. Where does Mrs. Markham want to go?

From *Main-Travelled Roads*   **1899**
Hamlin Garland

A Day's Pleasure

When Markham came in from shovelling his last wagon-load of corn into the crib he found that his wife had put the children to bed, and was kneading a batch of dough with the dogged action of a tired and sullen woman.

He slipped his soggy boots off his feet, and having laid a piece of wood on top of the stove, put his heels on it comfortably. His chair squeaked as he leaned back on its hinder legs, but he paid no attention; he was used to it, exactly as he was used to his wife's lameness and ceaseless toil.

"That closes up my corn," he said after a silence. "I guess I'll go to town to-morrow to git my horses shod."

"I guess I'll git ready and go along," said his wife, in a sorry attempt to be firm and confident of tone.

"What do you want to go to town fer?" he grumbled.

"What does anybody want to go to town fer?" she burst out, facing him. "I ain't been out o' this house fer six months, while you go an' go!"

"Oh, it ain't six months. You went down that day I got the mower."

"When was that? The tenth of July, and you know it."

"Well, mebbe 'twas. I didn't think it was so long ago. I ain't no objection to your goin', only I'm goin' to take a load of wheat."

"Well, jest leave off a sack, an' that'll balance me an' the baby," she said spiritedly.

"All right," he replied good-naturedly, seeing she was roused. "Only that wheat ought to be put up to-night if you're goin'. You won't have any time to hold sacks for me in the morning with them young ones to get off to school."

"Well, let's go do it then," she said, sullenly resolute.

"I hate to go out agin; but I s'pose we'd better."

He yawned dismally and began pulling his boots on again, stamping his swollen feet into them with grunts of pain. She put on his coat and one of the boy's caps, and they went out to the granary. The night was cold and clear.

"Don't look so much like snow as it did last night," said Sam. "It may turn warm."

Laying out the sacks in the light of the lantern, they sorted out those which were whole, and Sam climbed into the bin with a tin pail in his hand, and the work began.

He was a sturdy fellow, and he worked desperately fast; the shining tin pail dived deep into the cold wheat and dragged heavily on the woman's tired hands as it came to the mouth of the sack, and she trembled with fatigue, but held on and dragged the sacks away when filled, and brought others, till at last Sam climbed out, puffing and wheezing, to tie them up.

"I guess I'll load 'em in the morning," he said. "You needn't wait for me. I'll tie 'em up alone."

"Oh, I don't mind," she replied, feeling a little touched by his unexpectedly easy acquiescence to her request. When they went back to the house the moon had risen.

It had scarcely set when they were wakened by the crowing roosters. The man rolled stiffly out of bed and began rattling at the stove in the dark, cold kitchen.

His wife arose lamer and stiffer than usual, and began twisting her thin hair into a knot.

Sam did not stop to wash, but went out the barn. The woman, however, hastily soused her face into the hard limestone water at the sink, and put the kettle on. Then she called the children. She knew it was early, and they would need several callings. She pushed breakfast forward, running over in her mind the things she must have: two spools of thread, six yards of cotton flannel, a can of coffee, and mittens for Kitty. These she must have—there were oceans of things she needed.

The children soon came scudding down out of the darkness of the upstairs to dress tumultuously at the kitchen stove. They humped and shivered, holding up their bare feet from the cold floor, like chickens in new fallen snow. They were irritable, and snarled and snapped and struck like cats and dogs. Mrs. Markham stood it for a while with mere commands to "hush up," but at last her patience gave out, and she charged down on the struggling mob and cuffed them right and left.

They ate their breakfast by lamplight, and when Sam went back to his work around the barnyard it was scarcely dawn. The children, left alone with their mother, began to tease her to let them go to town also.

"No, sir—nobody goes but baby. Your father's goin' to take a load of wheat."

She was weak with the worry of it all when she had sent the older children away to school and the kitchen work was finished. She went into the cold bedroom off the little sitting room and put on her best dress. It had never been a good fit, and now she was getting so thin it hung in wrinkled folds everywhere about the shoulders and waist. She lay down on the bed a moment to ease that dull pain in her back. She had a moment's distaste for going out at all. The thought of sleep was more alluring. Then the thought of the long, long day, and the sickening sameness of her life, swept over her again, and she rose and prepared the baby for the journey.

It was but little after sunrise when Sam drove out into the road and started for Belleplain. His wife sat perched upon the wheat-sacks behind him, holding the baby in her lap, a cotton quilt under her, and a cotton horse-blanket over her knees.

Sam was disposed to be very good-natured, and he talked back at her occasionally, though she could only understand him when he turned his face toward her. The baby stared out at the passing fence-posts, and wiggled his hands out of his mittens at every opportunity. He was merry at least.

It grew warmer as they went on, and a strong south wind arose. The dust settled upon the woman's shawl and hat. Her hair loosened and blew unkemptly about her face. The road which led across the high, level prairie was quite smooth and dry, but still it jolted her, and the pain in her back increased. She had nothing to lean against, and the weight of the child grew greater, till she was forced to place him on the sacks beside her, though she could not loose her hold for a moment.

The town drew in sight—a cluster of small frame houses and stores on the dry prairie beside a railway station. There were no trees yet which could be called shade trees. The pitilessly severe light of the sun flooded everything. A few teams were hitched about, and in the lee of the stores a few men could be seen seated comfortably, their broad hat-rims flopping up and down, their faces brown as leather.

Markham put his wife out at one of the grocery-stores, and drove off down toward the elevators to sell his wheat.

The grocer greeted Mrs. Markham in a perfunctorily kind manner, and offered her a chair, which she took gratefully. She sat for a quarter of an hour almost without moving, leaning against the back of the high chair. At last the child began to get restless and troublesome, and she spent half an hour helping him amuse himself around the nail-kegs.

At length she rose and went out on the walk, carrying the baby. She went into the dry-goods store and took a seat on one of the little revolving stools. A woman was buying some woollen goods for a dress. It was worth twenty-seven cents a yard, the clerk said, but he would knock off two cents if she took ten yards. It looked warm, and Mrs. Markham wished she could afford it for Mary.

A pretty young girl came in and laughed and chatted with the clerk, and bought a pair of gloves. She was the daughter of the grocer. Her happiness made the wife and mother sad. When Sam came back she asked him for some money.

"What you want to do with it?" he asked.

"I want to spend it," she said.

She was not to be trifled with, so he gave her a dollar.

"I need a dollar more."

"Well, I've got to go take up that note at the bank."

"Well, the children's got to have some new underclo'es," she said.

He handed her a two-dollar bill and then went out to pay his note.

She bought her cotton flannel and mittens and thread, and then sat leaning against the counter. It was noon, and she was hungry. She went out to the wagon, got the lunch she had brought, and took it into the grocery to eat it—where she could get a drink of water.

The grocer gave the baby a stick of candy and handed the mother an apple.

"It'll kind o' go down with your doughnuts," he said.

After eating her lunch she got up and went out. She felt ashamed to sit there any longer. She entered another dry-goods store, but when the clerk came toward her saying, "Anything to-day, Mrs. ——?" she answered, "No, I guess not," and turned away with foolish face.

She walked up and down the street, desolately homeless. She did not know what to do with herself. She knew no one except the grocer. She grew bitter as she saw a couple of ladies pass, holding their demi-trains in the latest city fashion. Another woman went by pushing a baby carriage, in which sat a child just about as big as her own. It was bouncing itself up and down on the long slender springs, and laughing and shouting. Its clean round face glowed from its pretty fringed hood. She looked down at the dusty clothes and grimy face of her own little one, and walked on savagely.

She went into the drug store where the soda fountain was, but it made her thirsty to sit there and she went out on the street again. She heard Sam laugh, and saw him in a group of men over by the blacksmith shop. He was having a good time and had forgotten her.

Her back ached so intolerably that she concluded to go in and rest once more in the grocer's chair. The baby was growing cross and fretful. She bought five cents' worth of candy to take home to the children, and gave baby a little piece to keep him quiet. She wished Sam would come. It must be getting late. The grocer said it was not much after one. Time seemed terribly long. She felt that she ought to do something while she was in town. She ran over her purchases—yes, that was all she had planned to buy. She fell to figuring on the things she needed. It was terrible. It ran away up into twenty or thirty dollars at the least. Sam, as well as she, needed underwear for the cold winter, but they would have to wear the old ones, even if they were thin and ragged. She would not need a dress, she thought bitterly, because she never went anywhere. She rose and went out on the street once more, and wandered up and down, looking at everything in the hope of enjoying something.

A man from Boon Creek backed a load of apples up to the sidewalk, and as he stood waiting for the grocer he noticed Mrs. Markham and the baby, and gave the baby an apple. This was a pleasure. He had such a hearty way about him. He on his part saw an ordinary farmer's wife with dusty dress, unkempt hair, and tired face. He did not know exactly why she appealed to him, but he tried to cheer her up.

The grocer was familiar with these bedraggled and weary wives. He was accustomed to see them sit for hours in his big wooden chair, and nurse tired and fretful children. Their forlorn, aimless, pathetic wandering up and down the street was a daily occurrence, and had never possessed any special meaning to him.

II

In a cottage around the corner from the grocery store two men and a woman were finishing a dainty luncheon. The woman was dressed in cool, white garments, and she seemed to make the day one of perfect comfort.

The home of the Honorable Mr. Hall was by no means the costliest in the town, but his wife made it the most attractive. He was one of the leading lawyers of the county, and a man of culture and progressive views. He was entertaining a friend who had lectured the night before in the Congregational church.

They were by no means in serious discussion. The talk was rather frivolous. Hall had the ability to caricature men with a few gestures and attitudes, and was giving to his Eastern friend some descriptions of the old-fashioned Western lawyers he had met in his practice. He was very amusing, and his guest laughed heartily for a time.

But suddenly Hall became aware that Otis was not listening. Then he perceived that he was peering out of the window at some one, and that on his face a look of bitter sadness was falling.

Hall stopped. "What do you see, Otis?"

Otis replied, "I see a forlorn, weary woman."

Mrs. Hall rose and went to the window. Mrs. Markham was walking by the house, her baby in her arms. Savage anger and weeping were in her eyes and on her lips, and there was hopeless tragedy in her shambling walk and weak back.

In the silence Otis went on: "I saw the poor, dejected creature twice this morning. I couldn't forget her."

"Who is she?" asked Mrs. Hall, very softly.

"Her name is Markham; she's Sam Markham's wife," said Hall.

The young wife led the way into the sitting room, and the men took seats and lit their cigars. Hall was meditating a diversion when Otis resumed suddenly:

"That woman came to town to-day to get a change, to have a little play-spell, and she's wandering around like a starved and weary cat. I wonder if there is a woman in this town with sympathy enough and courage enough to go out and help that woman? The saloon-keepers, the politicians, and the grocers make it pleasant for the man—so pleasant that he forgets his wife. But the wife is left without a word."

Mrs. Hall's work dropped, and on her pretty face was a look of pain. The man's harsh words had wounded her—and wakened her. She took up her hat and hurried out on the walk. The men looked at each other, and then the husband said:

"It's going to be a little sultry for the men around these diggings. Suppose we go out for a walk."

Delia felt a hand on her arm as she stood at the corner.

"You look tired, Mrs. Markham; won't you come in a little while? I'm Mrs. Hall."

Mrs. Markham turned with a scowl on her face and a biting word on her tongue, but something in the sweet, round little face of the other woman silenced her, and her brow smoothed out.

"Thank you kindly, but it's most time to go home. I'm looking fer Mr. Markham now."

"Oh, come in a little while, the baby is cross and tired out; please do."

Mrs. Markham yielded to the friendly voice, and together the two women reached the gate just as two men hurriedly turned the other corner.

"Let me relieve you," said Mrs. Hall.

The mother hesitated: "He's so dusty."

"Oh, that won't matter. Oh, what a big fellow he is! I haven't any of my own," said Mrs. Hall, and a look passed like an electric spark between the two women, and Delia was her willing guest from that moment.

They went into the little sitting room, so dainty and lovely to the farmer's wife, and as she sank into an easy-chair she was faint and drowsy with the pleasure of it. She submitted to being brushed. She gave the baby into the hands of the Swedish girl, who washed its face and hands and sang it to sleep, while its mother sipped some tea. Through it all she lay back in her easy-chair, not speaking a word, while the ache passed out of her back, and her hot, swollen head ceased to throb.

But she saw everything—the piano, the pictures, the curtains, the wall-paper, the little tea-stand. They were almost as grateful to her as the food and fragrant tea. Such housekeeping as this she had never seen. Her mother had worn her kitchen floor thin as brown paper in keeping a speckless house, and she had been in houses that were larger and costlier, but something of the charm of her hostess was in the arrangement of vases, chairs, or pictures. It was tasteful.

Mrs. Hall did not ask about her affairs. She talked to her about the sturdy little baby, and about the things upon which Delia's eyes dwelt. If she seemed interested in a vase she was told what it was and where it was made. She was shown all the pictures and books. Mrs. Hall seemed to read her visitor's mind. She kept as far from the farm and her guest's affairs as possible, and at last she opened the piano and sang to her—not slow-moving hymns, but catchy love-songs full of sentiment, and then played some simple melodies, knowing that Mrs. Markham's eyes were studying her hands, her rings, and the flash of her fingers on the keys—seeing more than she heard—and through it all Mrs. Hall conveyed the impression that she, too, was having a good time.

The rattle of the wagon outside roused them both. Sam was at the gate for her. Mrs. Markham rose hastily. "Oh, it's almost sundown!" she gasped in astonishment as she looked out of the window.

"Oh, that won't kill anybody," replied her hostess. "Don't hurry. Carrie, take the baby out the wagon for Mrs. Markham while I help her with her things."

"Oh, I've had such a good time," Mrs. Markham said as they went down the little walk.

"So have I," replied Mrs. Hall. She took the baby a moment as her guest climbed in. "Oh, you big, fat fellow!" she cried as she gave him a squeeze. "You must bring your wife in oftener, Mr. Markham," she said, as she handed the baby up.

Sam was staring with amazement.

"Thank you, I will," he finally managed to say.

"Good-night," said Mrs. Markham.

"Good-night, dear," called Mrs. Hall, and the wagon began to rattle off.

The tenderness and sympathy in her voice brought the tears to Delia's eyes—not hot or bitter tears, but tears that cooled her eyes and cleared her mind.

The wind had gone down, and the red sunlight fell mistily over the world of corn and stubble. The crickets were still chirping and the feeding cattle were drifting toward the farmyards. The day had been made beautiful by human sympathy.

Glossary	"A Day's Pleasure"
acquiescence	agreement, consent
alluring	attractive, tempting
astonishment	great amazement
batch	amount of dough needed for one baking

bedraggled	wet and dirty
bin	box for storing grain
caricature	to imitate with exaggeration and humor
catchy	catching attention, easily remembered
crib	framework for storing grain
cuffed	slapped with open hand
dainty	delicious and choice
demi-trains	half trains, material that hangs down behind a dress
desolately	forlornly, wretchedly
diggings	lodgings, house
dogged	persistent
dough	mixture of flour, liquid, and other ingredients for baking bread
drowsy	sleepy, half asleep
dry-goods	cloth, cloth products, thread
dwelt	lived
elevators	warehouses for storing grain
fer	for
forlorn	pitiful, miserable, hopeless
fretful	irritable, discontented
frivolous	trivial, not important or serious
git	get
granary	building for storing grain
grimy	dirty
hearty	extremely warm and friendly
hinder	rear, back
hitched	fastened, tied, harnessed
hymns	songs in praise or honor of God
intolerable	unbearable, painful
kneading	mixing dough by pressing and squeezing with hands
knock off	to subtract
lameness	having an injured leg or foot that makes one limp
lee	shelter, protection
mebbe	maybe
meditating	planning, intending, thinking about
mistily	blurred by or covered by mist
pathetic	arousing pity, sorrow, compassion; pitiful
perfunctorily	indifferently, without caring
progressive	favoring political progress or reform
resolute	determined, resolved
roused	awakened
savagely	wildly, fiercely, furiously
scowl	frown
scudding	running quickly
shambling	shuffling, clumsy
shod	fitted with shoes
shovelling	lifting and moving with a shovel

soggy	full of moisture, soaked
soused	plunged into liquid
speckless	extremely clean, without a stain
stubble	short stumps of grain left after harvesting
sullen	showing resentment and bad humor, morose, unsociable
sultry	extremely hot and moist
throb	to beat strongly
toil	hard, exhausting work
trifled with	not treated seriously
tumultuously	wildly, noisily
'twas	it was
unkemptly	not combed, untidily

Discussion

1. Summarize the plot of "A Day's Pleasure." Is it simple or complicated?
2. What is the dominant mood of "A Day's Pleasure"? How does Garland create this mood?
3. What kind of life do Sam and Delia Markham have?
4. What makes the characters seem realistic?
5. Have you ever been in a situation like Delia's, where you felt lonely and out of place?
6. Do you enjoy reading short stories? Who are your favorite short story authors?
7. How did this story make you feel? Cheerful? Depressed? Write a few sentences explaining your response to the story, and share your reaction with the class.

Comprehension

1. Why does Mrs. Markham want to go to town?
2. What is her husband's response?
3. What kind of man is Mr. Markham?
4. What kind of woman is Mrs. Markham?
5. What does Mrs. Markham buy?
6. How does Mrs. Markham feel after she eats lunch?
7. Who is Mr. Hall?
8. What question does Mr. Hall's friend Otis ask?
9. How does Mrs. Hall respond to what Otis says?
10. What is the meaning of the look that passes between the two women?
11. How does Mrs. Markham feel while she is visiting Mrs. Hall?
12. What does Mrs. Hall tell Mr. Markham?
13. What is the theme of this story?

Style and Language

Understanding the style and tone of an author is essential to understanding what the author has written. Therefore, this activity helps you analyze the author's style, tone, and language. It also asks you to identify some of the basic elements of a short story: setting, point of view, and theme. Circle the letter next to the correct answer(s). More than one answer may be correct. Be prepared to justify your choices by giving specific examples from the reading selection.

1. Style refers to the author's manner of writing. Garland's style can be characterized as
    a. personal.
    b. impersonal.
    c. realistic.
    d. romantic.

2. Tone reveals the author's attitude toward his or her subject and audience and helps create the mood of a poem or story. The tone of "A Day's Pleasure" can be described as
    a. serious.
    b. humorous.
    c. subjective.
    d. objective.

3. Analysis of an author's language centers on sentence structure, word choice, and figures of speech. Garland's language contains
    a. detailed physical descriptions.
    b. abstract religious symbolism.
    c. authentic regional dialect.
    d. complex philosophical arguments.

4. Point of view refers to who is telling the story, the voice that the reader hears. This voice may be a character in the story or the author. Thus, a story can be narrated in the first person (I) or the third person (he or she). This story is told from the point of view of
    a. Mrs. Markham.
    b. Mr. Markham.
    c. Mrs. Hall.
    d. the third-person narrator (omniscient author).

5. Authors set their stories in a particular time and place or environment. This story is set in the late nineteenth century in
    a. a large western city.
    b. a village in New England.
    c. a small town on the prairie.
    d. a big town in the desert.

6. The theme of a story is its major or central idea: the message the author gives the reader. The theme of "A Day's Pleasure" is
    a. stated in the introduction.
    b. stated in the conclusion.
    c. stated in the first paragraph of part II.
    d. not stated explicitly.

Underline the sentence containing the theme.

Writing Assignments

1. Write a two-paragraph summary of the ideas and actions in "A Day's Pleasure."

2. Write a letter from Mrs. Hall to Mrs. Markham, discussing their first visit and inviting Mrs. Markham to come visit her again.

3. Describe a day that was made beautiful through human kindness and sympathy. Draw on your personal experience, and limit your description to three or four paragraphs.

Group Work

A proverb is a short, popular saying that expresses a common truth. Working with a partner or in a small group, read the following proverbs and discuss their meanings. Which ones relate to "A Day's Pleasure"?   Write a brief summary of your discussion.

Father and mother are kind, but God is kinder.	Danish proverb
Kindness grows old fast.	French proverb
He who does kindly deeds becomes rich.	Hindu proverb
One kind word can warm three Winter months.	Japanese proverb
God is merciful to those who are kind.	Moroccan proverb
A kind word is better than a big pie.	Russian proverb
The gardens of kindness never fade.	Greek proverb
Always repay kindness with even more kindness.	Welsh proverb

Analysis

"A Day's Pleasure" (1899), by Hamlin Garland, is an example of the prose written during the American Realistic Movement (1841–1900). Hamlin Garland was a member of the "Chicago realist" writers. His novels and stories about middlewestern farm families are characterized by careful attention to detail and lifelike portrayals of setting and characters. Revealing the deadening boredom of farm life, his plots turn on simple ideas and events and contain little dramatic action.

In "A Day's Pleasure," Garland paints a truly bleak picture of the hardships facing poor families living on farms in the Midwest frontier. In fact, the generally pessimistic mood of the story makes it an early example of naturalistic writing, which dominated American prose after 1890. His plot is basic: A farmer takes his wife and baby on a one-day trip into town. Garland emphasizes character rather than plot. His characters are depicted honestly, without romantic idealism. Sam and Delia Markham are victims of their harsh environment, barely able to exert their wills or change their lives for the better. However, Mrs. Hall, the other major character, is instrumental in transforming the mood of the story, and her "human sympathy" makes the day "beautiful." Garland's theme is, thus, the primary importance of and need for human interaction and caring relationships.

The style of "A Day's Pleasure" is clear and simple. Garland uses plain words, commonplace images, and carefully chosen physical details. The story is told from the point of view of the omniscient author (third-person narrator), and the tone is impersonal and unemotional. The dialogue, which contains authentic country dialect, reveals the emotions and thoughts of Garland's characters, while also helping to develop the plot. The language is highly descriptive, with a few figures of speech ("their faces brown as leather," and "she's wandering around like a starved and weary cat") that are drawn from daily life.

Because Garland's depressing story concludes with an optimistic tone, he holds out the possibility of moral choice and offers a belief in the essential goodness of human beings. His message is that life contains simple pleasures, such as a visit with a friend, and it is these pleasures that make the bleakness of life bearable.

Answers to Exercises

Discussion (Answers will vary.)

1. The plot is simple but realistic. It concerns a day in the life of a poor farm woman whose lonely life revolves around taking care of her children and doing her farm chores ("the sickening sameness of her life"). Mrs. Markham goes to town with her husband and baby. She is lonely and unhappy, but a kind woman, Mrs. Hall, invites her to come into her home and visit for a few hours. Mrs. Hall's kindness gives Mrs. Markham great pleasure and makes her day beautiful.
2. The dominant mood is one of sadness, loneliness, and depression. Garland creates this mood through his detailed descriptions. He reveals the thoughts of the characters, the harshness of their lives, and the bleakness of setting.
3. The Markhams have a hard and lonely life on their farm. They are very poor and have few comforts or pleasures.
4. Garland's characters are realistic in their actions, emotions, and words. They experience universal human emotions of boredom, loneliness, and desire for friendship and personal relationships. They talk in a country dialect ("git," "fer").

Comprehension

1. Mrs. Markham hasn't been out of her farmhouse for six months.
2. He has no strong objection, but he asks her to help put up the wheat.
3. He is "a sturdy fellow" and good-natured.
4. She is an angry, worn-out, lonely, shy, and depressed woman.
5. She buys cotton flannel, mittens, and thread.
6. She feels ashamed about sitting in the store and "desolately homeless." She is bitter and angry because she has no money, nothing to do, and her back aches.
7. Mr. Hall is "one of the leading lawyers of the county, and a man of culture and progressive views."
8. Otis asks if there is "a woman in the town with sympathy enough and courage enough to go out and help that woman."

9. Mrs. Hall invites Mrs. Markham to come to her house.
10. Mrs. Markham understands that Mrs. Hall wishes she had a baby.
11. Mrs. Markham feels very comfortable, relaxed, and happy.
12. Mrs. Hall tells Mr. Markham to bring his wife to town more often.
13. The theme is the importance of caring about other people ("human sympathy"), which can add beauty to a difficult and boring life.

Style and Language

1. b: impersonal. The story is told by a third-person narrator using "he," "she," "they."
   c: realistic. Garland makes his characters and setting true-to-life with carefully chosen, authentic details.
2. a: serious. The author is serious in his attitude toward the subject and shows no humor.
   d: objective. There are no explicitly subjective opinions of the author. He tells the story without comment.
3. a: detailed physical descriptions. The characters and setting are described in great detail.
   c: authentic regional dialect. The dialogue contains the dialect of midwestern farmers.
4. d: third-person narrator (omniscient author)
5. c: a small town on the prairie
6. b: stated in the conclusion. "The day had been made beautiful by human sympathy."

Chapter 2

Nineteenth-Century American Prose: The Short Story

"Plot is very imperfectly understood, and has never been rightly defined. Many persons regard it as mere complexity of incident . . . it is that from which no component atom can be removed, and in which none of the component atoms can be displaced, without ruin to the whole."
Edgar Allan Poe, *Marginalia,* 1844–49

"I should, upon the whole, be disposed to rank American short stories only below those of such Russian writers as I have read, and I should praise rather than blame their free use of our different local parlances, or 'dialects,' as people call them. I like this because I hope that our inherited English may be constantly freshened and revived from the native sources."
William Dean Howells, *Criticism and Fiction*, 1891

"One might say that every fine story must leave in the mind of the sensitive reader an intangible residuum of pleasure."
Willa Cather, *Not under Forty*, 1936

"The short story continues to be a rich and fertile strain of literary expression. At its best, it achieves a degree of perfection rarely attained by the novel. Indeed, the distinctive power and beauty of the short story are involved in its very brevity, the discipline of its strict limits challenging the writer to ever more brilliant inventiveness in such areas as symbolism, suggestiveness and plotting."
Douglas Angus, introduction to *The Best Short Stories of the Modern Age*, 1962

"The short story is the most democratic of all the arts; anyone may tell a story, and if it is an absorbing one someone will listen."
Hallie Burnett, *On Writing the Short Story*, 1983

Shorter than a novel or a novella, the short story usually has one main theme and is limited in number of characters and scope. It originated in the fables, folktales, parables, and tales of earlier ages and cultures.

In the nineteenth century, the short story began in the United States with the early tales of Nathaniel Hawthorne and the works of Edgar Allan Poe. In Europe the great masters of the short story were Guy de Maupassant (1850–93) in France and Alexander Pushkin (1799–1837) and Anton Chekhov (1860–1904) in Russia. These nineteenth-century writers have had an immense and lasting impact on the short story writers who came after them.

The American short story has moved through various literary periods from the symbolism and fantasy of Hawthorne and Poe to Crane's impressionism to twentieth-century realism and surrealism. Today it is a major literary genre throughout the world. Perhaps its conciseness makes the short story particularly well suited to the rush and time pressures of the modern age.

Nathaniel Hawthorne   "The Canterbury Pilgrims"

"I read no newspapers, and hardly remember who is President; and feel as if I had no more concern with what other people trouble themselves about than if I dwelt in another planet."
Nathaniel Hawthorne, "Brook Farm," *Journal,* April 28, 1841

"The style is purity itself. Force abounds. High imagination gleams from every page. Mr. Hawthorne is a man of the highest imagination."
Edgar Allan Poe, *Hawthorne's Twice-Told Tales*, 1842

"There is Hawthorne, with genius so shrinking and rare
That you hardly at first see the strength that is there."
James Russell Lowell, *A Fable for Critics*, 1847–48

"Although a Yankee, he partakes of none of the characteristics of a Yankee. His thinking and his style have an antique air. His roots strike down through the visible mold of the present, and draw sustenance from the generations under ground."
Alexander Smith, *Dreamthorp,* 1863

Nathaniel Hawthorne (1804–64) was born in Salem, Massachusetts, into an old New England seafaring family. He devoted himself to writing after graduating from college but was not successful until later in his life. He is best known for his novels *The Scarlet Letter, The House of Seven Gables, Blithedale Romance,* and *The Marble Faun.* He also wrote many collections of short stories, published in *Twice-Told Tales, Mosses from an Old Manse,* and *The Snow Image and Other Twice-Told Tales.*

One of the greatest nineteenth-century American writers, Hawthorne was perhaps the first major short story writer. Most of his stories concern the question of evil and, as Edgar Allan Poe said, have a general tone of "melancholy and mysticism." Hawthorne was a moralist who explored American Puritanism, especially the mysteries of sin and redemption. However, as a democratic Christian humanist, he wrote from a religious point of view that was critical of the harshness of Puritanism.

Hawthorne once described his complex tales as "flowers that blossomed in too retired a shade." His works are symbolic and often contain allegories. They are mixtures of the abstract and the concrete, the symbolic and the realistic, almost always containing images of guilt, secrecy, isolation, and death. Hawthorne's major themes are the sin of pride and the conflict between the head and the heart, or the conscious and the unconscious minds. His overall philosophy was antiromantic; his stories portray the existence of evil rather than the romantic belief in the natural goodness of human beings. His works are characterized by ambiguity, just as real life is, and he gives no clear answers to the questions he raises.

Preview

Skimming: Skim the reading to gain a general impression.
1. Read the title and first sentence of the story.
2. Skim the story to get an idea of its form and length.

Questioning: Answer the following question and discuss your answers in class.
How easy was it for you to leave the security of your home environment and travel to the outside world?

Scanning: Scan to answer the following questions to get an idea of the content and style.
1. Where are Josiah and Miriam going?
2. Whom do Josiah and Miriam meet while they are sitting at the spring?

The Canterbury Pilgrims   1835
Nathaniel Hawthorne

The summer moon, which shines in so many a tale, was beaming over a broad extent of uneven country. Some of its brightest rays were flung into a spring of water, where no traveller, toiling, as the writer has, up the hilly road beside which it gushes, ever failed to quench his thirst. The work of neat hands and considerate art was visible about this blessed fountain. An open cistern, hewn and hollowed out of solid stone, was placed above the waters, which filled it to the brim, but by some invisible outlet were conveyed away without dripping down its sides. Though the basin had not room for another drop, and the continual gush of water made a tremor on the surface, there was a secret charm that forbade it to overflow. I remember, that when I had slaked my summer thirst, and sat panting by the cistern, it was my fanciful theory that Nature could not afford to lavish so pure a liquid, as she does the waters of all meaner fountains.

While the moon was hanging almost perpendicularly over this spot, two figures appeared on the summit of the hill, and came with noiseless footsteps down towards the spring. They were then in the first freshness of youth; nor is there a wrinkle now on either of their brows, and yet they wore a strange, old-fashioned garb. One, a young man with ruddy cheeks, walked beneath the canopy of a broad-brimmed gray hat; he seemed to have inherited his great-grandsire's square-skirted coat, and a waistcoat that extended its immense flaps to his knees; his brown locks, also, hung down behind, in a mode unknown to our times. By his side was a sweet young damsel, her fair features sheltered by a prim little bonnet, within which appeared the vestal muslin of a cap; her close, long-waisted gown, and indeed her whole attire, might have been worn by some rustic beauty who had faded half a century before. But that there was something too warm and life-like in them, I would here have compared this couple to the ghosts of two young lovers who had died long since in the glow of passion, and now were straying out of their graves, to renew the old vows, and shadow forth the unforgotten kiss of their earthly lips, beside the moonlit spring.

"Thee and I will rest here a moment, Miriam," said the young man, as they drew near the stone cistern, "for there is no fear that the elders know what we have done; and this may be the last time we shall ever taste this water."

Thus speaking, with a little sadness in his face, which was also visible in that of his companion, he made her sit down on a stone and was about to place himself very close to her side; she, however, repelled him, though not unkindly.

"Nay, Josiah," said she, giving him a timid push with her maiden hand, "thee must sit farther off, on that other stone, with the spring between us. What would the sisters say, if thee were to sit so close to me?"

"But we are of the world's people now, Miriam," answered Josiah.

The girl persisted in her prudery, nor did the youth, in fact, seem altogether free from a similar sort of shyness; so they sat apart from each other, gazing up the hill, where the moonlight discovered the tops of a group of buildings. While their attention was thus occupied, a party of travellers, who had come wearily up the long ascent, made a halt to refresh themselves at the spring. There were three men, a woman, and a little girl and boy. Their attire was mean, covered with the dust of the summer's day, and damp with the night-dew; they all looked woebegone, as if the cares and sorrows of the world had made their steps heavier as they climbed the hill; even the two little children appeared older in evil days than the young man and maiden who had first approached the spring.

"Good evening to you, young folks," was the salutation of the travellers; and "Good evening, friends," replied the youth and damsel.

"Is that white building the Shaker meeting-house?" asked one of the strangers. "And are those the red roofs of the Shaker village?"

"Friend, it is the Shaker village," answered Josiah, after some hesitation.

The travellers, who, from the first, had looked suspiciously at the garb of these young people, now taxed them with an intention which all the circumstances, indeed, rendered too obvious to be mistaken.

"It is true, friends," replied the young man, summoning up his courage. "Miriam and I have a gift to love each other, and we are going among the world's people to live after their fashion. And ye know that we do not transgress the law of the land; and neither ye, nor the elders themselves, have a right to hinder us."

"Yet you think it expedient to depart without leave-taking," remarked one of the travellers.

"Yea, ye-a," said Josiah, reluctantly, "because father Job is a very awful man to speak with; and being aged himself, he has but little charity for what he calls the iniquities of the flesh."

"Well," said the stranger, "we will neither use force to bring you back to the village, nor will we betray you to the elders. But sit you here awhile, and when you have heard what we shall tell you of the world which we have left, and into which you are going, perhaps you will turn back with us of your own accord. What say you?" added he, turning to his companions. "We have travelled thus far without becoming known to each other. Shall we tell our stories, here by this pleasant spring, for our own pastime, and the benefit of these misguided young lovers?"

In accordance with this proposal, the whole party stationed themselves round the stone cistern; the two children, being very weary, fell asleep upon the damp earth, and the pretty Shaker girl, whose feelings were those of a nun or a Turkish lady, crept as close as possible to the female travel-ler, and as far as she well could from the unknown men. The same person who had hitherto been the chief spokesman now stood up, waving his hat in his hand, and suffered the moonlight to fall full upon his front.

"In me," said he, with a certain majesty of utterance,—"in me, you behold a poet."

Though a lithographic print of this gentleman is extant, it may be well to notice that he was now nearly forty, a thin and stooping figure, in a black coat, out at elbows; notwithstanding the ill condition of his attire, there were about him several tokens of a peculiar sort of foppery, unworthy of a mature man, particularly in the arrangement of his hair, which was so disposed as to give all possible loftiness and breadth to his forehead. However, he had an intelligent eye, and, on the whole, a marked countenance.

"A poet!" repeated the young Shaker, a little puzzled how to understand such a designation, seldom heard in the utilitarian community where he had spent his life. "Oh, ay, Miriam, he means a varse-maker, thee must know."

This remark jarred upon the susceptible nerves of the poet; nor could he help wondering what strange fatality had put into this young man's mouth an epithet, which ill-natured people had affirmed to be more proper to his merit than the one assumed by himself.

"True, I am a verse-maker," he resumed, "but my verse is no more than the material body into which I breathe the celestial soul of thought. Alas! how many a pang has it cost me, this same insensibility to the ethereal essence of poetry, with which you have here tortured me again, at the moment when I am to relinquish my profession forever! O Fate! why hast thou warred with Nature, turning all her higher and more perfect gifts to the ruin of me, their possessor? What is the voice of song, when the world lacks the ear of taste? How can I rejoice in my strength and delicacy of feeling, when they have but made great sorrows out of little ones? Have I dreaded scorn like death, and yearned for fame as others pant for vital air, only to find myself in a middle state between obscurity and infamy? But I have my revenge! I could have given existence to a thousand bright creations. I crush them into my heart, and there let them putrefy! I shake off the dust of my feet against my countrymen! But posterity, tracing my footsteps up this weary hill, will cry shame upon the unworthy age that drove one of the fathers of American song to end his days in a Shaker village!"

During this harangue, the speaker gesticulated with great energy, and, as poetry is the natural language of passion, there appeared reason to apprehend his final explosion into an ode extempore. The reader must understand that, for all these bitter words, he was a kind, gentle, harmless, poor fellow enough, whom Nature, tossing her ingredients together without looking at her recipe, had sent into the world with too much of one sort of brain, and hardly any of another.

"Friend," said the young Shaker, in some perplexity, "thee seemest to have met with great troubles; and, doubtless, I should pity them, if—if I could but understand what they were."

"Happy in your ignorance!" replied the poet, with an air of sublime superiority. "To your coarser mind, perhaps, I may seem to speak of more important griefs when I add, what I had wellnigh forgotten, that I am out at elbows, and almost starved to death. At any rate, you have the advice and example of one individual to warn you back; for I am come hither, a disappointed man, flinging aside the fragments of my hopes, and seeking shelter in the calm retreat which you are so anxious to leave."

"I thank thee, friend," rejoined the youth, "but I do not mean to be a poet, nor, Heaven be praised! do I think Miriam ever made a varse in her life. So we need not fear thy disappointments. But, Miriam," he added, with real concern, "thee knowest that the elders admit nobody that has not a gift to be useful. Now, what under the sun can they do with this poor varse-maker?"

"Nay, Josiah, do not thee discourage the poor man," said the girl, in all simplicity and kindness. "Our hymns are very rough, and perhaps they may trust him to smooth them."

Without noticing this hint of professional employment, the poet turned away, and gave himself up to a sort of vague reverie, which he called thought. Sometimes he watched the moon, pouring a silvery liquid on the clouds, through which it slowly melted till they became all bright, then he saw the same sweet radiance dancing on the leafy trees which rustled as if to shake it off, or sleeping on the high tops of hills, or hovering down in distant valleys, like the material of unshaped dreams; lastly, he looked into the spring, and there the light was mingling with the water. In its crystal bosom, too, beholding all heaven reflected there, he found an emblem of a pure and tranquil breast. He listened to that most ethereal of all sounds, the song of crickets, coming in full choir upon the wind, and fancied that, if moonlight could be heard, it would sound just like that. Finally, he took a draught at the Shaker spring, and, as if it were the true Castalia, was forthwith moved to compose a lyric, a Farewell to his Harp, which he swore should be its closing strain, the last verse that an ungrateful world should have from him. This effusion, with two or three other little pieces, subsequently written, he took the first opportunity to send, by one of the Shaker brethren, to Concord, where they were published in the New Hampshire Patriot.

Meantime, another of the Canterbury pilgrims, one so different from the poet that the delicate fancy of the latter could hardly have conceived of him, began to relate his sad experience. He was a small man, of quick and unquiet gestures, about fifty years old, with a narrow forehead, all wrinkled and drawn together. He held in his hand a pencil, and a card of some commission-merchant in foreign parts, on the back of which, for there was light enough to read or write by, he seemed ready to figure out a calculation.

"Young man," said he, abruptly, "what quantity of land do the Shakers own here, in Canterbury?"

"That is more than I can tell thee, friend," answered Josiah, "but it is a very rich establishment, and for a long way by the roadside thee may guess the land to be ours, by the neatness of the fences."

"And what may be the value of the whole," continued the stranger, "with all the buildings and improvements, pretty nearly, in round numbers?"

"Oh, a monstrous sum,—more than I can reckon," replied the young Shaker.

"Well, sir," said the pilgrim, "there was a day, and not very long ago, neither, when I stood at my counting-room window, and watched the signal flags of three of my own ships entering the harbor, from the East Indies, from Liverpool, and from up the Straits, and I would not have given the invoice of the least of them for the title-deeds of this whole Shaker settlement. You stare. Perhaps, now, you won't believe that I could have put more value on a little piece of paper, no bigger than the palm of your hand, than all these solid acres of grain, grass, and pasture-land would sell for?"

"I won't dispute it, friend," answered Josiah, "but I know I had rather have fifty acres of this good land than a whole sheet of thy paper."

"You may say so now," said the ruined merchant, bitterly, "for my name would not be worth the paper I should write it on. Of course, you must have heard of my failure?"

And the stranger mentioned his name, which, however mighty it might have been in the commercial world, the young Shaker had never heard of among the Canterbury hills.

"Not heard of my failure!" exclaimed the merchant, considerably piqued. "Why, it was spoken of on 'Change in London, and from Boston to New Orleans men trembled in their shoes. At all events, I did fail, and you see me here on my road to the Shaker village, where, doubtless (for the Shakers are a shrewd sect), they will have a due respect for my experience, and give me the management of the trading part of the concern, in which case I think I can pledge myself to double their capital in four or five years. Turn back with me, young man; for though you will never meet with my good luck, you can hardly escape my bad."

"I will not turn back for this," replied Josiah, calmly, "any more than for the advice of the varse-maker, between whom and thee, friend, I see a sort of likeness, though I can't justly say where it lies. But Miriam and I can earn our daily bread among the world's people as well as in the Shaker village. And do we want anything more, Miriam?"

"Nothing more, Josiah," said the girl, quietly.

"Yea, Miriam, and daily bread for some other little mouths, if God send them," observed the simple Shaker lad.

Miriam did not reply, but looked down into the spring, where she encountered the image of her own pretty face, blushing within the prim little bonnet. The third pilgrim now took up the conversation. He was a sunburnt countryman, of tall frame and bony strength, on whose rude and manly face there appeared a darker, more sullen and obstinate despondency, than on those of either the poet or the merchant.

"Well, now, youngster," he began, "these folks have had their say, so I'll take my turn. My story will cut but a poor figure by the side of theirs; for I never supposed that I could have a right to meat and drink, and great praise besides, only for tagging rhymes together, as it seems this man does; nor ever tried to get the substance of hundreds into my own hands, like the trader there. When I was about of your years, I married me a wife,—just such a neat and pretty young woman as Miriam, if that's her name,—and all I asked of Providence was an ordinary blessing on the sweat of my brow, so that we might be decent and comfortable, and have daily bread for ourselves, and for some other little mouths that we soon had to feed. We had no very great prospects before us; but I never wanted to be idle; and I thought it a matter of course that the Lord would help me, because I was willing to help myself."

"And didn't He help thee, friend?" demanded Josiah, with some eagerness.

"No," said the yeoman, sullenly; "for then you would not have seen me here. I have labored hard for years; and my means have been growing narrower, and my living poorer, and my heart colder and heavier, all the time; till at last I could bear it no longer. I set myself down to calculate whether I had best go on the Oregon expedition, or come here to the Shaker village; but I had not hope enough left in me to begin the world over again; and, to make my story short, here I am. And now, youngster, take my advice, and turn back; or else, some few years hence, you'll have to climb this hill, with as heavy a heart as mine."

This simple story had a strong effect on the young fugitives. The misfortunes of the poet and merchant had won little sympathy from their plain good sense and unworldly feelings, qualities which made them such unprejudiced and inflexible judges, that few men would have chosen to take the opinion of this youth and maiden as to the wisdom or folly of their pursuits. But here was one whose simple wishes had resembled their own, and who, after efforts which almost gave him a right to claim success from fate, had failed in accomplishing them.

"But thy wife, friend?" exclaimed the younger man. "What became of the pretty girl, like Miriam? Oh, I am afraid she is dead!"

"Yea, poor man, she must be dead,—she and the children, too," sobbed Miriam.

The female pilgrim had been leaning over the spring, wherein latterly a tear or two might have been seen to fall, and form its little circle on the surface of the water. She now looked up, disclosing features still comely, but which had acquired an expression of fretfulness, in the same long course of evil fortune that had thrown a sullen gloom over the temper of the unprosperous yeoman.

"I am his wife," said she, a shade of irritability just perceptible in the sadness of her tone. "These poor little things, asleep on the ground, are two of our children. We had two more, but God has provided better for them than we could, by taking them to Himself."

"And what would thee advise Josiah and me to do?" asked Miriam, this being the first question which she had put to either of the strangers.

"'Tis a thing almost against nature for a woman to try to part true lovers," answered the yeoman's wife, after a pause; "but I'll speak as truly to you as if these were my dying words. Though my husband told you some of our troubles, he didn't mention the greatest, and that which makes all the rest so hard to bear. If you and your sweetheart marry, you'll be kind and pleasant to each other for a year or two, and while that's the case, you never will repent; but, by and by, he'll grow gloomy, rough, and hard to please, and you'll be peevish, and full of little angry fits, and apt to be complaining by the fireside, when he comes to rest himself from his troubles out of doors; so your love will wear away by little and little, and leave you miserable at last. It has been so with us; and yet my husband and I were true lovers once, if ever two young folks were."

As she ceased, the yeoman and his wife exchanged a glance, in which there was more and warmer affection than they had supposed to have escaped the frost of a wintry fate, in either of their breasts. At that moment, when they stood on the utmost verge of married life, one word fitly spoken, or perhaps one peculiar look, had they had mutual confidence enough to reciprocate it, might have renewed all their old feelings, and sent them back, resolved to sustain each other amid the struggles of the world. But the crisis passed and never came again. Just then, also, the children, roused by their mother's voice, looked up, and added their wailing accents to the testimony borne by all the Canterbury pilgrims against the world from which they fled.

"We are tired and hungry!" cried they. "Is it far to the Shaker village?"

The Shaker youth and maiden looked mournfully into each other's eyes. They had but stepped across the threshold of their homes, when lo! the dark array of cares and sorrows that rose up to warn them back. The varied narratives of the strangers had arranged themselves into a parable; they seemed not merely instances of woful fate that had befallen others, but shadowy omens of disappointed hope and unavailing toil, domestic grief and estranged affection, that would cloud the onward path of these poor fugitives. But after one instant's hesitation, they opened their arms, and sealed their resolve with as pure and fond an embrace as ever youthful love had hallowed.

"We will not go back," said they. "The world never can be dark to us, for we will always love one another."

Then the Canterbury pilgrims went up the hill, while the poet chanted a drear and desperate stanza of the Farewell to his Harp, fitting music for that melancholy band. They sought a home where all former ties of nature or society would be sundered, and all old distinctions levelled, and a cold and passionless security be substituted for mortal hope and fear, as in that other refuge of the world's weary outcasts, the grave. The lovers drank at the Shaker spring, and then, with chastened hopes, but more confiding affections, went on to mingle in an untried life.

Glossary	"The Canterbury Pilgrims"
array	impressive display
befallen	happened to
blushing	becoming red from shame or embarrassment
canopy	anything that covers or seems to cover like a canopy
capital	wealth (money or property) owned by persons or corporations
Castalia	a spring on Mount Parnassus, an ancient source of poetic inspiration
celestial	heavenly, divine
chastened	subdued, lessened

cistern	backward, in a reverse direction
comely	attractive, pleasant to look at
confiding	trustful or inclined to trust
countenance	appearance; the look on a person's face
damsel	a girl; maiden
designation	title, name of an office, post or position
despondency	loss of courage or hope; dejection
draught	drink
effusion	emotional expression in speaking or writing
elders	older persons or officers with authority in a community
epithet	phrase used to describe a person or thing, often negatively
estranged	alienated
ethereal	heavenly, celestial
expedient	advantageous, convenient, guided by self-interest
extant	still existing; not lost or destroyed
foppery	paying too much attention to clothes and appearance
forthwith	immediately, at once
fretfulness	irritability, discontent
fugitives	persons running away
garb	clothing
gesticulated	used gestures, especially with hands and arms
gushes	flows out suddenly and plentifully
hallowed	made holy or sacred, sanctified
harangue	long, noisy or scolding speech
hewn	made or shaped by or as by cutting or chopping with an axe
hinder	to stop, prevent, keep back
hither	here, to this place
hitherto	until this time, to now
infamy	disgrace; dishonor, having a very bad reputation
iniquities	wickedness; unrighteous acts
invoice	list of goods shipped or services rendered, with a request for payment
jarred	had a harsh, irritating effect
lavish	to give or spend generously
levelled	destroyed, demolished
lithographic	process of printing a picture from a flat stone or metal plate
locks	curls, tresses, or ringlets of hair
mean	poor in appearance, shabby
mingle	to join, unite or take part with others
misguided	led into error or misconduct
monstrous	huge, enormous
mouths	little children
nay	no; a negative answer
obscurity	not being well-known or famous
obstinate	stubborn, not yielding to reason
ode extempore	poem spoken without any preparation

of your own accord	willingly, without being asked
omens	things supposed to foretell a future event, either good or evil
pang	sudden, sharp and brief pain, physical or emotional
pant	to yearn eagerly, to strongly desire
parable	short, simple story, with a moral or religious lesson
pastime	recreation, diversion; pleasant way of spending time
peevish	irritated, annoyed, bad-tempered
perceptible	can be perceived by the senses; audible
perpendicularly	vertically; straight up
piqued	offended, provoked
posterity	future humankind; all succeeding generations
Providence	God, as the guiding power of the universe
prudery	the quality of being too modest or proper in behavior
putrify	to become rotten, decay
quench	to satisfy
reciprocate	to give in return, return in kind, interchange
relinquish	to abandon, give up
repelled	rejected; refused to accept
resolve	intention, decision, firm determination
reverie	daydreaming, dreamy thinking or imagining
roused	wakened
ruddy	having a healthy red color
rustic	simple or plain
sealed	confirmed the truth of
sect	small religious group that has broken away from established church
Shaker	a former religious sect observing a doctrine of celibacy, common property, and community living
shrewd	clever or sharp in practical affairs
slaked	satisfied
strain	tune, passage of music
sublime	noble, majestic
suffered	allowed, permitted
sullen	showing ill humor; gloomy, sad
sundered	broken apart, separated
susceptible	easily affected emotionally; having a sensitive nature
sustain	to support, comfort, encourage
sweat of my brow	hard work
taxed	charged
thee	you; used in place of "thou" by the Quakers
they	your
timid	shy; showing fear or lack of self-confidence
title	deeds, documents that establish ownership of property
toiling	working hard and continuously
tokens	signs, indications
transgress	to break or overstep a law
tremor	a vibratory or quivering motion
unavailing	useless, futile

utilitarian	stressing usefulness over beauty
utterance	style of speaking
varse-maker	verse-maker: person who writes verses
verge	edge, brink
wellnigh	very nearly, almost
wherein	in which
woebegone	looking sorrowful, mournful, or wretched
yeoman	small landowner who worked his own land

Discussion

1. Summarize the plot of "The Canterbury Pilgrims." What is the central conflict?

2. What irony does Hawthorne achieve by using "the summer moon" in the first sentence of the story? What does the moon suggest?

3. In what ways are Josiah and Miriam realistic characters, and in what ways are they symbols? What do they symbolize?

4. Who are the Canterbury pilgrims and what do each of them symbolize?

5. What makes the portrayal of the poet humorous? Read a few of his statements aloud.

6. What is your reaction to the yeoman's wife and her description of marriage?

Style and Language

1. Which sentence best describes Hawthorne's style?
   a. Hawthorne's style is a mixture of realism and symbolism.
   b. Hawthorne's style is characterized by romanticism and paradox.
   Justify your answer with examples from the text.

2. Choose the sentence that best describes the tone of the story:
   a. The tone of "The Canterbury Pilgrims" is harshly critical and very pessimistic.
   b. The tone of "The Canterbury Pilgrims" is rather melancholy but somewhat optimistic.

3. Hawthorne uses satire in the story to humorously criticize
   a. Josiah and Miriam.
   b. the poet.
   c. the merchant.
   d. the yeoman and his wife.
   Give quotations from the story that are examples of this satire.

4. The story is told from the point of view of
   a. the young lovers, Josiah and Miriam.
   b. the poet.
   c. the merchant.
   d. the third-person narrator.

5. Identify and explain the figure of speech used by Hawthorne on page 25 to describe the poet: "He was a kind, gentle, harmless, poor fellow enough, whom Nature, tossing her ingredients together without looking at her recipe, had sent into the world with too much of one sort of brain, and hardly any of another."

Writing Assignments

1. A symbol is a special kind of image (a person, scene or object) that represents an abstract idea or emotion. Reread "The Canterbury Pilgrims," focusing on Hawthorne's use of symbolism. Make a list of the symbols in the story, and explain their possible meanings.

2. Write an essay analyzing the conclusion to "The Canterbury Pilgrims." Is it primarily optimistic or pessimistic, idealistic or realistic? Is it ambiguous or clear? What is Hawthorne's message? Will Josiah and Miriam have a good life in the outside world?

3. Discuss Hawthorne's view of marriage, as presented in "The Canterbury Pilgrims." According to Hawthorne, what is the purpose of marriage, and what causes a marriage to fail or succeed?

Group Work

Working with a partner or in a small group, read the poem "Is Love" by the twentieth-century African American poet Maya Angelou (1928–). Then discuss the similarities between Angelou's ideas as seen in "Is Love" and Hawthorne's as seen in "The Canterbury Pilgrims." What is the main idea of Angelou's poem? Write a one-paragraph interpretation of this poem.

Is Love   1990
Maya Angelou

Midwives and winding sheets
know birthing is hard
and dying is mean
and living's a trial in between.

Why do we journey, muttering
like rumors among the stars?
Is a dimension lost?
Is it love?

Edgar Allan Poe   "The Cask of Amontillado"

"Poe is a kind of Hawthorne and delirium tremens." [1]
Leslie Stephen, *Hours in a Library,* 1879

"I have a distinct and pleasing remembrance of his looks, voice, manner, and matter; very kindly and human, but subdued, perhaps a little jaded."
Walt Whitman, *Specimen Days,* 1882

"With the exception of Henry James and Hawthorne, Poe is our only master of pure prose. He wrote the first perfect short stories in the English language."
Willa Cather, *Home Monthly,* May 1897

---

1. Delirium tremens is a violent mental disturbance caused by drinking too much alcohol.

Edgar Allan Poe

Virginia Poe (Mrs. Edgar Allan Poe)

"There is no more effective way of realizing the distinction of Poe's genius than by imagining American literature without him."
W. C. Brownell, *American Prose Masters*, 1909

"Poe gave the sense for the first time in America that literature is *serious,* not a matter of courtesy but of truth."
William Carlos Williams, "Edgar Allan Poe," *In the American Grain,* 1925

Edgar Allan Poe (1809–49) was born in Boston, Massachusetts. He had a troubled life, marked by poverty, ill health, and alcoholism. Orphaned as a young child, he was adopted by John Allan and taken to England for five years. He later joined the U.S. Army but received a dishonorable discharge. Poe's marriage to his thirteen-year-old cousin Virginia brought him some happiness until she died eleven years later, and Poe gave way to depression and drinking.

Poe is highly regarded for his psychological stories of violence, terror, revenge, mystery, and murder that combine elements of realism and romanticism. As a Romantic writer, Poe created fantasies of the imagination. His characters and plots are not realistic, and his settings are usually European or Oriental. However, his realistic themes of inner conflict and death, which reflect his own self-destructive conflicts, seem strikingly modern although he was an early-nineteenth-century writer.

Struggling throughout his life to earn money and gain recognition as a writer, Poe finally succeeded in 1845, with the publication of *The Raven and Other Poems*. He died at the age of forty, having helped to determine the direction of twentieth-century literature. After his death, Poe became influential in French literature when the poet Baudelaire translated his works into French. Today he is considered the father of the modern short story and is among the most well-known American writers in Europe.

Poe's famous works include "The Fall of the House of Usher," "The Pit and the Pendulum," "The Murders in the Rue Morgue," and "The Tell-Tale Heart." He also wrote musical poetry: "The Raven," "Ulalume," "Annabel Lee," and "The Bells."

Preview

Skimming: Skim the reading to gain a general impression.
1. Read the title and first sentence of the story.
2. Skim the story to get an idea of its form and length.

Questioning: Answer the following questions and discuss your answers in class.
Have you ever wanted to take revenge on someone? For what reason?

Scanning: Scan to answer the following questions to get an idea of the content and style.
1. What was Fortunato's weak point?
2. In what season of the year does the story take place?

The Cask of Amontillado   1846

Edgar Allan Poe

The thousand injuries of Fortunato I had borne as I best could, but when he ventured upon insult I vowed revenge. You, who so well know the nature of my soul, will not suppose, however, that I gave utterance to a threat. *At length* I would be avenged; this was a point definitely settled—but the very definitiveness with which it was resolved precluded the idea of risk. I must not only punish but punish with impunity. A wrong is unredressed when retribution overtakes its redresser. It is equally unredressed when the avenger fails to make himself felt as such to him who has done the wrong.

It must be understood that neither by word nor deed had I given Fortunato cause to doubt my good will. I continued, as was my wont, to smile in his face, and he did not perceive that my smile *now* was at the thought of his immolation.

He had a weak point—this Fortunato—although in other regards he was a man to be respected and even feared. He prided himself on his connoisseurship in wine. Few Italians have the true virtuoso spirit. For the most part their enthusiasm is adopted to suit the time and opportunity, to practise imposture upon the British and Austrian *millionaires.* In painting and gemmary, Fortunato, like his countrymen, was a quack, but in the matter of old wines he was sincere. In this respect I did not differ from him materially;—I was skilful in the Italian vintages myself, and bought largely whenever I could.

It was about dusk, one evening during the supreme madness of the carnival season, that I encountered my friend. He accosted me with excessive warmth, for he had been drinking much. The man wore motley. He had on a tight-fitting parti-striped dress, and his head was surmounted by the conical cap and bells. I was so pleased to see him that I thought I should never have done wringing his hand.

I said to him—"My dear Fortunato, you are luckily met. How remarkably well you are looking to-day. But I have received a pipe of what passes for Amontillado, and I have my doubts."

"How?" said he. "Amontillado? A pipe? Impossible! And in the middle of the carnival!"

"I have my doubts," I replied; "and I was silly enough to pay the full Amontillado price without consulting you in the matter. You were not to be found, and I was fearful of losing a bargain."

"Amontillado!"

"I have my doubts."

"Amontillado!"

"And I must satisfy them."

"Amontillado!"

"As you are engaged, I am on my way to Luchresi. If any one has a critical turn it is he. He will tell me —"

"Luchresi cannot tell Amontillado from Sherry."

"And yet some fools will have it that his taste is a match for your own."

"Come, let us go."

"Whither?"

"To your vaults."

"My friend, no; I will not impose upon your good nature. I perceive you have an engagement. Luchresi —"

"I have no engagement;—come."

"My friend, no. It is not the engagement, but the severe cold with which I perceive you are afflicted. The vaults are insufferably damp. They are encrusted with nitre."

"Let us go, nevertheless. The cold is merely nothing. Amontillado! You have been imposed upon. And as for Luchresi, he cannot distinguish Sherry from Amontillado."

Thus speaking, Fortunato possessed himself of my arm; and putting on a mask of black silk and drawing a *roquelaire* closely about my person, I suffered him to hurry me to my palazzo.

There were no attendants at home; they had absconded to make merry in honour of the time. I had told them that I should not return until the morning, and had given them explicit orders not to stir from the house. These orders were sufficient, I well knew, to insure their immediate disappearance, one and all, as soon as my back was turned.

I took from their sconces two flambeaux, and giving one to Fortunato, bowed him through several suites of rooms to the archway that led into the vaults. I passed down a long and winding staircase, requesting him to be cautious as he followed. We came at length to the foot of the descent, and stood together upon the damp ground of the catacombs of the Montresors.

The gait of my friend was unsteady, and the bells upon his cap jingled as he strode.

"The pipe," he said.

"It is farther on," said I; "but observe the white web-work which gleams from these cavern walls."

He turned towards me, and looked into my eyes with two filmy orbs that distilled the rheum of intoxication.

"Nitre?" he asked, at length.

"Nitre," I replied. "How long have you had that cough?"

"Ugh! ugh! ugh!—ugh! ugh! ugh!—ugh! ugh! ugh!—ugh! ugh! ugh!—ugh! ugh! ugh!"

My poor friend found it impossible to reply for many minutes.

"It is nothing," he said, at last.

"Come," I said, with decision, "we will go back; your health is precious. You are rich, respected, admired, beloved; you are happy, as once I was. You are a man to be missed. For me it is no matter. We will go back; you will be ill, and I cannot be responsible. Besides, there is Luchresi —"

"Enough," he said; "the cough is a mere nothing; it will not kill me. I shall not die of a cough."

"True—true," I replied; "and, indeed, I had no intention of alarming you unnecessarily—but you should use all proper caution. A draught of this Medoc will defend us from the damps."

Here I knocked off the neck of a bottle which I drew from a long row of its fellows that lay upon the mould.

"Drink," I said, presenting him the wine.

He raised it to his lips with a leer. He paused and nodded to me familiarly, while his bells jingled.

"I drink," he said, "to the buried that repose around us."

"And I to your long life."

He again took my arm, and we proceeded.

"These vaults," he said, "are extensive."

"The Montresors," I replied, "were a great and numerous family."

"I forget your arms."

"A huge human foot d'or, in a field azure; the foot crushes a serpent rampant whose fangs are imbedded in the heel."

"And the motto?"

"Nemo me impune lacessit."

"Good!" he said.

The wine sparkled in his eyes and the bells jingled. My own fancy grew warm with the Medoc. We had passed through long walls of piled skeletons, with casks and puncheons intermingling, into the inmost recesses of the catacombs. I paused again, and this time I made bold to seize Fortunato by an arm above the elbow.

"The nitre!" I said; "see, it increases. It hangs like moss upon the vaults. We are below the river's bed. The drops of moisture trickle among the bones. Come, we will go back ere it is too late. Your cough—"

"It is nothing," he said; "let us go on. But first, another draught of the Medoc."

I broke and reached him a flagon of De Grâve. He emptied it at a breath. His eyes flashed with a fierce light. He laughed and threw the bottle upwards with a gesticulation I did not understand.

I looked at him in surprise. He repeated the movement—a grotesque one.

"You do not comprehend?" he said.

"Not I," I replied.

"Then you are not of the brotherhood."

"How?"

"You are not of the masons."

"Yes, yes," I said, "yes, yes."

"You? Impossible! A mason?"

"A mason," I replied.

"A sign," he said, "a sign."

"It is this," I answered, producing from beneath the folds of my *roquelaire* a trowel.

"You jest," he exclaimed, recoiling a few paces. "But let us proceed to the Amontillado."

"Be it so," I said, replacing the tool beneath the cloak and again offering him my arm. He leaned upon it heavily. We continued our route in search of the Amontillado. We passed through a range of low arches, descended, passed on, and descending again, arrived at a deep crypt, in which the foulness of the air caused our flambeaux rather to glow than flame.

At the most remote end of the crypt there appeared another less spacious. Its walls had been lined with human remains, piled to the vault overhead, in the fashion of the great catacombs of Paris. Three sides of this interior crypt were still ornamented in this manner. From the fourth side the bones had been thrown down, and lay promiscuously upon the earth, forming at one point a mound of some size. Within the wall thus exposed by the displacing of the bones, we perceived a still interior crypt or recess, in depth about four feet, in width three, in height six or seven. It seemed to have been constructed for no especial use within itself, but formed merely the interval between two of the colossal supports of the roof of the catacombs, and was backed by one of their circumscribing walls of solid granite.

It was in vain that Fortunato, uplifting his dull torch, endeavoured to pry into the depth of the recess. Its termination the feeble light did not enable us to see.

"Proceed," I said; "herein is the Amontillado. As for Luchresi—"

"He is an ignoramus," interrupted my friend, as he stepped unsteadily forward, while I followed immediately at his heels. In an instant he had reached the extremity of the niche, and finding his progress arrested by the rock, stood stupidly bewildered. A moment more and I had fettered him to the granite. In its surface were two iron staples, distant from each other about two feet, horizontally. From one of these depended a short chain, from the other a padlock. Throwing the links about his waist, it was but the work of a few seconds to secure it. He was too much astounded to resist. Withdrawing the key I stepped back from the recess.

"Pass your hand," I said, "over the wall; you cannot help feeling the nitre. Indeed, it is *very* damp. Once more let me *implore* you to return. No? Then I must positively leave you. But I must first render you all the little attentions in my power."

"The Amontillado!" ejaculated my friend, not yet recovered from his astonishment.

"True," I replied; "the Amontillado."

As I said these words I busied myself among the pile of bones of which I have before spoken. Throwing them aside, I soon uncovered a quantity of building stone and mortar. With these materials and with the aid of my trowel, I began vigorously to wall up the entrance of the niche.

I had scarcely laid the first tier of the masonry when I discovered that the intoxication of Fortunato had in a great measure worn off. The earliest indication I had of this was a low moaning cry from the depth of the recess. It was *not* the cry of a drunken man. There was then a long and obstinate silence. I laid the second tier, and the third, and the fourth; and then I heard the furious vibrations of the chain. The noise lasted for several minutes, during which, that I might hearken to it with the more satisfaction, I ceased my labours and sat down upon the bones. When at last the clanking subsided, I resumed the trowel, and finished without interruption the fifth, the sixth, and the seventh tier. The wall was now nearly upon a level with my breast. I again paused, and holding the flambeaux over the mason-work, threw a few feeble rays upon the figure within. A succession of loud and shrill screams, bursting suddenly from the throat of the chained form, seemed to thrust me violently back. For a brief moment I hesitated, I trembled. Unsheathing my rapier, I began to grope with it about the recess; but the thought of an instant reassured me. I placed my hand upon the solid fabric of the catacombs, and felt satisfied. I reapproached the wall; I replied to the yells of him who clamoured. I re-echoed, I aided, I surpassed them in volume and in strength. I did this, and the clamourer grew still.

It was now midnight, and my task was drawing to a close. I had completed the eighth, the ninth and the eleventh; there remained but a single stone to be fitted and plastered in. I struggled with its weight; I placed it partially in its destined position. But now there came from out the niche a low laugh that erected the hairs upon my head. It was succeeded by a sad voice, which I had difficulty in recognizing as that of the noble Fortunato. The voice said—

"Ha! ha! ha!—he! he! he!—a very good joke, indeed—an excellent jest. We will have many a rich laugh about it at the palazzo—he! he! he!—over our wine—he! he! he!"

"The Amontillado!" I said.

"He! he! he!—he! he! he!—yes, the Amontillado. But is it not getting late? Will not they be awaiting us at the palazzo, the Lady Fortunato and the rest? Let us be gone."

"Yes," I said, "let us be gone."

"For the love of God, Montresor!"

"Yes," I said, "for the love of God!"

But to these words I hearkened in vain for a reply. I grew impatient. I called aloud—

"Fortunato!"

No answer. I called again—

"Fortunato!"

No answer still. I thrust a torch through the remaining aperture and let it fall within. There came forth in return only a jingling of the bells. My heart grew sick; it was the dampness of the catacombs that made it so. I hastened to make an end of my labour. I forced the last stone into its position; I plastered it up. Against the new masonry I re-erected the old rampart of bones. For the half of a century no mortal has disturbed them. *In pace requiescat!*

Glossary   "The Cask of Amontillado"

absconded   ran away secretly and quickly
accosted   greeted first, before being greeted

afflicted	suffering
Amontillado	a pale, relatively dry sherry
aperture	opening, hole, gap
avenger	person who gets revenge for a wrong
azure	sky blue color
be avenged	to get revenge for a wrong; to inflict deserved punishment
bed	bottom of river
borne	put up with, tolerated, endured
Carnival	a time of festivity, feasting, merrymaking
cask	a barrel of any size, especially for liquids
catacombs	series of vaults in an underground burial place
circumscribing	encircling, confining, limiting
clamoured	cried out noisily
colossal	huge, gigantic, enormous
conical	shaped like a cone
connoisseurship	expert knowledge and discrimination in matters of taste
crypt	underground vault serving as a burial place
d'or	of gold
distilled	dripped, trickled
encrusted	covered with a crust
engaged	occupied, busy
explicit	clearly stated, leaving nothing implied; definite
fangs	long, grooved teeth
feeble	weak, without force or effectiveness
fettered	chained, shackled, bound
flagon	container for liquids
flambeaux	lighted torches
gait	way of walking
gave utterance to	expressed by voice
gemmary	precious stones used in jewelry
grope	to feel one's way; to search about blindly or hesitantly
grotesque	bizarre, strange, ridiculous, absurd
hearken	listen carefully
ignoramus	ignorant and stupid person
immolation	sacrifice; killing as a sacrifice
impose	to force oneself on another without right or invitation
imposture	fraud, deception
impunity	exemption from punishment, penalty, or harm
in pace requiescat	rest in peace (Latin)
in vain	useless, futile
intoxication	drunkenness
jest	to joke, jeer, mock
leer	sly, sidelong look showing malicious triumph
masonry	brickwork or stonework
masons	international secret society based on brotherliness, charity, and aid

Medoc	red Bordeaux wine made in Medoc region in France
mortal	human being, person
motley	a garment of various colors
motto	phrase or sentence expressing goals or ideals of a family
nemo me impune lacessit	no one wounds me without punishment (Latin)
niche	a recess or hollow in a wall
nitre	potassium nitrate; sodium nitrate
orbs	eyes
padlock	removable lock with a link to be passed through a staple
palazzo	palace or palatial building
pipe	large cask for wine, having a capacity of 126 gallons
precluded	made impossible, prevented
promiscuously	without plan or purpose; casually
pry	to look closely and curiously
puncheons	large casks of varying capacities for beer, wine
quack	person who pretends to have knowledge he or she does not have
rampart	defense against attack
rapier	light, sharp-pointed sword
redresser	person who remedies a wrong or sees that justice is done
repose	to rest in death
retribution	punishment for evil done
rheum	watery discharge from eyes
roquelaire	heavy cloak, usually knee-length and fur-trimmed
sconces	brackets attached to wall for holding candles
serpent	snake, especially a large, poisonous one
skeletons	bony frameworks of human beings remaining after death
staples	u-shaped metal pieces, driven into a surface to keep a hook
suffered	allowed, permitted
surmounted	topped
tier	row, layer
trowel	tool with a thin, flat, pointed blade for applying mortar
unredressed	not set right, not remedied
unsheathing	drawing or removing (a sword) from a sheath
vaults	cellar rooms used for storage, as of wine; a burial chamber
ventured	undertook the risk of
virtuoso	having a general or broad interest in the arts and sciences
whither	where
wringing	clasping a person's hand forcefully in greeting

Discussion

1. Summarize the plot of "The Cask of Amontillado." What is the central conflict?
2. In what ways are Fortunato and Montresor portrayed realistically?
3. Describe the dominant mood of the story. How did this story affect you?
4. Why is the story titled "The Cask of Amontillado"? Does the story justify this title? What other titles could be given to this story?

5. Were you surprised by the conclusion? What is your response to this ending? Can you suggest an alternative that would be as effective?

6. Why do people enjoy reading tales of horror and terror? Do you like reading horror stories?

Style and Language

1. Choose the sentence that best describes Poe's style:
   a. Poe's style can be described as a mixture of psychological realism and romanticism.
   b. Poe's style can be described as a mixture of humorous satire and idealism.

2. Which sentence best describes the tone in this story?
   a. The tone of "The Cask of Amontillado" is matter-of-fact and calm.
   b. The tone of "The Cask of Amontillado" is dramatic and angry.
   How does Poe create this tone, and how does it contrast with the action of the plot?

3. The story is told from the point of view of
   a. Fortunato.
   b. Montresor.
   c. Luchresi.
   d. the omniscient author.
   What is the effect of using this point of view?

4. Irony is a difference between what is said and what is meant. Identify Poe's uses of irony throughout the story, and explain the effects he achieves with irony.

5. Poe's use of language is characterized by
   a. poetic imagery.
   b. religious symbolism.
   c. realistic dialogue.
   d. detailed description.
   Give quotations from the text that are examples of this language.

6. What is the setting for the story? Underline the words in the story that describe the setting.

7. Foreshadowing is a literary technique in which the author gives clues about what will happen later. Identify the foreshadowing in this story, and explain how it creates suspense.

Writing Assignments

1. Write an essay in which you explain your response to this story of revenge. Why do you like / dislike this tale? Develop your essay according to cause-effect method of organization.

2. Poe's story is full of terror. Describe and analyze the methods Poe uses to develop the terrifying atmosphere. You may use the following thesis: The terrifying atmosphere in "The Cask of Amontillado" results from the frightening setting, the suspenseful plot, and the first-person narration by Montresor. Choose specific quotations from the story to support the thesis and major points.

3. Rewrite the last paragraphs of the conclusion to "The Cask of Amontillado." In your conclusion, allow Fortunato to escape from Montresor.

Group Work

Although Poe is known primarily for his short stories, he also wrote beautiful poetry. Working with a partner or in a small group, read and discuss Poe's poem "Alone." What is the theme of the poem? How does the theme relate to the writer of "The Cask of Amontillado"? What kind of person was Poe? Write a one-paragraph interpretation of this poem.

Alone   1829
Edgar Allan Poe

From childhood's hour I have not been
As others were—I have not seen
As others saw—I could not bring
My passions from a common spring—
From the same source I have not taken
My sorrow—I could not awaken
My heart to joy at the same tone—
And all I loved—*I* loved alone—
Then—in my childhood, in the dawn
Of a most stormy life—was drawn
From every depth of good and ill
The mystery which binds me still—
From the torrent, or the fountain—
From the red cliff of the mountain—
From the sun that round me rolled
In its autumn tint of gold—
From the lightning in the sky
As it pass'd me flying by—
From the thunder and the storm—
And the cloud that took the form
When the rest of Heaven was blue
Of a demon in my view.

Kate Chopin   "Madame Célestin's Divorce"

"In creating *The Awakening* and her short stories, Chopin unflinchingly depicted her vision of the paradoxes, complexities, and conflicts of human experience, treating them as no one else had in American fiction. Critics and readers were not yet ready to confront her challenging views."
Barbara Solomon, introduction to *The Awakening and Selected Stories of Kate Chopin*, 1976

"There is a rich emotional content that enlarges these stories, that elevates and ennobles them."
Roxana Robinson, introduction to *A Matter of Prejudice and Other Stories by Kate Chopin*, 1992

Kate O'Flaherty Chopin (1851–1904) was born in St. Louis, Missouri, to a wealthy Irish-American father and an aristocratic Creole mother. (Creoles were descendants of the original French settlers of Louisiana.) She married a Creole and moved to New Orleans. After his death in 1882, she supported herself and her six children by writing short stories for popular magazines. These stories established her reputation as a local-color writer who described the Cajun and Creole societies in Louisiana.

Chopin was an early feminist whose themes center on the conflict between unconventional heroines and the traditional, male-dominated society of the later nineteenth century. Her realistic style, complex characters, and woman-centered plots show the influence of the European realists such as de Maupassant, Tolstoy (*Anna Karenina*), Flaubert (*Madame Bovary*), and Jane Austen (*Emma*).

The Awakening (1899), Chopin's masterpiece, is a novel about a married woman who struggles to assert her right to freedom and independence by having a passionate love affair with a young man. Considered shocking in its time because of its honest portrayal of a woman's sexuality, it was banned from libraries and bookstores. However, *The Awakening* has received much recognition in recent years.

Today, Kate Chopin has been rediscovered as one of America's best woman authors. Her other works include her first novel, *At Fault,* which is on the subject of divorce, and her short story collections *Bayou Folk* and *A Night in Acadie*.

"Madame Célestin's Divorce" is set in a small town in Louisiana where Chopin once lived. It centers on the relationship between a Creole married woman and her friend, lawyer Paxton, and contains authentic Creole dialect as well as French words, as the Creoles spoke both French and English.

Preview

Skimming: Skim the reading to gain a general impression.
1. Read the title and first sentence of the story.
2. Skim the story to get an idea of its form and length.

Questioning: Answer the following questions and discuss your answers.
1. Do you know anyone who has gotten a divorce?
2. Is the divorce rate high in your country? How easy is it to get a divorce?

Scanning: Scan to answer the following questions to get an idea of the content and style.
1. What had Madame Célestin talked to lawyer Paxton about?
2. How did Madame Célestin's family and friends feel about the divorce?

Madame Célestin's Divorce   1893
Kate Chopin

Madame Célestin always wore a neat and snugly fitting calico wrapper when she went out in the morning to sweep her small gallery. Lawyer Paxton thought she looked very pretty in the gray one that was made with a graceful Watteau fold at the back: and with which she invariably wore a bow of pink ribbon at the throat. She was always sweeping her gallery when lawyer Paxton passed by in the morning on his way to his office in St. Denis Street.

Sometimes he stopped and leaned over the fence to say good-morning at his ease; to criticise or admire her rosebushes; or, when he had time enough, to hear what she had to say. Madame Célestin usually had a good deal to say. She would gather up the train of her calico wrapper in one hand, and balancing the broom gracefully in the other, would go tripping down to where the lawyer leaned, as comfortably as he could, over her picket fence.

Of course, she had talked to him of her troubles. Every one knew Madame Célestin's troubles.

"Really, madame," he told her once, in his deliberate, calculating, lawyer-tone, "it's more than human nature—woman's nature—should be called upon to endure. Here you are, working your fingers off"—she glanced down at two rosy finger-tips that showed through the rents in her baggy doeskin gloves—"taking in sewing; giving music lessons; doing God knows what in the way of manual labor to support yourself and those two little ones"—Madame Célestin's pretty face beamed with satisfaction at this enumeration of her trials.

"You right, Judge. Not a picayune, not one, not one, have I lay my eyes on in the pas' fo' months that I can say Célestin give it to me or sen' it to me."

"The scoundrel!" muttered lawyer Paxton in his beard.

"An' *pourtant,*" she resumed, "they say he's making money down roun' Alexandria w'en he wants to work."

"I dare say you haven't seen him for months?" suggested the lawyer.

"It's good six month' since I see a sight of Célestin," she admitted.

"That's it, that's what I say; he has practically deserted you; fails to support you. It wouldn't surprise me a bit to learn that he has ill treated you."

"Well, you know, Judge," with an evasive cough, " a man that drinks—w'at can you expec'? An' if you would know the promises he has made me! Ah, If I had as many dolla' as I had promises from Célestin, I wouldn' have to work, *je vous garantis.*"

"And in my opinion, Madame, you would be a foolish woman to endure it longer, when the divorce court is there to offer you redress."

"You spoke about that befo', Judge: I'm goin' think about that divo'ce. I believe you right."

Madame Célestin thought about the divorce and talked about it, too; and lawyer Paxton grew deeply interested in the theme.

"You know, about that divo'ce, Judge," Madame Célestin was waiting for him that morning, "I been talking to my family an' my frien's, an' it's me that tells you, they all plumb agains' that divo'ce."

"Certainly, to be sure; that's to be expected, Madame, in this community of Creoles. I warned you that you would meet with opposition, and would have to face it and brave it."

"Oh, don't fear, I'm going to face it! Maman says it's a disgrace like it's neva been in the family. But it's good for Maman to talk, her. W'at trouble she ever had? She says I mus' go by all means consult with Pére Duchéron—it's my confessor, you undastan'—Well, I'll go, Judge, to please Maman. But all the confessor' in the worl' ent goin' make me put up with that conduc' of Célestin any longa."

A day or two later, she was there waiting for him again. "You know, Judge, about that divo'ce."

"Yes, yes," responded the lawyer, well pleased to trace a new determination in her brown eyes and in the curves of her pretty mouth. "I suppose you saw Pére Duchéron and had to brave it out with him, too."

"Oh, fo' that, a perfec' sermon, I assho you. A talk of giving scandal an' bad example that I thought would neva en'! He says, fo' him, he wash' his hands; I mus' go see the bishop."

"You won't let the bishop dissuade you, I trust," stammered the lawyer more anxiously than he could well understand.

"You don't know me yet, Judge," laughed Madame Célestin with a turn of the head and a flirt of the broom which indicated that the interview was at an end.

"Well, Madame Célestin! And the bishop!" Lawyer Paxton was standing there holding to a couple of the shaky pickets. She had not seen him. "Oh, it's you, Judge?" and she hastened towards him with an *empressement* that could not but have been flattering.

"Yes, I saw Monseigneur," she began. The lawyer had already gathered from her expressive countenance that she had not wavered in her determination. "Ah, he's a eloquent man. It's not a mo' eloquent man in Natchitoches parish. I was fo'ced to cry, the way he talked to me about my troubles; how he undastan's them, an' feels for me. It would move even you, Judge, to hear how he talk' about that step I want to take; its danga, its temptation. How it is the duty of a Catholic to stan' everything till the las' extreme. An' that life of retirement an' self-denial I would have to lead,—he tole me all that."

"But he hasn't turned you from your resolve, I see," laughed the lawyer complacently.

"For that, no," she returned emphatically. "The bishop don't know w'at it is to be married to a man like Célestin, an' have to endu' that conduc' like I have to endu' it. The Pope himse'f can't make me stan' that any longer, if you say I got the right in the law to sen' Célestin sailing."

A noticeable change had come over lawyer Paxton. He discarded his work-day coat and began to wear his Sunday one to the office. He grew solicitous as to the shine of his boots, his collar, and the set of his tie. He brushed and trimmed his whiskers with a care that had not before been apparent. Then he fell into a stupid habit of dreaming as he walked the streets of the old town. It would be very good to take unto himself a wife, he dreamed. And he could dream of no other than pretty Madame Célestin filling that sweet and sacred office as she filled his thoughts, now. Old Natchitoches would not hold them comfortably, perhaps; but the world was surely wide enough to live in, outside of Natchitoches town.

His heart beat in a strangely irregular manner as he neared Madame Célestin's house one morning, and discovered her behind the rosebushes, as usual plying her broom. She had finished the gallery and steps and was sweeping the little brick walk along the edge of the violet border.

"Good-morning, Madame Célestin."

"Ah, it's you, Judge? Good-morning." He waited. She seemed to be doing the same. Then she ventured, with some hesitancy, "You know, Judge, about that divo'ce. I been thinking,—I reckon you betta neva mine about that divo'ce." She was making deep rings in the palm of her gloved hand with the end of the broomhandle, and looking at them critically. Her face seemed to the lawyer to be unusually rosy; but maybe it was only the reflection of the pink bow at the throat. "Yes, I reckon you need n' mine. You see, Judge, Célestin came home las' night. An' he's promise me on his word an' honor he's going to turn ova a new leaf."

Glossary   "Madame Célestin's Divorce"

agains'	against
assho	to assure
befo'	before
betta	better
brave	to face with courage; to defy
calculating	shrewd or cunning; scheming
calico	printed cotton fabric
complacently	with satisfaction, contentment
conduc'	conduct, behavior

confessor	a priest authorized to hear confession
countenance	face; the look on a person's face
Creoles	descendants of early French or Spanish settlers of Louisiana
danga'	danger
discarded	threw away, got rid of
doeskin	leather made from skin of female deer
dolla	dollars
empressement	eagerness (French)
endu'	to endure
ent	ain't (are not)
evasive	not straightforward, tricky
fo'	four; for
gallery	veranda or porch
je vous garantis	I assure you (French)
las'	last
longa'	longer
neva mine	never mind
neva	never
office	function, position
opposition	resistance, hostility
pas'	past
perfec'	perfect
picayune	coin of small value; former Spanish half-real of Louisiana
pickets	pointed slates used in a fence
plumb	entirely, absolutely
pourtant	yet (French)
reckon	to think
redress	to set right; to remedy a wrong
rents	holes or torn places in cloth
scoundrel	an immoral or wicked person
sen' sailing	send away
sen'	sent
snuggly	tightly, neatly
solicitous	showing care, attention, concern
stammered	spoke with rapid repetition of syllables from excitement
stan'	to stand, endure, accept
tole	told
tripping	moving lightly and quickly
turn ova a new leaf	to turn over a new leaf; to change one's behavior
undastan'	to understand
ventured	expressed, offered
w'at	what
w'en	when
Watteau	named for the French painter Jean Antoine Watteau (1684–1721)
wavered	showed doubt or indecision
wrapper	dressing gown

Discussion

1. Explain the plot of "Madame Célestin's Divorce." What is the central conflict?
2. Describe the dominant mood of the story. How did this story affect you?
3. What are lawyer Paxton's feelings for Madame Célestin?
4. Why is Madame Célestin considering a divorce from her husband?
5. What causes Madame Célestin to change her mind? Is her decision a good one?
6. What is ironic about the story's ending? Can you suggest an alternative ending?
7. What do you predict will happen to the Célestins in the future?

Style and Language

1. Complete the sentence with the words below: Chopin's writing style in "Madame Célestin's

    Divorce" can be described as _____, _____, and _____.

romantic	vague	understated
realistic	precise	dramatic

2. Choose the sentence that best describes the tone in this story:
    a. The tone of "Madame Célestin's Divorce" can be characterized as gently ironic.
    b. The tone of "Madame Célestin's Divorce" can be characterized as harshly satirical.

3. The story is told from the point of view of
    a. Célestin.
    b. Madame Célestin.
    c. Lawyer Paxton.
    d. the omniscient author.

4. Chopin's language contains
    a. Creole dialect.
    b. figures of speech.
    c. realistic descriptions.
    d. philosophical arguments.
    Give quotations from the text that are specific examples of this language.

5. Explain the meaning of Madame's Célestin's statement about her husband: "An' he's promise me on his word an' honor he's going to turn ova a new leaf."

Writing Assignments

1. In "Madame Célestin's Divorce," Chopin depicts a nineteenth-century woman's conflict about whether to get a divorce from her husband. Write an essay in which you contrast Chopin's view of love and marriage as presented in this story with American poet Anne Bradstreet's view as she presents it in "To My Dear and Loving Husband," published in 1678. (Anne Bradstreet [1612–72], a Puritan, wrote the first collection of poems published in America.)

To My Dear and Loving Husband   1678
Anne Bradstreet

If ever two were one, then surely we.
If ever man were loved by wife, then thee;
If ever wife was happy in a man,
Compare with me ye women if you can.
I prize thy love more than whole mines of gold,
Or all the riches that the East doth hold.
My love is such that rivers cannot quench,
Nor ought but love from thee give recompense.
Thy love is such I can no way repay,
The heavens reward thee manifold I pray.
Then while we live, in love let's so persevere,
That when we live no more, we may live ever.

2. In "Madame Célestin's Divorce," Chopin realistically portrays a conflict within the central character. Write an essay analyzing the conflicting emotions Madame Célestin experiences and her resolution of these feelings. Include your opinion about her decision.

3. Irony involves the use of language and situations that are the opposite of what might be expected. In "Madame Célestin's Divorce," irony is one of the most important elements in the story. Identify and explain Chopin's uses of irony.

Group Work

Working with a partner or in a small group, read the following quotations and proverbs about marriage. Then discuss their meanings and whether they apply to "Madame Célestin's Divorce." Write a brief summary of your discussion.

"I don't think matrimony is consistent with the liberty of the subject."
George Farquhar, *The Twin Rivals,* 1702

"Women have become so highly educated that nothing should surprise them except happy marriages."
Oscar Wilde, *A Woman of No Importance*, 1893

"A marriage is likely to be what is called happy if neither party ever expected to get much happiness out of it."
Bertrand Russell, *Marriage and Morals*, 1929

"It is better for a woman to marry a man who loves her than a man she loves."
Arab proverb

"Marriage is a school in which the pupil learns too late."
German proverb

Marriage is the tomb of love.
Russian proverb

Marriage is the only evil that men pray for.
Greek proverb

Stephen Crane   "A Mystery of Heroism"

"A man is born into the world with his own pair of eyes, and he is not at all responsible for his vision—he is merely responsible for his quality of personal honesty. To keep close to this personal honesty is my supreme ambition."
Stephen Crane, *Letter*

"Yet this fellow Crane has written short stories equal to some of Maupassant's."
Willa Cather, *Pittsburg Leader,* June 3, 1899

"James and Crane were the only nineteenth century realists much concerned with the person of the observer, and even their impressionism did not hinder them from admitting the existence of the external, objective, sensuously-perceptible world, and defining realism, essentially, as the literary method which proposed to present it without distortion."
Wallace Stegner, introduction to *Selected American Prose: The Realistic Movement,* 1962

"I think no one will deny that compared with Hawthorne and Melville, or even with Henry James and Mark Twain, Stephen Crane is a *modern* writer—almost, one might say, a twentieth-century writer. His frankness, his bohemianism, his naturalism, his entire alienation from everything genteel, aristocratic, or puritan testify to his modernity."
Richard Chase, introduction to *The Red Badge of Courage and Other Writings by Stephen Crane,* 1960

Stephen Crane (1871–1900) was born in New Jersey. During his short life, he was a newspaper reporter, a war correspondent during the Spanish-American War, and an author. Most of Crane's major works were written in the 1890s and are examples of the "naturalist" school of writing, whose members included Jack London, Frank Norris, and Theodore Dreiser. The naturalists were writers of social protest who stressed Darwin's theory of the survival of the fittest in a violent and unjust universe. Their vision of life is pessimistic, ironic, and amoral, and centers on the power of environment and heredity as the determinants of people's lives, rather than free choice.

Crane's writing mixes realism with fantasy to describe the fear and bravery that cause men to act violently. Many of his stories explore the mysticism of death, often in a war setting. His themes concern the difference between reality and illusion, conventional morality and actual behavior, and the irrational world of battle. To Crane, the universe is a mystery, and life is ironic and absurd. With his emphasis on the visual, Crane's naturalistic prose style is impressionistic and poetic. Symbolism and imagery are used to convey his psychological analysis of the dark forces that motivate human beings. In both style and content, Crane's fiction marks the beginning of the modern age of American literature.

Crane's major works include many short stories, such as "The Blue Hotel," "The Bride Comes to Yellow Sky," and "The Open Boat." His best-known novels are *Maggie: A Girl of the Streets* (1893) and *The Red Badge of Courage* (1895), which is the story of an inexperienced soldier fighting in the American Civil War of 1861–65. His short story "A Mystery of Heroism" also describes an episode in the life of a young Civil War soldier.

Preview

Skimming: Skim the reading to gain a general impression.
1. Read the title and first sentence of the story.
2. Skim the story to get an idea of its form and length.

Questioning: Answer the following questions and discuss your answers in class.
1. What does the word *heroism* mean to you? Who is an example of a hero?
2. Have you served in the military? Do you want to?

Scanning: Scan to answer the following questions to get an idea of the content and style.
1. What did Fred Collins wish he had?
2. To whom did Collins give a drink of water?

A Mystery of Heroism   1898
Stephen Crane

The dark uniforms of the men were so coated with dust from the incessant wrestling of the two armies that the regiment almost seemed a part of the clay bank which shielded them from the shells. On the top of the hill a battery was arguing in tremendous roars with some other guns, and to the eye of the infantry the artillerymen, the guns, the caissons, the horses, were distinctly outlined upon the blue sky. When a piece was fired, a red streak as round as a log flashed low in the heavens, like a monstrous bolt of lightning. The men of the battery wore white duck trousers, which somehow emphasized their legs; and when they ran and crowded in little groups at the bidding of the shouting officers, it was more impressive than usual to the infantry.

Fred Collins, of A Company, was saying, "Thunder! I wisht I had a drink. Ain't there any water round here?" Then somebody yelled: "There goes th' bugler!"

As the eyes of half the regiment swept in one machinelike movement, there was an instant's picture of a horse in a great convulsive leap of a death wound and a rider leaning back with a crooked arm and spread fingers before his face. On the ground was the crimson terror of an exploding shell, with fibres of flame that seemed like lances. A glittering bugle swung clear of the rider's back as fell headlong the horse and the man. In the air was an odor as from a conflagration.

Sometimes they of the infantry looked down at a fair little meadow which spread at their feet. Its long green grass was rippling gently in a breeze. Beyond it was the grey form of a house half torn to pieces by shells and by the busy axes of soldiers who had pursued firewood. The line of an old fence was now dimly marked by long weeds and by an occasional post. A shell had blown the well-house to fragments. Little lines of grey smoke ribboning upward from some embers indicated the place where had stood the barn.

From beyond a curtain of green woods there came the sound of some stupendous scuffle, as if two animals of the size of islands were fighting. At a distance there were occasional appearances of swift-moving men, horses, batteries, flags, and with the crashing of infantry volleys were heard, often, wild and frenzied cheers. In the midst of it all Smith and Ferguson, two privates of A Company, were engaged in a heated discussion which involved the greatest questions of the national existence.

The battery on the hill presently engaged in a frightful duel. The white legs of the gunners scampered this way and that way, and the officers redoubled their shouts. The guns, with their demeanors of stolidity and courage, were typical of something infinitely self-possessed in this clamor of death that swirled around the hill.

One of a "swing" team was suddenly smitten quivering to the ground, and his maddened brethren dragged his torn body in their struggle to escape from this turmoil and danger. A young soldier astride one of the leaders swore and fumed in his saddle and furiously jerked at the bridle. An officer screamed out an order so violently that his voice broke and ended the sentence in a falsetto shriek.

The leading company of the infantry regiment was somewhat exposed, and the colonel ordered it moved more fully under the shelter of the hill. There was the clank of steel against steel.

A lieutenant of the battery rode down and passed them; holding his right arm carefully in his left hand. And it was as if this arm was not at all a part of him, but belonged to another man. His sober and reflective charger went slowly. The officer's face was grimy and perspiring, and his uniform was tousled as if he had been in direct grapple with an enemy. He smiled grimly when the men stared at him. He turned his horse toward the meadow.

Collins, of A Company, said: "I wisht I had a drink. I bet there's water in that there ol' well yonder!"

"Yes; but how you goin' to git it?"

For the little meadow which intervened was now suffering a terrible onslaught of shells. Its green and beautiful calm had vanished utterly. Brown earth was being flung in monstrous handfuls. And there was a massacre of the young blades of grass. They were being torn, burned, obliterated. Some curious fortune of the battle had made this gentle little meadow the object of the red hate of the shells, and each one as it exploded seemed like an imprecation in the face of a maiden.

The wounded officer who was riding across this expanse said to himself: "Why, they couldn't shoot any harder if the whole army was massed here!"

A shell struck the gray ruins of the house, and as, after the roar, the shattered wall fell in fragments, there was a noise which resembled the flapping of shutters during a wild gale of winter. Indeed, the infantry paused in the shelter of the bank appeared as men standing upon a shore contemplating a madness of the sea. The angel of calamity had under its glance the battery upon the hill. Fewer white-legged men labored about the guns. A shell had smitten one of the pieces, and after the flare, the smoke, the dust, the wrath of this blow were gone, it was possible to see white legs stretched horizontally upon the ground. And at that interval to the rear where it is the business of battery horses to stand with their noses to the fight, awaiting the command to drag their guns out of the destruction, or into it, or wheresoever these incomprehensible humans demanded with whip and spur—in this line of passive and dumb spectators, whose fluttering hearts yet would not let them forget the iron laws of man's control of them—in this rank of brute-soldiers there had been relentless and hideous carnage. From the ruck of bleeding and prostrate horses, the men of the infantry could see one animal raising its stricken body with its forelegs and turning its nose with mystic and profound eloquence toward the sky.

Some comrades joked Collins about his thirst. "Well, if yeh want a drink so bad, why don't yeh go git it?"

"Well, I will in a minnet, if yeh don't shut up!"

A lieutenant of artillery floundered his horse straight down the hill with as little concern as if it were level ground. As he galloped past the colonel of the infantry, he threw up his hand in swift salute. "We've got to get out of that," he roared angrily. He was a black-bearded officer, and his eyes, which resembled beads, sparkled like those of an insane man. His jumping horse sped along the column of infantry.

The fat major, standing carelessly with his sword held horizontally behind him and with his legs far apart, looked after the receding horseman and laughed. "He wants to get back with orders pretty quick, or there'll be no batt'ry left," he observed.

The wise young captain of the second company hazarded to the lieutenant-colonel that the enemy's infantry would probably soon attack the hill, and the lieutenant-colonel snubbed him.

A private in one of the rear companies looked out over the meadow, and then turned to a companion and said, "Look there, Jim!" It was the wounded officer from the battery, who some time before had started to ride across the meadow, supporting his right arm carefully with his left hand. This man had encountered a shell, apparently, at a time when no one perceived him, and he could now be seen lying face downward with a stirruped foot stretched across the body of his dead horse. A leg of the charger extended slantingly upward, precisely as stiff as a stake. Around this motionless pair the shells still howled.

There was a quarrel in A Company. Collins was shaking his fist in the faces of some laughing comrades. "Dern yeh! I ain't afraid t' go. If yeh say much, I will go!"

"Of course, yeh will! You'll run through that there medder, won't yeh?"

Collins said, in a terrible voice: "You see now!" At this ominous threat his comrades broke into renewed jeers.

Collins gave them a dark scowl, and went to find his captain. The latter was conversing with the colonel of the regiment.

"Captain," said Collins, saluting and standing at attention— in those days all trousers bagged at the knees—"Captain, I want t' get permission to go git some water from that there well over yonder!"

The colonel and the captain swung about simultaneously and stared across the meadow. The captain laughed. "You must be pretty thirsty, Collins?"

"Yes, sir, I am."

"Well—ah," said the captain. After a moment, he asked, "Can't you wait?"

"No, sir."

The colonel was watching Collins's face. "Look here, my lad," he said, in a pious sort of voice—"Look here, my lad"—Collins was not a lad—"don't you think that's taking pretty big risks for a little drink of water?"

"I dunno" said Collins uncomfortably. Some of the resentment toward his companions, which perhaps had forced him into this affair, was beginning to fade. "I dunno wether 'tis."

The colonel and the captain contemplated him for a time.

"Well," said the captain finally.

"Well," said the colonel, "if you want to go, why, go."

Collins saluted. "Much obliged t' yeh."

As he moved away the colonel called after him. "Take some of the other boys' canteens with you, an' hurry back, now."

"Yes, sir, I will."

The colonel and the captain looked at each other then, for it had suddenly occurred that they could not for the life of them tell whether Collins wanted to go or whether he did not.

They turned to regard Collins, and as they perceived him surrounded by gesticulating comrades, the colonel said: "Well, by thunder! I guess he's going."

Collins appeared as a man dreaming. In the midst of the questions, the advice, the warnings, all the excited talk of his company mates, he maintained a curious silence.

They were very busy in preparing him for his ordeal. When they inspected him carefully, it was somewhat like the examination that grooms give a horse before a race; and they were amazed, staggered, by the whole affair. Their astonishment found vent in strange repetitions.

"Are yeh sure a-goin'?" they demanded again and again.

"Certainly I am," cried Collins at last, furiously.

He strode sullenly away from them. He was swinging five or six canteens by their cords. It seemed that his cap would not remain firmly on his head, and often he reached and pulled it down over his brow.

There was a general movement in the compact column. The long animal-like thing moved slightly. Its four hundred eyes were turned upon the figure of Collins.

"Well, sir, if that ain't th' derndest thing! I never thought Fred Collins had the blood in him for that kind of business."

"What's he goin' to do, anyhow?"

"He's goin' to that well there after water."

"We ain't dyin' of thirst, are we? That's foolishness."

"Well, somebody put him up to it, an' he's doin' it."

"Say, he must be a desperate cuss."

When Collins faced the meadow and walked away from the regiment, he was vaguely conscious that a chasm, the deep valley of all prides, was suddenly between him and his comrades. It was provisional, but the provision was that he return as a victor. He had blindly been led by quaint emotions, and laid himself under an obligation to walk squarely up to the face of death.

But he was not sure that he wished to make a retraction, even if he could do so without shame. As a matter of truth, he was sure of very little. He was mainly surprised.

It seemed to him supernaturally strange that he had allowed his mind to manœuvre his body into such a situation. He understood that it might be called dramatically great.

However, he had no full appreciation of anything, excepting that he was actually conscious of being dazed. He could feel his dulled mind groping after the form and color of this incident. He wondered why he did not feel some keen agony of fear cutting his sense like a knife. He wondered at this, because human expression had said loudly for centuries that men should feel afraid of certain things, and that all men who did not feel this fear were phenomena—heroes.

He was, then, a hero. He suffered that disappointment which we would all have if we discovered that we were ourselves capable of those deeds which we most admire in history and legend. This, then, was a hero. After all, heroes were not much.

No, it could not be true. He was not a hero. Heroes had no shames in their lives, and, as for him, he remembered borrowing fifteen dollars from a friend and promising to pay it back the next day, and then avoiding that friend for ten months. When, at home, his mother had aroused him for the early labor of his life on the farm, it had often been his fashion to be irritable, childish, diabolical; and his mother had died since he had come to the war.

He saw that, in this matter of the well, the canteens, the shells, he was an intruder in the land of fine deeds.

He was now about thirty paces from his comrades. The regiment had just turned its many faces toward him.

From the forest of terrific noises there suddenly emerged a little uneven line of men. They fired fiercely and rapidly at distant foliage on which appeared little puffs of white smoke. The spatter of skirmish firing was added to the thunder of the guns on the hill. The little line of men ran forward. A color-sergeant fell flat with his flag as if he had slipped on ice. There was hoarse cheering from this distant field.

Collins suddenly felt that two demon fingers were pressed into his ears. He could see nothing but flying arrows, flaming red. He lurched from the shock of this explosion, but he made a mad rush for the house, which he viewed as a man submerged to the neck in a boiling surf might view the shore. In the air little pieces of shell howled, and the earthquake explosions drove him insane with the menace of their roar. As he ran the canteens knocked together with a rhythmical tinkling.

As he neared the house, each detail of the scene became vivid to him. He was aware of some bricks of the vanished chimney lying on the sod. There was a door which hung by one hinge.

Rifle bullets called forth by the insistent skirmishers came from the far-off bank of foliage. They mingled with the shells and the pieces of shells until the air was torn in all directions by hootings, yells, howls. The sky was full of fiends who directed all their wild rage at his head.

When he came to the well, he flung himself face downward and peered into its darkness. There were furtive silver glintings some feet from the surface. He grabbled one of the canteens and, unfastening its cap, swung it down by the cord. The water flowed slowly in with an indolent gurgle.

And now, as he lay with his face turned away, he was suddenly smitten with the terror. It came upon his heart like the grasp of claws. All the power faded from his muscles. For an instant he was no more than a dead man.

The canteen filled with a maddening slowness, in the manner of all bottles. Presently he recovered his strength and addressed a screaming oath to it. He leaned over until it seemed as if he intended to try to push water into it with his hands. His eyes as he gazed down into the well shone like two pieces of metal, and in their expression was a great appeal and a great curse. The stupid water derided him.

There was the blaring thunder of a shell. Crimson light shone through the swift-boiling smoke, and made a pink reflection on part of the wall of the well. Collins jerked out his arm and canteen with the same motion that a man would use in withdrawing his head from a furnace.

He scrambled erect and glared and hesitated. On the ground near him lay the old well bucket, with a length of rusty chain. He lowered it swiftly into the well. The bucket struck the water and then, turning lazily over, sank. When, with hand reaching tremblingly over hand, he hauled it out, it knocked often against the walls of the well and spilled some of its contents.

In running with a filled bucket, a man can adopt but one kind of gait. So, through this terrible field over which screamed practical angels of death, Collins ran in the manner of a farmer chased out of a dairy by a bull.

His face went staring white with anticipating—anticipation of a blow that would whirl him around and down. He would fall as he had seen other men fall, the life knocked out of them so suddenly that their knees were no more quick to touch the ground than their heads. He saw the long blue line of the regiment, but his comrades were standing looking at him from the edge of an impossible star. He was aware of some deep wheelruts and hoofprints in the sod beneath his feet.

The artillery officer who had fallen in this meadow had been making groans in the teeth of the tempest of sound. These futile cries, wrenched from him by his agony, were heard only by shells, bullets. When wild-eyed Collins came running, this officer raised himself. His face contorted and blanched from pain, he was about to utter some great beseeching cry. But suddenly his face straightened, and he called: "Say, young man, give me a drink of water, will you?"

Collins had no room amid his emotions for surprise. He was mad from the threats of destruction.

"I can't!" he screamed, and in his reply was a full description of his quaking apprehension. His cap was gone and his hair was riotous. His clothes made it appear that he had been dragged over the ground by the heels. He ran on.

The officer's head sank down, and one elbow crooked. His foot in its brass-bound stirrup still stretched over the body of his horse, and the other leg was under the steed.

But Collins turned. He came dashing back. His face had now turned grey, and in his eyes was all terror. "Here it is! here it is!"

The officer was as a man gone in drink. His arm bent like a twig. His head drooped as if his neck were of willow. He was sinking to the ground, to lie face downward.

Collins grabbed him by the shoulder. "Here it is. Here's your drink. Turn over. Turn over, man, for God's sake!"

With Collins hauling at his shoulder, the officer twisted his body and fell with his face turned toward that region where lived the unspeakable noises of the swirling missiles. There was the faintest shadow of a smile on his lips as he looked at Collins. He gave a sigh, a little primitive breath like that from a child.

Collins tried to hold the bucket steadily, but his shaking hands caused the water to splash all over the face of the dying man. Then he jerked it away and ran on.

The regiment gave him a welcoming roar. The grimed faces were wrinkled in laughter.

His captain waved the bucket away. "Give it to the men!"

The two genial, skylarking young lieutenants were the first to gain possession of it. They played over it in their fashion.

When one tried to drink, the other teasingly knocked his elbow. "Don't Billie! You'll make me spill it," said the one. The other laughed.

Suddenly there was an oath, the thud of wood on the ground, and a swift murmur of astonishment among the ranks. The two lieutenants glared at each other. The bucket lay on the ground empty.

Glossary	"A Mystery of Heroism"
apprehension	dread, anxious feeling of foreboding
artillerymen	soldiers who are in charge of large, mounted guns
astride	with a leg on either side of a horse
battery	basic unit of artillery; an infantry company
beseeching	entreating, begging
blanched	whitened, turned pale
brethren	brothers; fellow soldiers
bugler	person in army who blows a bugle for military calls
caissons	two-wheeled wagons for transporting ammunition
calamity	disaster, extreme misfortune
canteens	small metal flasks for carrying drinking water
carnage	bloody slaughter, massacre, bloodshed
chasm	gap, wide divergence of feelings
clamor	loud, sustained noise
coated	covered
conflagration	big, destructive fire

contorted	deformed, violently twisted out of its usual form
convulsive	having a violent, involuntary contracting of muscles
cuss	person regarded as strange or annoying
dazed	stunned, bewildered, as by a shock
demeanors	outward appearances and behavior
demon	devilish, evil
derided	made fun of, ridiculed
dern	darn; a euphemism for damn (the curse)
derndest	darndest; a euphemism for damndest (the curse)
diabolical	very wicked, devilish
duel	fight between two groups of soldiers
dunno	don't know
embers	smoldering remains of a fire
falsetto	higher register than the natural voice
fiends	devils, evil spirits
floundered	plunged about in a stumbling manner
foliage	mass of leaves of trees
frenzied	showing a frantic, wild outburst of feeling or action
futile	useless, hopeless
gait	way of moving on foot
gale	strong wind
genial	cheerful, friendly, amiable
gesticulating	making gestures with the hands or arms
grabbled	seized
grapple	hand-to-hand combat, fight
grimed	very dirty or grimy
groans	deep sounds expressing pain or distress
grooms	men whose work is tending horses
gurgle	bubbling or rippling sound like water flowing
hazarded	ventured a guess
headlong	with the head first; with uncontrolled speed
heated	exciting, emotional
howled	made a long, loud wailing cry
imprecation	curse
incessant	constant, unending, continual
incomprehensible	cannot be understood
indolent	lazy
jeers	sarcastic, rude comments
lances	weapons with sharp metal spearheads
lurched	rolled or swayed suddenly forward or sideways
mad	insane, mentally ill
manoeuvre	to move, lead, put by some scheme
massacre	slaughter, merciless killing
medder	meadow; a piece of level grassland
oath	swear word, curse used to express anger
obliterated	destroyed

onslaught	violent attack
ordeal	difficult, dangerous experience; severe trial
paces	units of length, equal to the length of a step
perspiring	sweating
phenomena	extremely unusual or extraordinary persons or occurrences
pious	having devotion and loyalty to religion and family
prostrate	lying flat; fallen to the ground
provision	requirement, condition
provisional	having the nature of a temporary provision
quaint	unusual, strange, old-fashioned
quaking	shaking from fear
regiment	military unit consisting of two or more battalions
retraction	withdrawal of statement or promise
scuffle	rough, confused fight or struggle
shell	explosive artillery projectile containing explosives
skirmish	brief fight between small groups
skylarking	playing boisterously
smitten	struck with a hard blow
snubbed	treated with scorn; ignored
staggered	affected strongly with astonishment, horror
steed	horse
stolidity	lack of emotion
stupendous	astonishingly large
supernaturally	exceeding normal bounds; extremely
thud	dull sound of a heavy object dropping to the ground
tousled	disordered, disheveled
twig	small, slender branch of a tree
vent	to release expression
volleys	bullets fired at the same time
willow	wood of willow trees, having flexible twigs
wrestling	struggling in opposition, fighting
yeh	you
yonder	over there, at that place

Discussion

1. How fully are the feelings and motivations of Crane's characters revealed?
2. Why does Collins decide to go get the water?
3. Why does Collins come back to give the dying officer a drink of water?
4. Do the two lieutenants drop the bucket of water accidentally or on purpose?
5. Do you think Collins wants to be a hero? How does he react to his own courage?
6. Is Collins a hero? Would you do what he did? Why or why not?
7. What is the meaning of the conclusion? In what way is it ironic?
8. Do you believe that human beings have free will, or is a person's fate predetermined?

Style and Language

1. Circle the words which best describe Crane's style.

   complex   academic   realistic   modern
   simple   impressionistic   romantic   old-fashioned

2. Complete this sentence with the words below: The tone of this story is

   _____, _____, and _____.

   humorous   balanced   objective
   ironic   disapproving   subjective

   What specific words or phrases create this tone?

3. Crane's language contains
   a. pictorial descriptions.
   b. abstract philosophy.
   c. realistic dialogue.
   d. moral judgments.
   Give specific examples of this language.

4. The story is told from the point of view of
   a. the Colonel.
   b. the Captain.
   c. Fred Collins.
   d. the omniscient author.

5. Choose the best paraphrase of the following statement: "The angel of calamity had under its glance the battery upon the hill." (page 51, paragraph 9).
   a. The angel of fate was protecting the soldiers on the hill.
   b. A tragic battle had taken place on the hill.

6. Crane often uses symbols to suggest abstract ideas. Explain the possible symbolism of the blades of grass in the meadow ("And there was a massacre of the young blades of grass") and the bucket of water carried by Collins ("The bucket lay on the ground empty").

Writing Assignments

1. Why is this story titled "A Mystery of Heroism"? Write an essay analyzing the story's plot, theme, and characters. You may use the following thesis: The meaning of the title "A Mystery of Heroism" is explained by the plot, theme, and characters of Crane's story. Choose specific quotations from the story to support the thesis and major points.

2. Impressionism is a term taken from French painting of the late nineteenth century. When applied to literature, impressionism means a highly descriptive and personal style. Crane's impressionistic writing style is full of pictorial details and color. Underline the adjectives, color words, and visual images, and explain how these words create the scene of the story.

3. Write an essay defining heroism. Begin with the dictionary definition and then extend it to consider these points: When does heroism exist? Who is an example of a hero to you?

Group Work

Although known primarily for his prose, Crane published two books of poetry. Working with a partner or in a small group, read the poem from *War Is Kind* (1899) by Crane, and discuss the similarities in style, content, and theme between this poem and "A Mystery of Heroism." Then make a list of all these similarities, and include a one-sentence statement of the main idea of the poem.

From *War Is Kind*   1899
Stephen Crane

A slant of sun on dull brown walls,
A forgotten sky of bashful blue.

Toward God a mighty hymn,
A song of collisions and cries,
Rumbling wheels, hoof-beats, bells,
Welcomes, farewells, love-calls, final moans,
Voices of joy, idiocy, warning, despair,
The unknown appeals of brutes,
The chanting of flowers,
The screams of cut trees,
The senseless babble of hens and wise men—
A cluttered incoherency that says at the stars:
"O God, save us!"

Chapter Synthesis

Discuss the conflict that is at the center of the plot in Hawthorne's "The Canterbury Pilgrims," Poe's "The Cask of Amontillado," Chopin's "Madame Célestin's Divorce," and Crane's "A Mystery of Heroism." How is the conflict resolved in each story? Is the resolution definite or ambiguous (open to different interpretations)? Thesis: Although most short stories are built around a conflict and its resolution, the resolution is sometimes ambiguous.

Chapter 3

Nineteenth- and Early-Twentieth-Century American Prose: Autobiography/Essay

"Some turn over all books, and are equally searching in all papers; they write out of what they presently find or meet, without choice. Such are all essayists, even their master Montaigne."
Ben Jonson, *Discoveries*, c. 1615

"It is a hard and a nice subject for a man to write of himself. It pains his own heart to say any thing of disparagement, and the reader's ears to hear any thing of praise from him."
Abraham Cowley, *Of Myself*, 1665

"The next thing like living one's life over again seems to be a recollection of that life, and to make that recollection as durable as possible by putting it down in writing."
Benjamin Franklin, *Autobiography*, 1798

"There is one great trouble about dictating an autobiography and that is the multiplicity of texts that offer themselves when you sit down and let your mouth fall open and are ready to begin."
Mark Twain, *The Autobiography of Mark Twain*, 1917

As in Europe, the nineteenth century in American literature is known as the Age of Romanticism. It was a rebellion against the eighteenth-century Age of Reason. America, a young country, was expanding and experiencing tremendous growth in science and technology, population, and wealth. Until the Civil War (1861–65), the overall mood of the country was optimistic, and the pursuit of business success and material goals was highly valued. However, just as important as the ideals of self-reliance and hard work was the emphasis on love of nature, the emotions and feelings, and individualism.

Literature was seen as an expression of the individual; therefore, it was often personal and autobiographical. Writers described their private experiences rather than the universal experiences of humankind, as the classical and neoclassical writers had done. These works ranged from slave narratives recounting African Americans' escape from slavery into freedom to essays on the controversies of the times, such as women's rights and the abolition of slavery. The prose style of this period became more lyrical, subjective, and emotional in contrast to the formal, objective, and rational style of the eighteenth century. At the same time, the Puritan tradition of common sense and restraint underlay the new ideals of romanticism and resulted in an American prose style that combined intellect, feelings, and imagination. The American Transcendentalists Ralph Waldo Emerson and Henry David Thoreau best expressed this mixture of Romantic self-expression and intellectual discipline.

Nineteenth-century America was a complex period of history, combining not only industrial growth but also social turbulence. This conflict culminated in 1861 in the War between the States (the Civil War), caused in great part by the question of slavery. The Southern states, where slavery formed the basis of the agricultural economy, refused to abolish the slave system, which had become increasingly powerful. After the election of President Abraham Lincoln in November 1860, the South rose up against the North, seceding from the United States to form the Confederacy.

Although the North originally fought to preserve the Union, abolition of slavery was the underlying issue. This tragic war ended with the surrender of the South at the Battle of Appomattox in 1865. Even before the war had ended, President Abraham Lincoln's historic Emancipation Proclamation on January 1, 1863, abolished slavery: "I do order and declare that all persons held as slaves within said designated states and parts of states are and henceforward shall be free." However, the nation was divided by bitter lines of racial hatred that have still not been completely erased.

Washington Irving   From *The Sketch Book*

"We are a young people, necessarily an imitative one, and must take our examples and models, in a great degree, from the existing nations of Europe. There is no country more worthy of our study than England. . . . Let it be the pride of our writers to speak of the English nation without prejudice, and with determined candor."
Washington Irving, "English Writers on America," *The Sketch Book*, 1819–20

"In the four quarters of the globe, who reads an American book or goes to an American play?"
Sydney Smith, *Edinburgh Review*, Jan.–May 1820

"I do not go to bed two nights out of the seven without taking Washington Irving under my arm."
Charles Dickens, speech in New York, Feb. 18, 1842

"There is no room for the impurities of literature in an essay."
Virginia Woolf, "The Modern Essay," *The Common Reader*, 1925

Washington Irving (1783–1859) was born in New York and educated to be a lawyer, but he never practiced law. Having taken a trip to England in 1815, he wrote *The Sketch Book of Geoffrey Crayon, Gent.*, which made him famous. Irving remained abroad for seventeen years, working as a writer. He also published *Tales of a Traveller* (1822), *The History of the Life and Voyages of Christopher Columbus* (1828), and *The Alhambra* (1832) after living in Spain as a diplomat.

Irving was very successful as a writer during his lifetime, in both America and England, and was the first American writer to become popular and highly respected in Europe. He writes in the tradition of the eighteenth-century English novelists Henry Fielding and Laurence Sterne. His prose style, which is a mixture of Romantic richness and neoclassic order and clarity, reveals his good-natured, somewhat sentimental attitude toward life.

The Sketch Book is a combination of sketches of English life, essays on American topics, and adaptations of German folktales, such as the well-known "Rip Van Winkle" and "The Legend of Sleepy Hollow." Irving uses the pseudonym (pen name) of Geoffrey Crayon, Gent. because his collection of stories is like an artist's sketch book, and he is the tourist traveling through England sketching pictures (in words) with his crayon (pen).

Preview

Skimming: Skim the reading to gain a general impression.
1. Read the title and first sentence of each chapter.
2. Skim each chapter to get an idea of its form and length.

Questioning: Answer the following questions and discuss your answers in class.
1. Do you enjoy traveling to unfamiliar places? What countries have you visited?
2. How did you feel when you first arrived in the United States?

Scanning: Scan to answer the following questions to get an idea of the content and style.
1. "The Author's Account of Himself": What did Irving have an earnest desire to see?
2. "The Voyage": What does a sea voyage make you conscious of?

From *The Sketch Book*   **1819–20**
Washington Irving

The Author's Account of Himself

> I am of this mind with Homer, that as the snaile that crept out of her shel was turned eftsoons into a toad, and thereby was forced to make a stoole to sit on; so the traveller that stragleth from his owne country is in a short time transformed into so monstrous a shape, that he is faine to alter his mansion with his manners, and to live where he can, not where he would.
>
>   LYLY'S EUPHUES

I was always fond of visiting new scenes, and observing strange characters and manners. Even when a mere child I began my travels, and made many tours of discovery into foreign parts and unknown regions of my native city, to the frequent alarm of my parents and the emolument of the town crier. As I grew into boyhood, I extended the range of my observations. My holiday afternoons were spent in rambles about the surrounding country. I made myself familiar with all its places famous in history or fable. I knew every spot where a murder or robbery had been committed, or a ghost seen. I visited the neighboring villages, and added greatly to my stock of knowledge by noting their habits and customs and conversing with their sages and great men. I even journeyed one long summer's day to the summit of the most distant hill, whence I stretched my eye over many a mile of terra incognita, and was astonished to find how vast a globe I inhabited.

This rambling propensity strengthened with my years. Books of voyages and travels became my passion, and in devouring their contents, I neglected the regular exercises of the school. How wistfully would I wander about the pier heads in fine weather and watch the parting ships, bound to distant climes—with what longing eyes would I gaze after their lessening sails and waft myself in imagination to the ends of the earth!

Further reading and thinking, though they brought this vague inclination into more reasonable bounds, only served to make it more decided. I visited various parts of my own country, and had I been merely a lover of fine scenery I should have felt little desire to seek elsewhere its gratification, for on no country have the charms of nature been more prodigally lavished. Her mighty lakes, like oceans of liquid silver; her mountains, with their bright aerial tints; her valleys, teeming with wild fertility; her tremendous cataracts, thundering in their solitudes; her boundless plains, waving with spontaneous verdure; her broad, deep rivers, rolling in solemn silence to the ocean; her trackless forests, where vegetation puts forth all its magnificence; her skies, kindling with the magic of summer clouds and glorious sunshine—no, never need an American look beyond his own country for the sublime and beautiful of natural scenery.

But Europe held forth the charms of storied and poetical association. There were to be seen the masterpieces of art, the refinements of highly cultivated society, the quaint peculiarities of ancient and local custom. My native country was full of youthful promise: Europe was rich in the accumulated treasures of age. Her very ruins told the history of times gone by, and every moldering stone was a chronicle. I longed to wander over the scenes of renowned achievement—to tread, as it were, in the footsteps of antiquity, to loiter about the ruined castle, to meditate on the falling tower, to escape, in short, from the commonplace realities of the present and lose myself among the shadowy grandeurs of the past.

I had, besides all this, an earnest desire to see the great men of the earth. We have, it is true, our great men in America: not a city but has an ample share of them. I have mingled among them in my time, and been almost withered by the shade into which they cast me, for there is nothing so baleful to a small man as the shade of a great one, particularly the great man of a city. But I was anxious to see the great men of Europe, for I had read in the works of various philosophers that all animals degenerated in America, and man among the number. A great man of Europe, thought I, must therefore be as superior to a great man of America as a peak of the Alps to a highland of the Hudson; and in this idea I was confirmed by observing the comparative importance and swelling magnitude of many English travelers among us, who, I was assured, were very little people in their own country. I will visit this land of wonders, thought I, and see the gigantic race from which I am degenerated.

It has been either my good or evil lot to have my roving passion gratified. I have wandered through different countries, and witnessed many of the shifting scenes of life. I cannot say that I have studied them with the eye of a philosopher, but rather with the sauntering gaze with which humble lovers of the picturesque stroll from the window of one print shop to another, caught sometimes by the delineations of beauty, sometimes by the distortions of caricature, and sometimes by the loveliness of landscape. As it is the fashion for modern tourists to travel pencil in hand and bring home their portfolios filled with sketches, I am disposed to get up a few for the entertainment of my friends. When, however, I look over the hints and memorandums I have taken down for the purpose, my heart almost fails me at finding how my idle humor has led me aside from the great objects studied by every regular traveler who would make a book. I fear I shall give equal disappointment with an unlucky landscape painter, who had traveled on the continent, but, following the bent of his vagrant inclination, had sketched in nooks and corners and byplaces. His sketch book was accordingly crowded with cottages and landscapes and obscure ruins, but he had neglected to paint St. Peter's, or the Coliseum; the cascade of Terni, or the bay of Naples; and had not a single glacier or volcano in his whole collection.

The Voyage

Ships, ships, I will descrie you
Amidst the main,
I will come and try you,
What you are protecting,
And projecting,
What's your end and aim.
One goes abroad for merchandise and trading,
Another stays to keep his country from invading,
A third is coming home with rich and wealthy lading.
Halloo! my fancie, whither wilt thou go?
OLD POEM

To an American visiting Europe, the long voyage he has to make is an excellent preparative. The temporary absence of worldly scenes and employments produces a state of mind peculiarly fitted to receive new and vivid impressions. The vast space of waters that separates the hemispheres is like a blank page in existence. There is no gradual transition, by which, as in Europe, the features and population of one country blend almost imperceptibly with those of another. From the moment you lose sight of the land you have left, all is vacancy until you step on the opposite shore and are launched at once into the bustle and novelties of another world.

In traveling by land, there is a continuity of scene and a connected succession of persons and incidents that carry on the story of life and lessen the effect of absence and separation. We drag, it is true, "a lengthening chain" at each remove of our pilgrimage; but the chain is unbroken: we can trace it back link by link, and we feel that the last still grapples us to home. But a wide sea voyage severs us at once. It makes us conscious of being cast loose from the secure anchorage of settled life, and sent adrift upon a doubtful world. It interposes a gulf, not merely imaginary but real, between us and our homes—a gulf subject to tempest and fear and uncertainty, rendering distance palpable and return precarious.

Such, at least, was the case with myself. As I saw the last blue line of my native land fade away like a cloud in the horizon, it seemed as if I had closed one volume of the world and its concerns, and had time for meditation before I opened another. That land, too, now vanishing from my view, which contained all most dear to me in life; what vicissitudes might occur in it, what changes might take place in me before I should visit it again! Who can tell, when he sets forth to wander, whither he may be driven by the uncertain currents of existence, or when he may return, or whether it may ever be his lot to revisit the scenes of his childhood?

I said that at sea all is vacancy; I should correct the expression. To one given to daydreaming and fond of losing himself in reveries, a sea voyage is full of subjects for meditation; but then they are the wonders of the deep and of the air, and rather tend to abstract the mind from worldly themes. I delighted to loll over the quarter railing, or climb to the maintop, of a calm day, and muse for hours together on the tranquil bosom of a summer's sea; to gaze upon the piles of golden clouds just peering above the horizon, fancy them some fairy realms, and people them with a creation of my own; to watch the gentle undulating billows, rolling their silver volumes, as if to die away on those happy shores.

There was a delicious sensation of mingled security and awe with which I looked down from my giddy height on the monsters of the deep at their uncouth gambols. Shoals of porpoises tumbling about the bow of the ship; the grampus slowly heaving his huge form above the surface, or the ravenous shark, darting, like a specter, through the blue waters. My imagination would conjure up all that I had heard or read of the watery world beneath me, of the finny herds that roam its fathomless valleys, of the shapeless monsters that lurk among the very foundations of the earth, and of those wild phantasms that swell the tales of fishermen and sailors.

Sometimes a distant sail, gliding along the edge of the ocean, would be another theme of idle speculation. How interesting this fragment of a world, hastening to rejoin the great mass of existence! What a glorious monument of human invention, which has in a manner triumphed over wind and wave; has brought the ends of the world into communion; has established an interchange of blessings, pouring into the sterile regions of the north all the luxuries of the south; has diffused the light of knowledge and the charities of cultivated life; and has thus bound together those scattered portions of the human race, between which nature seemed to have thrown an insurmountable barrier.

We one day descried some shapeless object drifting at a distance. At sea, everything that breaks the monotony of the surrounding expanse attracts attention. It proved to be the mast of a ship that must have been completely wrecked, for there were the remains of handkerchiefs by which some of the crew had fastened themselves to this spar to prevent their being washed off by the waves. There was no trace by which the name of the ship could be ascertained. The wreck had evidently drifted about for many months; clusters of shellfish had fastened about it, and long seaweeds flaunted at its sides. But where, thought I, is the crew? Their struggle has long been over—they have gone down amidst the roar of the tempest—their bones lie whitening among the caverns of the deep. Silence, oblivion, like the waves, have closed over them, and no one can tell the story of their end. What sighs have been wafted after that ship! What prayers offered up at the deserted fireside of home! How often the mistress, the wife, the mother, pored over the daily news, to catch some casual intelligence of this rover of the deep! How has expectation darkened into anxiety—anxiety into dread— and dread into despair! Alas! Not one memento may ever return for love to cherish. All that may ever be known is that she sailed from her port, "and was never heard of more!"

The sight of this wreck, as usual, gave rise to many dismal anecdotes. This was particularly the case in the evening, when the weather, which had hitherto been fair, began to look wild and threatening, and gave indications of one of those sudden storms which will sometimes break in upon the serenity of a summer voyage. As we sat around the dull light of a lamp in the cabin that made the gloom more ghastly, everyone had his tale of shipwreck and disaster. I was particularly struck with a short one related by the captain.

"As I was once sailing," said he, "in a fine, stout ship across the banks of Newfoundland, one of those heavy fogs which prevail in those parts rendered it impossible for us to see far ahead even in the daytime; but at night the weather was so thick that we could not distinguish any object at twice the length of the ship. I kept lights at the masthead, and a constant watch forward to look out for fishing smacks, which are accustomed to lie at anchor on the banks. The wind was blowing a smacking breeze, and we were going at a great rate through the water. Suddenly the watch gave the alarm of 'a sail ahead!' It was scarcely uttered before we were upon her. She was a small schooner, at anchor, with her broadside toward us. The crew were all asleep, and had neglected to hoist a light. We struck her just amidships. The force, the size, the weight of our vessel bore her down below the waves; we passed over her and were hurried on our course. As the crashing wreck was sinking beneath us, I had a glimpse of two or three half-naked wretches rushing from her cabin; they just started from their beds to be swallowed shrieking by the waves. I heard their drowning cry mingling with the wind. The blast that bore it to our ears swept us out of all farther hearing. I shall never forget that cry! It was some time before we could put the ship about, she was under such headway. We returned, as nearly as we could guess, to the place where the smack had anchored. We cruised about for several hours in the dense fog. We fired signal guns and listened if we might hear the halloo of any survivors, but all was silent—we never saw or heard anything of them more."

I confess these stories, for a time, put an end to all my fine fancies. The storm increased with the night. The sea was lashed into tremendous confusion. There was a fearful, sullen sound of rushing waves and broken surges. Deep called unto deep. At times the black column of clouds overhead seemed rent asunder by flashes of lightning, which quivered along the foaming billows and made the succeeding darkness doubly terrible. The thunders bellowed over the wild waste of waters, and were echoed and prolonged by the mountain waves. As I saw the ship staggering and plunging among these roaring caverns, it seemed miraculous that she regained her balance or preserved her buoyancy. Her yards would dip into the water: her bow was almost buried beneath the waves. Sometimes an impending surge appeared ready to overwhelm her, and nothing but a dexterous movement of the helm preserved her from the shock.

When I retired to my cabin, the awful scene still followed me. The whistling of the wind through the rigging sounded like funereal wailings. The creaking of the masts, the straining and groaning of bulkheads as the ship labored in the weltering sea were frightful. As I heard the waves rushing along the sides of the ship and roaring in my very ear, it seemed as if Death were raging around this floating prison, seeking for his prey: the mere starting of a nail, the yawning of a seam, might give him entrance.

A fine day, however, with a tranquil sea and favoring breeze, soon put all these dismal reflections to flight. It is impossible to resist the gladdening influence of fine weather and fair wind at sea. When the ship is decked out in all her canvas, every sail swelled, and careering gaily over the curling waves, how lofty, how gallant she appears—how she seems to lord it over the deep!

I might fill a volume with the reveries of a sea voyage, for with me it is almost a continual reverie—but it is time to get to shore.

It was a fine sunny morning when the thrilling cry of "land!" was given from the masthead. None but those who have experienced it can form an idea of the delicious throng of sensations which rush into an American's bosom when he first comes in sight of Europe. There is a volume of associations with the very name. It is the land of promise, teeming with everything of which his childhood has heard or on which his studious years have pondered.

From that time until the moment of arrival, it was all feverish excitement. The ships of war that prowled like guardian giants along the coast; the headlands of Ireland, stretching out into the channel; the Welsh mountains, towering into the clouds; all were objects of intense interest. As we sailed up the Mersey, I reconnoitered the shores with a telescope. My eye dwelt with delight on neat cottages, with their trim shrubberies and green grass plots. I saw the moldering ruin of an abbey overrun with ivy, and the taper spire of a village church rising from the brow of a neighboring hill—all were characteristic of England.

The tide and wind were so favorable that the ship was enabled to come at once to the pier. It was thronged with people; some, idle lookers-on, others, eager expectants of friends or relatives. I could distinguish the merchant to whom the ship was consigned. I knew him by his calculating brow and restless air. His hands were thrust into his pockets; he was whistling thoughtfully, and walking to and fro, a small space having been accorded him by the crowd, in deference to his temporary importance. There were repeated cheerings and salutations interchanged between the shore and the ship as friends happened to recognize each other. I particularly noticed one young woman of humble dress but interesting demeanor. She was leaning forward from among the crowd; her eye hurried over the ship as it neared the shore to catch some wished-for countenance. She seemed disappointed and agitated, when I heard a faint voice call her name. It was from a poor sailor who had been ill all the voyage and had excited the sympathy of everyone on board. When the weather was fine, his messmates had spread a mattress for him on deck in the shade, but of late his illness had so increased that he had taken to his hammock, and only breathed a wish that he might see his wife before he died. He had been helped on deck as we came up the river, and was now leaning against the shrouds, with a countenance so wasted, so pale, so ghastly that it was no wonder even the eye of affection did not recognize him. But at the sound of his voice, her eye darted on his features; it read, at once, a whole volume of sorrow; she clasped her hands, uttered a faint shriek, and stood wringing them in silent agony.

All now was hurry and bustle. The meetings of acquaintances—the greetings of friends—the consultations of men of business. I alone was solitary and idle. I had no friend to meet, no cheering to receive. I stepped upon the land of my forefathers—but felt that I was a stranger in the land.

Glossary	From *The Sketch Book*
aerial	like air; unreal; imaginary
agitated	disturbed, perturbed, shaken
amidships	in the middle of a ship, between bow and stern
ample	abundant, more than enough
anchorage	stability, something that can be held on to
anecdotes	short, personal stories
ascertained	learned, found out
baleful	harmful, deadly
bent	tendency
billows	large waves
bound	ready to go or going; headed
bounds	limits; boundaries
buoyancy	ability to float in water
caricature	imitation of a person or thing that exaggerates its features
cataracts	large waterfalls
climes	regions or realms, especially with reference to its climate
consigned	delivered, handed over
continent	all of Europe except the British Isles
countenance	face
cultivated	refined, cultured
darted	moved suddenly
degenerated	deteriorated, lost former higher qualities
delineations	changes from usual or normal shape
demeanor	outward behavior, conduct
descried	saw in the distance, caught sight of
devouring	taking in greedily with the eyes, ears, or mind
dexterous	skillful and precise
earnest	devious, intense, and sincere
emolument	payment received for work; salary, wages
fathomless	too deep to be measured
gambols	play; jumping and skipping about

giddy	causing a dizzy, lightheaded sensation
grampus	small, black toothed whale, related to dolphins
grandeurs	splendors
grapples	ties, connects
gulf	wide gap, separation
hammock	length of netting swung from ropes at both ends
hitherto	until this time, until now
humor	temperament, inclination
idle	useless, lazy, not turned to appropriate use
imperceptibly	not easily perceived, not distinctly
in deference to	out of respect for
insurmountable	cannot be overcome
kindling	making bright; causing to light up
launched	started on a new course, sent off
lavished	very abundantly given
loiter	to spend time idly
loll	to lounge about in a relaxed or lazy manner
lurk	to stay hidden, ready to attach
moldering	crumbling into dust; decaying
oblivion	the condition of being forgotten
obscure	not famous, not well-known
palpable	tangible, evident, obvious, perceptible
phantasms	ghosts, fantasies
pondered	thought deeply about
portfolios	cases for carrying drawings
precarious	uncertain, insecure
prodigally	extremely generously
propensity	a natural inclination or tendency
prowled	roamed about secretly
rambles	aimless strolls through the streets of a village or town
reconnoitered	examined, surveyed
rent asunder	torn apart
reveries	dreamy thinking or imagining
rover	wanderer
roving	wandering
sages	elderly men respected for their wisdom and experience
sauntering	leisurely and aimless
schooner	ship with two or more masts, fore and aft
shoals	large groups, crowds
smacks	boats
spar	mast of a ship
stock	supply
sublime	inspiring awe or admiration through grandeur and beauty
teeming	full of, overflowing
terra incognita	unexplored territory; an unknown land (Latin)
town crier	person who formally cried public announcements

tread	to walk in
uncouth	awkward, clumsy
undulating	having a wavy form
vagrant	wandering from place to place, roaming
verdure	green vegetation
vicissitudes	difficulties, unpredictable changes
waft	to float, as on the wind
wafted	carried lightly through the air or over water
weltering	tossing of waves, tumbling, rolling
wistfully	longing pensively; showing or expressing vague yearnings
withered	dried up, decayed
wretches	persons in deep distress or misfortune

Discussion

1. Why does Irving like to travel? How young were you when you began to enjoy traveling?
2. Have you ever been on an ocean voyage? If so, describe your feelings.
3. What are the different emotions that Irving experiences during his voyage?
4. Irving felt like a stranger in England. When have you felt like "a stranger in the land"?
5. Which of these chapters do you find the most interesting? Why?

Style and Language

1. Choose the sentence that best describes Irving's style:
    a. Irving's style in *The Sketch Book* is impersonal, artificial, and complex.
    b. Irving's style in *The Sketch Book* is personal, natural, and clear.

2. Circle the words that best describe the tone in *The Sketch Book*.
    rather humorous   gently ironic
    very journalistic   harshly argumentative
    somewhat melancholy   subjective
    deeply religious   objective
    Give quotations from the text to support your choices.

3. The language of *The Sketch Book* contains
    a. figures of speech.
    b. absurd exaggerations.
    c. authentic dialogues.
    d. concrete examples.
    Give specific examples of this language.

4. Choose the best paraphrase of Irving's statement about the difference between Europe and America in "The Author's Account of Himself" (paragraph 4): "My native country was full of youthful promise: Europe was rich in the accumulated treasures of age."
    a. America had more young people: Europe had more older people.
    b. America offered new opportunites: Europe offered history and culture.

5. Irving uses dramatic expressions in *The Sketch Book*. Write a paraphrase of the following statement in "The Author's Account of Himself" (paragraph 6): "my heart almost fails me at finding how my idle humor has led me aside from the great objects studied by every regular traveler who would make a book." Share your paraphrase with the class.

Writing Assignments

1. In "The Voyage" Irving says that when he arrived in England, he was "solitary and idle," he had "no friends to meet, no cheering to receive." He felt he was "a stranger in the land." Write a four-paragraph essay describing a time when you felt you were "a stranger in the land."

2. Irving uses irony in "The Author's Account of Himself" when he says that he has "an earnest desire to see the great men of the earth. . . . and see the gigantic race from which I am degenerated." Explain Irving's use of irony and exaggeration throughout this paragraph.

3. After underlining the words and phrases that describe or relate to the setting of "The Voyage," write an essay analyzing Irving's realistic creation of the setting of an ocean voyage.

Group Work

In Irving's essay "English Writers on America" from *The Sketch Book* (1819–20), he writes: "Everyone knows the all-pervading influence of literature at the present day, and how much the opinions and passions of mankind are under its control. . . . Over no nation does the press hold a more absolute control than over the people of America, for the universal education of the poorest classes makes every individual a reader."

Find a newspaper or magazine article that shows the power of the press (print journalists) to control the opinions of Americans, and bring it to class. Working with a partner or in a small group, read each other's articles and discuss how the journalists attempt to influence public opinion. Then write a one-paragraph summary of your article.

Richard Henry Dana, Jr.   From *Two Years Before the Mast*

Lord, Lord! methought what pain it was to drown:
What dreadful noises of water in mine ears!
What sights of ugly death within mine eyes!
Methought I saw a thousand fearful wracks;
A thousand men that fishes gnawed upon.
William Shakespeare, *Richard III*, 1591

There is a pleasure in the pathless woods,
There is a rapture on the lonely shore;
There is society where none intrudes,
By the deep sea, and music in its roar.
Lord Byron, *Childe Harold*, 1818

"I never saw the use of the sea. Many a sad heart it has caused, and many a sick stomach it has occasioned. The boldest sailor climbs on board with a heavy soul, and leaps on land with a light spirit."
Benjamin Disraeli, *Vivian Grey,* 1837

"The voice of the sea speaks to the soul. The touch of the sea is sensuous, enfolding the body in its soft, close embrace."
Kate Chopin, *The Awakening,* 1899

Richard Henry Dana, Jr. (1815–82), was born in Massachusetts, the son of a poet. He attended Harvard University and became a lawyer. Because of an attack of measles in 1833, which damaged his eyesight, he had to interrupt his studies; therefore, he enlisted as a sailor on the *Pilgrim,* which sailed around Cape Horn to California. He sailed back to Boston and in 1840 wrote an account of his voyage, *Two Years Before the Mast.* It was an extremely popular book in his lifetime and had an influence on the writing of Herman Melville, the author of *Moby Dick* and other works about the sea.

Dana was a follower of Ralph Waldo Emerson, the founder of American Transcendentalism, and a neighbor of the writer Henry David Thoreau. The Transcendentalist belief in the mystical powers of nature can be seen in his book. But more importantly, Dana realistically evokes the atmosphere of sea life. Although his book originally was written to convey his sense of injustice at the life of a seaman in the Merchant Marine and to improve working conditions for the average sailor, today it is read as an adventure tale. Dana's factual yet poetic "personal narrative" is a moving portrayal of the drama of living "before the mast."

As Wright Morris wrote in his 1964 afterword to the book: "It seems hard, more than a century later to think of *Two Years Before the Mast* as one of the first books of its kind: a book that opened the sea to the landlocked seafaring mind. Until Dana this mind had been free to sail, but not actually to inhabit the ship in question."

Preview

Skimming: Skim the reading to gain a general impression.
1. Read the title and first sentence of the chapter.
2. Skim the chapter to get an idea of its form and length.

Questioning: Answer the following question and discuss your answers in class.
Would you consider working as a sailor on a ship traveling around the world?

Scanning: Scan to answer the following questions to get an idea of the content and style.
1. What happened on November 19?
2. What is a sailor's life a mixture of?

From *Two Years Before the Mast*   **1840**
Richard Henry Dana, Jr.

Chapter VI

Monday, November 19th. This was a black day in our calendar. At seven o'clock in the morning, it being our watch below, we were aroused from a sound sleep by the cry of "All hands ahoy! A man overboard!" This unwonted cry sent a thrill through the heart of everyone, and, hurrying on deck, we found the vessel hove flat aback, with all her studding sails set; for, the boy who was at the helm leaving it to throw something overboard, the carpenter, who was an old sailor, knowing that the wind was light, put the helm down and hove her aback. The watch on deck were lowering away the quarter boat, and I got on deck just in time to fling myself into her as she was leaving the side; but it was not until out upon the wide Pacific, in our little boat, that I knew whom we had lost. It was George Ballmer, the young English sailor, whom I have before spoken of as the life of the crew. He was prized by the officers as an active and willing seaman, and by the men as a lively, hearty fellow, and a good shipmate. He was going aloft to fit a strap round the maintop masthead, for ringtail halyards, and had the strap and block, a coil of halyards, and a marlinespike about his neck. He fell from the starboard futtock shrouds, and, not knowing how to swim, and being heavily dressed, with all those things round his neck, he probably sank immediately. We pulled astern, in the direction in which he fell, and though we knew that there was no hope of saving him, yet no one wished to speak of returning, and we rowed about for nearly an hour, without an idea of doing anything, but unwilling to acknowledge to ourselves that we must give him up. At length we turned the boat's head and made toward the brig.

Death is at all times solemn, but never so much so as at sea. A man dies on shore; his body remains with his friends, and "the mourners go about the streets"; but when a man falls overboard at sea and is lost, there is a suddenness in the event, and a difficulty in realizing it, which give to it an air of awful mystery. A man dies on shore—you follow his body to the grave, and a stone marks the spot. You are often prepared for the event. There is always something which helps you to realize it when it happens, and to recall it when it has passed. A man is shot down by your side in battle, and the mangled body remains an object, and a real evidence; but at sea, the man is near you—at your side—you hear his voice, and in an instant he is gone, and nothing but a vacancy shows his loss. Then, too, at sea—to use a homely but expressive phrase—you *miss* a man so much. A dozen men are shut up together in a little bark upon the wide, wide sea, and for months and months see no forms and hear no voices but their own, and one is taken suddenly from among them, and they miss him at every turn. It is like losing a limb. There are no new faces or new scenes to fill up the gap. There is always an empty berth in the forecastle, and one man wanting when the small night watch is mustered. There is one less to take the wheel, and one less to lay out with you upon the yard. You miss his form, and the sound of his voice, for habit had made them almost necessary to you, and each of your senses feels the loss.

All these things make such a death peculiarly solemn, and the effect of it remains upon the crew for some time. There is more kindness shown by the officers to the crew, and by the crew to one another. There is more quietness and seriousness. The oath and the loud laugh are gone. The officers are more watchful, and the crew go more carefully aloft. The lost man is seldom mentioned, or is dismissed with a sailor's rude eulogy—"Well, poor George is gone! His cruise is up soon! He knew his work, and did his duty, and was a good shipmate." Then usually follows some allusion to another world, for sailors are almost all believers, in their way, though their notions and opinions are unfixed and at loose ends. They say, "God won't be hard upon the poor fellow," and

seldom get beyond the common phrase which seems to imply that their sufferings and hard treatment here will be passed to their credit in the books of the Great Captain hereafter—"*To work hard,
live hard, die hard, and go to hell after would be hard indeed!*" Our cook, a simplehearted old
African, who had been through a good deal in his day, and was rather seriously inclined, always
going to church twice a day when on shore, and reading his Bible on a Sunday in the galley, talked
to the crew about spending the Lord's Days badly, and told them that they might go as suddenly as
George had, and be as little prepared.

Yet a sailor's life is at best but a mixture of a little good with much evil, and a little pleasure
with much pain. The beautiful is linked with the revolting, the sublime with the commonplace, and
the solemn with the ludicrous.

Not long after we had returned on board with our sad report, an auction was held of the poor
man's effects. The captain had first, however, called all hands aft and asked them if they were
satisfied that everything had been done to save the man, and if they thought there was any use in
remaining there longer. The crew all said that it was in vain, for the man did not know how to swim,
and was very heavily dressed. So we then filled away and kept the brig off to her course.

The laws regulating navigation make the captain answerable for the effects of a sailor who dies
during the voyage, and it is either a law or a custom, established for convenience, that the captain
should soon hold an auction of his things, in which they are bid off by the sailors, and the sums
which they give are deducted from their wages at the end of the voyage In this way the trouble and
risk of keeping his things through the voyage are avoided, and the clothes are usually sold for more
than they would be worth on shore. Accordingly, we had no sooner got the ship before the wind,
than his chest was brought up upon the forecastle, and the sale began. The jackets and trousers in
which we had seen him dressed so lately were exposed and bid off while the life was hardly out of
his body, and his chest was taken aft and used as a store chest, so that there was nothing left which
could be called *his*. Sailors have an unwillingness to wear a dead man's clothes during the same
voyage, and they seldom do so, unless they are in absolute want.

As is usual after a death, many stories were told about George. Some had heard him say that he
repented never having learned to swim, and that he knew that he should meet his death by drowning.
Another said that he never knew any good to come of a voyage made against the will, and the
deceased man shipped and spent his advance, and was afterward very unwilling to go, but, not being
able to refund, was obliged to sail with us. A boy, too, who had become quite attached to him, said
that George talked to him, during most of the watch on the night before, about his mother and family
at home, and this was the first time that he had mentioned the subject during the voyage.

The night after this event, when I went to the galley to get a light, I found the cook inclined to
be talkative, so I sat down on the spars, and gave him an opportunity to hold a yarn. I was the more
inclined to do so, as I found that he was full of the superstitions once more common among seamen,
and which the recent death had waked up in his mind. He talked about George's having spoken of
his friends, and said he believed few men died without having a warning of it, which he supported
by a great many stories of dreams, and of unusual behavior of men before death. From this he went
on to other superstitions, the Flying Dutchman, &c., and talked rather mysteriously, having something evidently on his mind. At length he put his head out of the galley and looked carefully about
to see if anyone was within hearing, and, being satisfied on that point, asked me in a low tone:

"I say! You know what countryman 'e carpenter be?"

"Yes," said I, "he's a German."

"What kind of a German!" said the cook.

"He belongs to Bremen," said I.

"Are you sure o' dat?" said he.

I satisfied him on that point by saying that he could speak no language but the German and English.

"I'm plaguy glad o' dat," said the cook. "I was mighty 'fraid he was a Finn. I tell you what, I been plaguy civil to that man all the voyage."

I asked him the reason of this, and found that he was fully possessed with the notion that Finns are wizards, and especially have power over winds and storms. I tried to reason with him about it, but he had the best of all arguments, that from experience, at hand, and was not to be moved. He had been to the Sandwich Islands in a vessel in which the sailmaker was a Finn, and could do anything he was of a mind to. This sailmaker kept a junk bottle in his berth, which was always just half full of rum, though he got drunk upon it nearly every day. He had seen him sit for hours together, talking to this bottle, which he stood up before him on the table. The same man cut his throat in his berth and everybody said he was possessed.

He had heard of ships, too, beating up the Gulf of Finland against a head wind, and having a ship heave in sight astern overhaul and pass them, with as fair a wind as could blow and all studding sails out, and find she was from Finland.

"Oh, no!" said he. "I've seen too much o' dem men to want to see 'em 'board a ship. If dey can't have dare own way, they'll play the d——l with you."

As I still doubted, he said he would leave it to John, who was the oldest seaman aboard, and would know, if anybody did. John, to be sure, was the oldest, and at the same time the most ignorant, man in the ship; but I consented to have him called. The cook stated the matter to him, and John as I anticipated, sided with the cook, and said that he himself had been in a ship where they had a head wind for a fortnight, and the captain found out at last that one of the men with whom he had had some hard words a short time before was a Finn, and immediately told him if he didn't stop the head wind he would shut him down in the forepeak. The Finn would not give in, and the captain shut him down in the forepeak, and would not give him anything to eat. The Finn held out for a day and a half, when he could not stand it any longer, and did something or other which brought the wind round again, and they let him up.

"Dar," said the cook, "what you tink o' dat?"

I told him I had no doubt it was true, and that it would have been odd if the wind had not changed in fifteen days, Finn or no Finn.

"Oh," says he, "go 'way! You tink, 'cause you been to college, you know better dan anybody. You know better dan dem as 'as seen it wid der own eyes. You wait till you've been to sea as long as I have, and den you'll know."

Glossary   From *Two Years Before the Mast*

aft	the rear end (stern) of a ship
allusion	indirect reference; casual mention
aloft	high above the deck of a ship; especially at the masthead
astern	at or toward the back of a ship
bark	any boat, especially a small sailing boat
brig	two-masted ship with square sails
civil	polite or courteous, especially in a merely formal way
dan	slang for "than"
dare	slang for "their" or "there"

dat	slang for "that"
deceased	dead
deck	platform in a ship forming the floor for its compartments
dem	slang for "them"
dey	slang for "they"
effects	belongings; property
eulogy	formal speech praising a person who has recently died
Finn	person from Finland
Flying Dutchman	a fabled Dutch sailor, condemned to sail the seas until Judgment Day; his ghostly ship, considered a bad omen by sailors who think they see it
forecastle	upper deck of a ship in front of the foremast
forepeak	part of a ship's hold in the angle of the bow
fortnight	two weeks
futtock shrouds	short iron rods to brace the topmast where it joins the lower mast
galley	ship's kitchen
halyards	ropes for raising or lowering sails
head wind	wind blowing in the direction directly opposite the course of a ship
heave	to raise or lift, especially with effort
helm	wheel or tiller by which a ship is steered
hove	moved, tugged, hauled on a rope
jack-tar	sailor
limb	arm or leg of a human being
ludicrous	laughably absurd or ridiculous
mangled	mutilated or disfigured
marlinespike	iron instrument for separating the strands of a rope
mast	tall poles rising vertically from the deck of a ship to support sails
masthead	top part of a ship's mast, especially of the lower mast
mustered	to assemble, to come together
overhaul	to gain on, catch up with, or overtake
plaguy	annoyingly; disagreeably
possessed	controlled as if by an evil spirit; crazed; mad
repented	felt sorry or self-reproachful for what one had done or failed to do
revolting	disgusting, repulsive
sided	supported or sympathized with
solemn	serious, grave, deeply earnest
spars	any poles, as masts, supporting or extending a sail of a ship
starboard	right-hand side of a ship as one faces forward, toward the bow
sublime	noble, exalted, majestic
superstitions	beliefs based on fear or ignorance that are inconsistent with the known laws of science
tink	slang for "think"
unwonted	not common, usual, or habitual; infrequent, rare
vessel	boat or ship
want	need

watch	the ship's sailors required to be on duty at a particular time
wid	slang for "with"
wizards	magicians, sorcerers
yarn	tale or story, especially one that seems exaggerated or hard to believe

Discussion

1. Describe the death at sea of the young English sailor.
2. How does the death of a sailor affect the crew and officers?
3. What makes Dana's writing effective in paragraph 4 of chapter VI? "Yet a sailor's life is at best but a mixture of a little good with much evil, and a little pleasure with much pain. The beautiful is linked with the revolting, the sublime with the commonplace, and the solemn with the ludicrous."
4. Would you like to interrupt your studies to travel for a year? Where would you go?
5. Are you superstitious? What superstitions do you believe in?

Style and Language

1. True or false: Dana's style is impersonal and very informal.

2. Complete this sentence with the words below: The tone of *Two Years Before the Mast* is

   generally _____, _____, and _____.

humorous	balanced	realistic
factual	critical	romantic

3. Dana's language can be described as
   a. very scholarly.
   b. sometimes poetic.
   c. often detailed.
   d. quite satirical.
   Give specific examples from the text of this language.

4. Explain the meaning of the sailors' statement in paragraph 3 on page 73: "God won't be hard upon the poor fellow."

5. Choose the best paraphrase of the first sentence in chapter VI: "This was a black day in our calendar."
   a. This was a stormy day in our year.
   b. This was a terrible day in our year.

6. Interpret the meaning of the simile Dana uses in paragraph 2 on page 73: ". . . one is taken suddenly from among them, and they miss him at every turn. It is like losing a limb." What is being compared? How does the simile clarify the meaning for the reader?

Writing Assignments

1. Dana left Harvard University and became a sailor for two years. Have you ever wanted to interrupt your studies for the purpose of travel? If so, write an essay describing where you would like to travel and why.

2. In chapter VI, paragraph 2 on page 73, Dana uses contrast and exemplification to clarify the differences between death "at sea" and "on shore." Analyze these differences (contrasts) and Dana's use of examples in a four-paragraph essay.

3. Henry David Thoreau, the transcendental writer, was a contemporary of Dana's. He wrote about their period of history: "I felt this was the heroic age itself, though we know it not, for the hero is commonly the simplest and obscurest of men." Write an essay explaining how Dana could be considered a hero of his age.

Group Work

Working with a partner or in a small group, read "Nocturne of the Wharves" by the twentieth-century African American poet Arna Bontemps (1902–73). Then compare and contrast Bontemps's poem with Dana's description of life at sea. Find at least three similarities and three differences in these works in regard to their form, content, and style.

Nocturne of the Wharves   1931
Arna Bontemps

All night they whine upon their ropes and boom
against the dock with helpless prows:
these little ships that are too worn for sailing
front the wharf but do not rest at all.
Tugging at the dim gray wharf they think
no doubt of China and of bright Bombay,
and they remember islands of the East,
Formosa and the mountains of Japan.
They think of cities ruined by the sea
and they are restless, sleeping at the wharf.

Tugging at the dim gray wharf they think
no less of Africa. An east wind blows
and salt spray sweeps the unattended decks.
Shouts of dead men break upon the night.
The captain calls his crew and they respond—
the little ships are dreaming—land is near.
But mist comes up to dim the copper coast,
mist dissembles images of the trees.
The captain and his men alike are lost
and their shouts go down in the rising sound of waves.

Ah little ships, I know your weariness!
I know the sea-green shadows of your dream.
For I have loved the cities of the sea,
and desolations of the old days I
have loved: I was a wanderer like you
and I have broken down before the wind.

Henry David Thoreau   **From *Walden***
                           From *Journals*

"He thought everything a discovery of his own, from moonlight to the planting of acorns and nuts by squirrels. This is a defect in his character, but one of his chief charms as a writer."
J. R. Lowell, "Thoreau," *North American Review,* Oct. 1865

"With his almost acid sharpness of insight, with his almost animal dexterity in act, there went none of that large, unconscious geniality of heroes. He was not easy, not ample, not urbane, not even kind."
R. L. Stevenson, *Familiar Studies of Men and Books,* 1882

I will arise and go now, and go to Innisfree,
And a small cabin build there, of clay and wattles made:
Nine bean-rows will I have there, a hive for the honey bee,
And live alone in the bee-loud glade.
William Butler Yeats, "The Lake Isle of Innisfree," 1893

"The Transcendentalists were good conversationalists; that in fact was their principal accomplishment."
Willa Cather, *Home Monthly,* May 1897

Henry David Thoreau (1817–62) was born and lived almost all of his life in Concord, Massachusetts, as a teacher, land surveyor, philosopher, and writer. He was a follower and friend of Ralph Waldo Emerson, the leader of the American Transcendentalists, whose writings contained a mixture of Romantic self-expression and intellectual discipline. The Transcendental movement of the 1830s was a religious, philosophical, social, and economic movement influenced by European Romanticism. The Transcendentalists turned against Puritan rationalism and stressed belief in spiritual, not material, values.

Thoreau believed that "the mass of men lead lives of quiet desperation," but he wanted to create a poetic form of life. As he wrote in his August 28, 1841 *Journal:* "My life hath been the poem I would have writ, / But I could not both live, and live to utter it." *Walden, or Life in the Woods* describes his solitary and primitive life amid nature at Walden Pond, where he moved on July 4, 1845. There he built a small cabin for a home and grew his own food. Although not popular during Thoreau's lifetime, today *Walden* is considered a literary classic. The basic structure of *Walden* is a metaphorical journey in which Thoreau explores his own surroundings, seeking self-knowledge through his study of nature. To Thoreau, studying nature was much more valuable than studying books.

While strongly influenced by the European tradition, Thoreau remained affected by his New England Puritan past. He was an idealist and a true nonconformist who valued simplicity and self-sufficiency, as he showed in his two-year experiment living at Walden Pond. In *Walden,* he writes beautifully about the life of nature and criticizes the pursuit of materialistic goals, meaningless social conventions, and hypocrisy. Thus, he says : "I went to the woods because I wished to live life deliberately, to front only the essential facts of life, and see if I could not learn what it had to teach, and not, when I came to die, discover that I had not lived."

Besides *Walden*, Thoreau's famous works include *A Week on the Concord and Merrimac Rivers* (1849) and many essays published after his death (*Journals* and *Writings*).

Preview

Skimming: Skim the reading to gain a general impression.
1. Read the title and first sentence of the chapter and the first sentence of the journal entry.
2. Skim the chapter and the journal entry to get an idea of their form and length.

Questioning: Answer the following questions and discuss your answers in class.
1. Has life in the twentieth century become too materialistic?
2. Could you live alone in a cabin in the woods?
3. Can traveling abroad have a negative effect on a person?

Scanning: Scan to answer the following questions to get an idea of the content and style.
1. *Walden:* Where did Thoreau stroll (walk) every day?
2. *Walden:* Why was Thoreau put in jail?
3. *Journals:* With what city does Thoreau compare Concord?

From *Walden*   1854
Henry David Thoreau

The Village

After hoeing, or perhaps reading and writing, in the forenoon, I usually bathed again in the pond, swimming across one of its coves for a stint, and washed the dust of labor from my person, or smoothed out the last wrinkle which study had made, and for the afternoon was absolutely free. Every day or two I strolled to the village to hear some of the gossip which is incessantly going on there, circulating either from mouth to mouth, or from newspaper to newspaper, and which, taken in homeopathic doses, was really as refreshing in its way as the rustle of leaves and the peeping of frogs. As I walked in the woods to see the birds and squirrels, so I walked in the village to see the men and boys; instead of the wind among the pines I heard the carts rattle. In one direction from my house there was a colony muskrats in the river meadows; under the grove of elms and button-woods in the other horizon was a village of busy men, as curious to me as if they had been prairie dogs, each sitting at the mouth of its burrow, or running over to a neighbor's to gossip. I went there frequently to observe their habits. The village appeared to me a great news room; and on one side, to support it, as once at Redding & Company's on State Street, they kept nuts and raisins, or salt and meal and other groceries. Some have such a vast appetite for the former commodity, that is, the news, and such sound digestive organs, that they can sit forever in public avenues without stirring, and let it simmer and whisper through them like the Etesian winds, or as if inhaling ether, it only producing numbness and insensibility to pain—otherwise it would often be painful to hear—without affecting the consciousness. I hardly ever failed, when I rambled through the village, to see a row of such worthies, either sitting on a ladder sunning themselves, with their bodies inclined forward and their eyes glancing along the line this way and that, from time to time, with a voluptuous expression, or else leaning against a barn with their hands in their pockets, like caryatids, as if to prop it up. They, being commonly out of doors, heard whatever was in the wind. These are the coarsest mills, in which all gossip is first rudely digested or cracked up before it is emptied into finer and more delicate hoppers within doors. I observed that the vitals of the village were the grocery, the barroom, the post-office, and the bank; and, as a necessary part of the machinery, they kept a bell, a big gun, and a fire engine, at convenient places; and the houses were so arranged as to make the most of mankind, in lanes and fronting one another, so that every traveler had to run the gauntlet, and every man, woman, and child might get a lick at him. Of course, those who were stationed nearest to the head of the line, where they could most see and be seen, and have the first blow at him, paid the highest prices for their places; and the few straggling inhabitants in the outskirts, where long gaps in the line began to occur, and the traveler could get over walls or turn aside into cowpaths, and so escape, paid a very slight ground or window tax. Signs were hung out on all sides to allure him; some to catch him by the appetite, as the tavern and victualing cellar; some by the fancy, as the dry goods store and the jeweler's; and others by the hair or the feet or the skirts, as the barber, the shoemaker, or the tailor. Besides, there was a still more terrible standing invitation to call at every one of these houses, and company expected about these times. For the most part I escaped wonderfully from these dangers, either by proceeding at once boldly and without deliberation to the goal, as is recommended to those who run the gauntlet, or by keeping my thoughts on high things, like Orpheus, who, "loudly singing the praises of the gods to his lyre, drowned the voices of the Sirens, and kept out of danger." Sometimes I bolted suddenly, and nobody could tell my whereabouts, for I did not stand much about gracefulness, and never hesitated at a gap in a fence. I was even accustomed to make an irruption into some houses, where I was well entertained, and after learning the kernels and very last sieveful of news, what had subsided, the prospects of war and peace, and whether the world was likely to hold together much longer, I was let out through the rear avenues, and so escaped to the woods again.

It was very pleasant, when I stayed late in town, to launch myself into the night, especially if it was dark and tempestuous, and set sail from some bright village parlor or lecture room, with a bag of rye or Indian meal upon my shoulder, for my snug harbor in the woods, having made all tight without and withdrawn under hatches with a merry crew of thoughts, leaving only my outer man at the helm, or even tying up the helm when it was plain sailing. I had many a genial thought by the cabin fire "as I sailed." I was never cast away nor distressed in any weather, though I encountered some severe storms. It is darker in the woods, even in common nights, than most suppose. I frequently had to look up at the opening between the trees above the path in order to learn my route, and, where there was no cart-path, to feel with my feet the faint track which I had worn, or steer by the known relation of particular trees which I felt with my hands, passing between two pines for instance, not more than eighteen inches apart, in the midst of the woods, invariably in the darkest night. Sometimes, after coming home thus late in a dark and muggy night, when my feet felt the path which my eyes could not see, dreaming and absent-minded all the way, until I was aroused by having to raise my hand to lift the latch, I have not been able to recall a single step of my walk, and I have thought that perhaps my body would find its way home if its master should forsake it, as the hand finds its way to the mouth without assistance. Several times, when a visitor chanced to stay into evening, and it proved a dark night, I was obliged to conduct him to the cart-path in the rear of the house, and then point out to him the direction he was to pursue, and in keeping which he was to be guided rather by his feet than his eyes. One very dark night I directed thus on their way two young men who had been fishing in the pond. They lived about a mile off through the woods, and were quite used to the route. A day or two after one of them told me that they wandered about the greater part of the night, close by their own premises, and did not get home till toward morning, by which time, as there had been several heavy showers in the meanwhile, and the leaves were very wet, they were drenched to their skins. I have heard of many going astray even in the village streets, when the darkness was so thick that you could cut it with a knife, as the saying is. Some who live in the outskirts, having come to town a-shopping in their wagons, have been obliged to put up for the night; and gentlemen and ladies making a call have gone half a mile out of their way, feeling the sidewalk only with their feet, and not knowing when they turned. It is a surprising and memorable, as well as valuable experience, to be lost in the woods any time. Often in a snowstorm, even by day, one will come out upon a well-known road and yet find it impossible to tell which way leads to the village. Though he knows that he has traveled it a thousand times, he cannot recognize a feature in it, but it is as strange to him as if it were a road in Siberia. By night, of course, the perplexity is infinitely greater. In our most trivial walks, we are constantly, though unconsciously, steering like pilots by certain well-known beacons and headlands, and if we go beyond our usual course we still carry in our minds the bearing of some neighboring cape; and not till we are completely lost, or turned round—for a man needs only to be turned round once with his eyes shut in this world to be lost—do we appreciate the vastness and strangeness of Nature. Every man has to learn the points of compass again as often as he awakes, whether from sleep or any abstraction. Not till we are lost, in other words, not till we have lost the world, do we begin to find ourselves, and realize where we are and the infinite extent of our relations.

One afternoon, near the end of the first summer, when I went to the village to get a shoe from the cobbler's, I was seized and put into jail, because, as I have elsewhere related, I did not pay a tax to, or recognize the authority of, the state which buys and sells men, women, and children, like cattle at the door of its senate-house. I had gone down to the woods for other purposes. But, wherever a man goes, men will pursue and paw him with their dirty institutions, and, if they can, constrain him to belong to their desperate odd-fellow society. It is true, I might have resisted forcibly with more or less effect, might have run "amok" against society; but I preferred that society should run "amok" against me, it being the desperate party. However, I was released the next day, obtained my mended shoe, and returned to the woods in season to get my dinner of huckleberries on Fair Haven Hill. I was never molested by any person but those who represented the state. I had no lock nor bolt but for the desk which held my papers, not even a nail to put over my latch or windows. I never fastened my door night or day, though I was to be absent several days; not even when the next fall I spent a fortnight in the woods of Maine. And yet my house was more respected than if it had been sur-rounded by a file of soldiers. The tired rambler could rest and warm himself by my fire, the literary amuse himself with the few books on my table, or the curious, by opening my closet door, see what was left of my dinner, and what prospect I had of a supper. Yet, though many people of every class came this way to the pond, I suffered no serious inconvenience from these sources, and I never missed anything but one small book, a volume of Homer, which perhaps was improperly gilded, and this I trust a soldier of our camp has found by this time. I am convinced, that if all men were to live as simply as I then did, thieving and robbery would be unknown. These take place only in commu-nities where some have got more than is sufficient while others have not enough.

From *Journals*   **1856**
Henry David Thoreau

When it was proposed to me to go abroad, rub off some rust, and *better my condition* in a worldly sense, I fear lest my life will lose some of its homeliness. If these fields and streams and woods, the phenomena of nature here, and the simple occupations of the inhabitants should cease to interest and inspire me, no culture or wealth would atone for the loss. I fear the dissipation that travelling, going into society, even the best, the enjoyment of intellectual luxuries, imply. If Paris is much in your mind, if it is more and more to you, Concord is less and less, and yet it would be a wretched bargain to accept the proudest Paris in exchange for my native village. At best, Paris could only be a school in which to learn to live here, a stepping-stone to Concord, a school in which to fit for this university. I wish so to live ever as to derive my satisfactions and inspirations from the commonest events, every-day phenomena, so that what my senses hourly perceive, my daily walk, the conversation of my neighbors, may inspire me, and I may dream of no heaven but that which lies about me. A man may acquire a taste for wine or brandy, and so lose his love for water, but should we not pity him?

Glossary	From *Walden*
allure	to attract, tempt
astray	off the right path
beacons	lights for warning or guiding
bolted	ran away
burrow	hole or tunnel dug in the ground by an animal
caryatids	supporting columns in the form of a female figure
cobblers	a person whose work is mending shoes
compass	instrument for showing directions
constrain	to force, compel
coves	small bays or inlets
drenched	soaked, wet all over
Etesian Winds	Mediterranean winds that blow from the northwest every summer
ether	liquid used as an anesthetic
forsake	to abandon, leave
hatches	coverings for a ship's hathway
headlands	point of land or cape reaching out into the water
helm	wheel or tiller by which a ship is steered
hoeing	digging, cultivating, weeding with a hoe
homeopathic	very small doses
Homer	Greek epic poet of c. eighth century B.C.; writer of the *Iliad* and the *Odyssey*
hoppers	containers
incessantly	continually, endlessly
irruption	sudden or violent break in
kernels	the central, most important parts
launch	to send off
lick	a sharp blow
lyre	small harp used by the ancient Greeks
molested	harmed, annoyed by, interfered with

muskrats	North American rodents living in water
Orpheus	Greek mythological poet and musician with magical powers
peeping	short, high-pitched sound; chirp
perplexity	confusion, bewilderment
premises	land and house
run amok	to lose control and attempt or do violence
run the gauntlet	to go the entire distance
rustle	soft sound of leaves being moved by a breeze
Siberia	Asiatic section of Russia
Sirens	sea nymphs, part bird and part woman, who lured sailors to their deaths (Greek and Roman mythology)
stint	pause
tempestuous	violent, turbulent, stormy
victualing	food or other provisions
voluptuous	sensuous; expressing sensual pleasure

Glossary   From *Journals*

abroad	outside one's own country; to foreign countries
atone	to make amends, to make up
better my condition	to improve my life or situation
brandy	alcoholic liquor distilled from wine
but	except; other than
derive	to get or receive
dissipation	wasting; frivolous amusement or diversion
fit	to prepare
homeliness	simplicity, unpretentiousness
lest	that
wretched	very inferior; unfortunate

Discussion

1. Thoreau says in *Walden:* "But, wherever a man goes, men will constrain him to belong to their desperate odd-fellow society." Do you agree with him?
2. How effective is civil disobedience, such as Thoreau's refusal to pay tax to the state, in bringing about changes in government policy? What well-known political leaders have used this method?
3. Thoreau believed that a person could gain self-knowledge through the study of nature in his or her own surroundings. How is this possible?
4. In his 1856 *Journal,* Thoreau wrote that "traveling, going into society" would be bad for him. Why did he have that opinion?
5. Could you follow Thoreau's philosophy of living a simple, natural life? Do you know anyone who does this?

Style and Language

1. Complete this sentence with the words below: Thoreau's style can be characterized as

   _____, _____, and _____.

rather informal	simple	personal
very formal	complex	impersonal

2. Circle the words that describe the tone of Thoreau's writing in *Walden*.

objective	critical	persuasive	angry
subjective	tolerant	tentative	philosophical

3. Thoreau's language contains many
   a. abstract generalities.
   b. specific descriptions.
   c. figures of speech.
   d. romantic symbols.
   Give quotations from the text that are examples of this language.

4. In "The Village" (paragraph 1) why does Thoreau compare "a village of busy men" to "prairie dogs"?
   a. To show his approval of common men, who work as hard as animals
   b. To show his disapproval of common men, who are like animals
   c. To show his understanding of human and animal life
   d. To show his love for both humans and animals

5. Thoreau shows a sense of humor in much of his writing. Identify the passages that are witty, and explain what makes them humorous.

Writing Assignments

1. In "The Village" Thoreau writes that "not till we are completely lost . . . do we appreciate the vastness and strangeness of Nature." Have you ever been lost in the country or the outdoors? Write an essay describing your experience.

2. In his 1856 *Journal*, Thoreau said that traveling abroad and "the enjoyment of intellectual luxuries" would result in loss of appreciation for the simple, common events and natural phenomena of life at home. Write an essay in which you agree or disagree with his point of view.   Justify your position with specific examples.

3. Explain and analyze Thoreau's contrast of Concord with Paris in his 1856 *Journal*.

Group Work

Read the following excerpt from Thoreau's essay *Life without Principle,* in which Thoreau describes life in American society in 1861:

Let us consider the way in which we spend our lives.

This world is a place of business. What an infinite bustle! I am awaked almost every night by the panting of the locomotive. It interrupts my dreams. There is no sabbath. It would be glorious to see mankind at leisure for once. It is nothing but work, work, work. I cannot easily buy a blankbook to write thoughts in; they are commonly ruled for dollars and cents. An Irishman, seeing me making a minute in the fields, took it for granted that I was calculating my wages. If a man was tossed out of a window when an infant, and so made a cripple for life, or scared out of his wits by the Indians, it is regretted chiefly because he was thus incapacitated for—business! I think that there is nothing, not even crime, more opposed to poetry, to philosophy, ay, to life itself, than this incessant business.

Working with a partner or in a small group, discuss Thoreau's ideas about the value of business, and identify the six examples he uses to support his idea that business is opposed to a good life. Then write a response to his opinion, justifying the role of business in modern life.

Harriet Jacobs   From *Incidents in the Life of a Slave Girl*

"I was now my own master. It was a happy moment, the rapture of which can be understood only by those who have been slaves."
Frederick Douglass, *Narrative of the Life of Frederick Douglass, an American Slave*, 1845

"Reader, be assured this narrative is no fiction. I am aware that some of my adventures may seem incredible; but they are, nevertheless, strictly true. I have not exaggerated the wrongs inflicted by Slavery; on the contrary, my descriptions fall far short of the facts."
Harriet Jacobs/"Linda Brent," preface to *Incidents in the Life of a Slave Girl*, 1861

"I have not added any thing to the incidents, or changed the import of her very pertinent remarks. With trifling exceptions, both the ideas and the language are her own."
L. Maria Child, introduction to *Incidents in the Life of a Slave Girl*, 1861

"Slave narrators . . . did, indeed, have pretentions to literature. They were both readers and self-conscious producers of narratives that were intended as literary works of art."
Houston A. Baker, Jr., introduction to *Narrative of the Life of Frederick Douglass, An American Slave*, 1982

Harriet Jacobs/"Linda Brent" (c. 1813–97) was born into slavery in North Carolina. Her mother died when she was six, and Jacobs went to live with her mistress. Jacobs remained a slave for twenty-seven years and then escaped to the North. *Incidents in the Life of a Slave Girl* describes her dangerous journey out of slavery to freedom. It is an example of a unique genre in American literature, the slave narrative, which was an important type of abolitionist (anti-slavery) writing in the years before the Civil War.

Jacobs wrote *Incidents in the Life of a Slave Girl* to expose the evils of slavery to the world. It is now considered one of the most noteworthy slave narratives of the period. Although over one hundred slave narratives were published before the Civil War, most authors were males. Jacobs's

Incidents is unusual because it tells the story of slavery from a woman's point of view. It is also unusual in its sophisticated use of language, which led to attempts to discredit its authenticity. Until the abolition of slavery, African Americans were prevented from learning to read and write. According to W. E. B. Du Bois, in *The Souls of Black Folk:* "The South believed an educated Negro to be a dangerous Negro." However, Jacobs was taught to read and write by her first mistress. As she says in her book: "While I was with her, she taught me to read and spell; and for this privilege, which so rarely falls to the lot of a slave, I blessed her memory."

After running away from her master, who attacked her sexually, and hiding in a garret (attic) for nearly seven years, Jacobs succeeded in 1842 in crossing into the free states, with the help of several kind people. Once she reached the North, Jacobs worked to support and educate her two children and also wrote her narrative, which was edited by Lydia Child, a white feminist. As Jacobs says in the preface: "But I do earnestly desire to arouse the women of the North to a realizing sense of the condition of two millions of women at the South, still in bondage, suffering what I endured, and most of them far worse. I want to add my testimony to that of abler pens to convince the people of the Free States what Slavery really is. Only by experience can any one realize how deep, and dark, and foul is that pit of abominations. May the blessing of God rest on this imperfect effort in behalf of my persecuted people."

Preview

Skimming: Skim the reading to gain a general impression.
1. Read the title and first sentence of the chapter.
2. Skim the chapter to get an idea of its form and length.

Questioning: Answer the following questions and discuss your answers in class.
1. In which countries of the world has slavery existed?
2. Has your country ever had a system of slavery? If so, when?

Scanning: Scan to answer the following questions to get an idea of the content and style.
1. How did Linda escape from the Flints' house?
2. How much money did Dr. Flint offer as a reward for catching Linda?

From *Incidents in the Life of a Slave Girl*   **1861**
Harriet Jacobs

The Flight

Mr. Flint was hard pushed for house servants, and rather than lose me he had restrained his malice. I did my work faithfully, though not, of course, with a willing mind. They were evidently afraid I should leave them. Mr. Flint wished that I should sleep in the great house instead of the servants' quarters. His wife agreed to the proposition, but said I mustn't bring my bed into the house, because it would scatter feathers on her carpet. I knew when I went there that they would never think of such a thing as furnishing a bed of any kind for me and my little one. I therefore carried my own bed, and now I was forbidden to use it. I did as I was ordered. But now that I was certain my children were to be put in their power, in order to give them a stronger hold on me, I resolved to leave them that night. I remembered the grief this step would bring upon my dear old grandmother; and nothing less than the freedom of my children would have induced me to disregard her advice. I went about my evening work with trembling steps. Mr. Flint twice called from his chamber door to inquire why the house was not locked up. I replied that I had not done my work. "You have had time enough to do it," said he. "Take care how you answer me!"

I shut all the windows, locked all the doors, and went up to the third story, to wait till midnight. How long those hours seemed, and how fervently I prayed that God would not forsake me in this hour of utmost need! I was about to risk every thing on the throw of a die; and if I failed, O what would become of me and my poor children? They would be made to suffer for my fault.

At half past twelve I stole softly down stairs. I stopped on the second floor, thinking I heard a noise. I felt my way down into the parlor, and looked out of the window. The night was so intensely dark that I could see nothing. I raised the window very softly and jumped out. Large drops of rain were falling and the darkness bewildered me. I dropped on my knees, and breathed a short prayer to God for guidance and protection. I groped my way to the road, and rushed towards the town with almost lightning speed. I arrived at my grandmother's house, but dared not see her. She would say, "Linda, you are killing me"; and I knew that would unnerve me. I tapped softly at the window of a room, occupied by a woman, who had lived in the house several years. I knew she was a faithful friend, and could be trusted with my secret. I tapped several times before she heard me. At last she raised the window, and I whispered, "Sally, I have run away. Let me in, quick." She opened the door softly, and said in low tones, "For God's sake, don't. Your grandmother is trying to buy you and de chillern. Mr. Sands was here last week. He tole her he was going away on business, but he wanted her to go ahead about buying you and de chillern, and he would help her all he could. Don't run away, Linda. Your grandmother is all bowed down wid trouble now."

I replied, "Sally, they are going to carry my children to the plantation to-morrow; and they will never sell them to any body so long as they have me in their power. Now, would you advise me to go back?"

"No, chile, no," answered she. "When dey finds you is gone, dey won't want de plague ob de chillern; but where is you going to hide? Dey knows ebery inch ob dis house."

I told her I had a hiding-place, and that was all it was best for her to know. I asked her to go into my room as soon as it was light, and take all my clothes out of my trunk, and pack them in hers; for I knew Mr. Flint and the constable would be there early to search my room. I feared the sight of my children would be too much for my full heart; but I could not go out into the uncertain future without one last look. I bent over the bed where lay my little Benny and baby Ellen. Poor little ones! fatherless and motherless! Memories of their father came over me. He wanted to be kind to them; but they were not all to him, as they were to my womanly heart. I knelt and prayed for the innocent little sleepers. I kissed them lightly and turned away.

As I was about to open the street door, Sally laid her hand on my shoulder, and said, "Linda, is you gwine all alone? Let me call your uncle."

"No, Sally," I replied, "I want no one to be brought into trouble on my account."

I went forth into the darkness and rain. I ran on till I came to the house of the friend who was to conceal me.

Early the next morning Mr. Flint was at my grandmother's inquiring for me. She told him she had not seen me, and supposed I was at the plantation. He watched her face narrowly, and said, "Don't you know any thing about her running off?" She assured him that she did not. He went on to say, "Last night she ran off without the least provocation. We had treated her very kindly. My wife liked her. She will soon be found and brought back. Are her children with you?" When told that they were, he said, "I am very glad to hear that. If they are here, she cannot be far off. If I find out that any of my niggers have had any thing to do with this damned business, I'll give 'em five hundred lashes." As he started to go to his father's, he turned round and added, persuasively, "Let her be brought back, and she shall have her children to live with her."

The tidings made the old doctor rave and storm at a furious rate. It was a busy day for them. My grandmother's house was searched from top to bottom. As my trunk was empty, they concluded I had taken my clothes with me. Before ten o'clock every vessel northward bound was thoroughly examined, and the law against harboring fugitives was read to all on board. At night a watch was set over the town. Knowing how distressed my grandmother would be, I wanted to send her a message; but it could not be done. Every one who went in or out of her house was closely watched. The doctor said he would take my children, unless she became responsible for them; which of course she willingly did. The next day was spent in searching. Before night, the following advertisement was posted at every corner, and in every public place for miles round:—

"$300 REWARD! Ran away from the subscriber, an intelligent, bright, mulatto girl, named Linda, 21 years of age. Five feet four inches high. Dark eyes, and black hair inclined to curl; but it can be made straight. Has a decayed spot on a front tooth. She can read and write, and in all probability will try to get to the Free States. All persons are forbidden, under penalty of the law, to harbor or employ said slave. $150 will be given to whoever takes her in the state, and $300 if taken out of the state and delivered to me, or lodged in jail.

DR. FLINT"

Glossary	From *Incidents in the Life of a Slave Girl*
bewildered	confused
bowed down	overwhelmed; crushed
chile	child
chillern	children
constable	a policeman; a peace officer in a town
de	the
decayed	rotten
dey	they
dis	this
distressed	anxious, suffering, troubled
ebery	every
fervently	passionately; showing great feeling
Free State	any state in which slavery was forbidden before the Civil War
fugitives	persons fleeing from danger; runaway slaves
groped	felt or searched about blindly, uncertainly
gwine	going
harboring	sheltering, providing protection; hiding
hard pushed for	having trouble getting
induced	persuaded, convinced
lightning	very fast, like lightning
lodged	placed and firmly fixed
malice	ill will; desire to harm another; evil intent
mulatto	a person of mixed African American and white ancestry
narrowly	carefully, closely; thoroughly
niggers	used during author's time for *negroes,* but considered highly offensive today
ob	of
plague	problem

plantation	an estate cultivated by workers living on it
posted	put up on a wall or post
proposition	proposal
provocation	cause of resentment, irritation
rave	to rage; to talk wildy
resolved	made up one's mind; decided
restrained	held back; kept under control
slave	a person held in servitude as the property of another
stole	moved quietly, secretly
storm	to be violently angry
story	section of a house
subscriber	a person who signed the document or notice
tapped	struck lightly and rapidly
throw of a die	a gamble (A die is a small cube used in games of chance.)
tidings	news, information
tole	told
trembling	shaking from fear, excitement
unnerve	to cause to lose one's nerve, courage, self-confidence
vessel	ship or boat
wid	with

Discussion

1. How is a slave different from a servant?
2. What kind of person is Linda?
3. What kind of person is Dr. Flint?
4. Why does Linda decide to run away?
5. How important to Linda are her children?
6. Did you enjoy this reading? Would you like to read the rest of the book?

Style and Language

1. True or false: Harriet Jacobs's writing style is impersonal, complex, and romantic.

2. Choose the best words to complete the sentence: The tone in "The Flight" is

   _____, _____, and _____.

subjective	humorous	straightforward
objective	serious	ironic

3. The language in "The Flight" contains
   a. figures of speech.
   b. authentic dialogue.
   c. harsh satire.
   d. personal revelations.
   Give quotations from the text that are examples of this language.

4. The story is told from the point of view of
    a. Dr. Flint.
    b. Linda's grandmother.
    c. Linda.
    d. the omniscient author.

5. The setting for Linda's flight is a
    a. cold, snowy afternoon.
    b. cloudy, windy evening.
    c. hot, sunny morning.
    d. dark, rainy night.
    Underline the sentences that describe the setting.

Writing Assignments

1. Write a three-paragraph summary of "The Flight."

2. Imagine you are Linda Brent (Harriet Jacobs). Write a letter to your children explaining why you are running away from the Flints and what your future plans are for them and for yourself.

3. Look up the word *slavery* in an encyclopedia. Read and take notes on the entry on slavery in the United States. Then write ten factual statements about slavery in the United States.

Group Work

Working with a partner or in a small group, read "To the Right Honorable William, Earl of Dartmouth" by Phillis Wheatley (c. 1753–94), the first African American poet to be published in America, and "The Slave Auction" by Frances Harper (1825–1911), a nineteenth-century African American writer. Discuss how the ideas in these eighteenth- and nineteenth-century American poems relate to Harriet Jacobs's "The Flight," and write a one-sentence statement of the main idea of each poem.

From "To the Right Honorable William, Earl of Dartmouth"   1773
Phillis Wheatley

    Should you, my lord, while you pursue my song,
Wonder from whence my love of *Freedom* sprung,
Whence flow these wishes for the common good,
By feeling hearts alone best understood,
I, young in life, by seeming cruel fate
Was snatch'd from *Afric's* fancy'd happy seat:
What pangs excruciating must molest,
What sorrows labour in my parent's breast?
Steel'd was the soul and by no misery mov'd
That from a father seiz'd his babe belov'd.
Such, such my case. And can I then but pray
Others may never feel tryannic sway?

The Slave Auction   1857
Frances Harper

The sale began—young girls were there,
  Defenceless in their wretchedness,
Whose stifled sobs of deep despair
  Revealed their anguish and distress.

And mothers stood with streaming eyes,
  And saw their dearest children sold;
Unheeded rose their bitter cries,
  While tyrants bartered them for gold.

And woman, with her love and truth—
  For these in sable forms may dwell—
Gaz'd on the husband of her youth,
  With anguish none may paint or tell.

And men, whose sole crime was their hue,
  The impress of their Maker's hand,
And frail and shrinking children, too,
  Were gathered in that mournful band.

Ye who have laid your love to rest,
  And wept above their lifeless clay,
Know not the anguish of that breast,
  Whose lov'd are rudely torn away.

Ye may not know how desolate
  Are bosoms rudely forced to part,
And how a dull and heavy weight
  Will press the life-drops from the heart.

Harriet Beecher Stowe   From "Sojourner Truth: The Libyan Sibyl"

"This filthy enactment (the Fugitive Slave Law) was made in the nineteenth century, by people who
could read and write. I will not obey it, by God."
Ralph Waldo Emerson, *Journals*, 1851

"I am naturally anti-slavery. If slavery is not wrong, nothing is wrong."
Abraham Lincoln, letter to A. C. Hodges, April 4, 1864

Blest be the hand that dared be strong to save,
  And blest be she who in our weakness came—
  Prophet and priestess! At one stroke she gave
  A race to freedom and herself to fame.
Paul Laurence Dunbar, "Harriet Beecher Stowe," 1890s

Harriet Beecher Stowe (1811–96) was born in Connecticut. She was the seventh of nine children. Her father, Lyman Beecher, was the leading Calvanist minister of the age, and he was a major influence on her life. After teaching at the Western Female Institute in Cincinnati, Ohio, Harriet married Colvin Stowe, a professor with whom she had seven children.

Stowe began her writing career as a regionalist writer, and over the course of her life wrote ten novels, many short stories, and essays. Her most famous work is *Uncle Tom's Cabin* (1851–52), an extremely popular antislavery novel that she wrote because of her anger about the Fugitive Slave Law of 1850, which rewarded the capture of runaway slaves. The book became an international best seller, arousing controversy and making Stowe a celebrity. She even went to England, where Queen Victoria honored her.

In 1863 Sojourner Truth, the black traveling preacher, visited Harriet Beecher Stowe. Sojourner Truth (c. 1797–1883) was born a slave named Isabella. She ran away from her master in New York and was freed in 1827, with the emancipation of slaves in New York. In 1843, after finding Christ, Sojourner became a traveling preacher and later also worked for the abolition of slavery and for women's rights, particularly the right to vote (woman's suffrage). (American women were not given the right to vote until August 26, 1920, when the Nineteenth Amendment to the U.S. Constitution took effect.)

Sojourner explains to Stowe that she got her new name in the following way: "And the Lord gave me Sojourner, because I was to travel up an' down the land, showin' the people their sins, an bein' a sign unto them. Afterwards I told the Lord I wanted another name 'cause everybody else had two names; and the Lord gave me Truth, because I was to declare the truth to the people." Sojourner was illiterate (unable to read or write), so her words and ideas have been passed on to future generations by descriptions of her, such as this account by Harriet Beecher Stowe, which was published in the *Atlantic Monthly* in April 1863.

Preview

Skimming: Skim the reading to gain a general impression.
1. Read the title and first sentence of the reading.
2. Skim the reading to get an idea of its form and length.

Questioning: Answer the following questions and discuss your answers in class.
Have you had the opportunity to meet a famous person? Who was it?

Scanning: Scan to answer the following questions to get an idea of the content and style.
1. Who was with Sojourner when she came to Harriet Beecher Stowe's house?
2. Why can't Sojourner preach from the Bible?

From "Sojourner Truth: The Libyan Sibyl"   1863
Harriet Beecher Stowe

Many years ago, the few readers of radical abolitionist papers must often have seen the singular name of Sojourner Truth announced as a frequent speaker at anti-slavery meetings, and as traveling on a sort of self-appointed agency through the country. I had myself often remarked the name, but never met the individual. On one occasion, when our house was filled with company, several eminent clergymen being our guests, notice was brought up to me that Sojourner Truth was below and requested an interview. Knowing nothing of her but her singular name, I went down, prepared to make the interview short, as the pressure of many other engagements demanded.

When I went into the room, a tall, spare form arose to meet me. She was evidently a full-blooded African, and, though now aged and worn with many hardships, still gave the impression of a physical development which in early youth must have been as fine a specimen of the torrid zone as Cumberworth's celebrated statuette of the Negro Woman at the Fountain. Indeed, she so strongly reminded me of that figure, that, when I recall the events of her life, as she narrated them to me, I imagine her as a living, breathing impersonation of that work of art.

I do not recollect ever to have been conversant with anyone who had more of that silent and subtle power which we call personal presence than this woman. In the modern spiritualistic phraseology, she would be described as having a strong sphere. Her tall form, as she rose up before me, is still vivid to my mind. She was dressed in some stout, grayish stuff, neat and clean, though dusty from travel. On her head she wore a bright Madras handkerchief, arranged as a turban, after the manner of her race. She seemed perfectly self-possessed and at her ease,—in fact, there was almost an unconscious superiority, not unmixed with a solemn twinkle of humor, in the odd, composed manner in which she looked down on me. Her whole air had at times a gloomy sort of drollery which impressed one strangely.

"So this is *you?*" she said.

"Yes," I answered.

"Well, honey, de Lord bless ye! I jes' thought I'd like to come an' have a look at ye. You's heerd o' me, I reckon?" she added.

"Yes, I think I have. You go about lecturing, do you not?"

"Yes, honey, that's what I do. The Lord has made me a sign unto this nation, an' I go round a-testifyin', an' showin' on 'em their sins agin my people."

So saying, she took a seat, and, stooping over and crossing her arms on her knees, she looked down on the floor, and appeared to fall into a sort of reverie. Her great gloomy eyes and her dark face seemed to work with some undercurrent of feeling; she sighed deeply, and occasionally broke out,—

"O Lord! O Lord! O the tears, an' the groans, an' the moans! O Lord!"

I should have said that she was accompanied by a little grandson of ten years,—the fattest, jolliest woolly-headed little specimen of Africa that one can imagine. He was grinning and showing his glistening white teeth in a state of perpetual merriment, and at this moment broke out into an audible giggle, which disturbed the reverie into which his relative was falling.

She looked at him with an indulgent sadness, and then at me.

"Laws, ma'am, *he* don't know nothin' about it,—*he* don't. Why, I've seen them poor critturs, beat an' 'bused an' hunted, brought in all torn,—ears hangin' all in rags, where the dogs been a-bitin' of 'em!"

This set off our little African Puck into another giggle, in which he seemed perfectly convulsed.

She surveyed him soberly, without the slightest irritation.

"Well, you may bless the Lord you *can* laugh; but I tell you, 'twa'n't no laughin' matter."

By this time I thought her manner so original that it might be worthwhile to call down my friends; and she seemed perfectly well pleased with the idea. An audience was what she wanted,—it mattered not whether high or low, learned or ignorant. She had things to say, and was ready to say them at all times, and to anyone.

I called down Dr. Beecher [Harriet's father], Professor Allen, and two or three other clergymen, who, together with my husband and family, made a roomful. No princess could have received a drawing-room with more composed dignity than Sojourner her audience. She stood among them, calm and erect, as one of her own native palm-trees waving alone in the desert. I presented one after another to her, and at last said,—

"Sojourner, this is Dr. Beecher. He is a very celebrated preacher."

"*Is* he?" she said, offering her hand in a condescending manner, and looking down on his white head. "Ye dear lamb, I'm glad to see ye! De Lord bless ye! I loves preachers. I'm a kind o' preacher myself."

"You are?" said Dr. Beecher. "Do you preach from the Bible?"

"No, honey, can't preach from de Bible,—can't read a letter."

"Why, Sojourner, what do you preach from, then?"

Her answer was given with a solemn power of voice, peculiar to herself, that hushed everyone in the room.

"When I preaches, I has just one text to preach from, an' I always preaches from this one. *My* text is, 'WHEN I FOUND JESUS.' "

"Well, you couldn't have a better one," said one of the ministers.

She paid no attention to him, but stood and seemed swelling with her own thoughts, and then began this narration:—

"Well, now, I'll jest have to go back, an' tell ye all about it. Ye see, we was all brought over from Africa, father an' mother an' I, an' a lot more of us; an' we was sold up an' down, an' hither an' yon; an' I can 'member when I was a little thing, not bigger than this 'ere," pointing to her grandson, "how my ole mammy would sit out o' doors in the evenin', an' look up at the stars an' groan. She'd groan an' groan, an' says I to her,—

" 'Mammy, what makes you groan so?'

"An' she'd say,—

" 'Matter enough, chile! I'm groanin' to think o' my poor children: they don't know where I be, an' I don't know where they be; they looks up at the stars, an' I looks up at the stars, but I can't tell where they be.

" 'Now,' she said, 'chile, when you're grown up, you may be sold away from your mother an' all your ole friends, an' have great troubles come on ye; an' when you has these troubles come on ye, ye jes' go to God, an' He'll help ye.'

"An' says I to her,—

" 'Who is God anyhow, mammy?'

"An' says she,—

" 'Why, chile, you jes' look up *dar!* It's Him that made all *dem!'*

"Well, I didn't mind much 'bout God in them days. I grew up pretty lively an' strong, an' could row a boat, or ride a horse, or work round, an' do 'most anything.

"At last I got sold away to a real hard massa an' missis. Oh, I tell you, they *was* hard! 'Peard like I couldn't please 'em, nohow. An' then I thought o' what my old mammy told me about God; an' I thought I'd got into trouble, sure enough, an' I wanted to find God, an' I heerd someone tell a story about a man that met God on a threshin'-floor, an' I thought, 'Well an' good, I'll have a threshin'-floor, too.' So I went down in the lot, an' I threshed down a place real hard, an' I used to go down there every day an' pray an' cry with all my might, a-prayin' to the Lord to make my massa an' missis better, but it didn't seem to do no good; an' so says I, one day,—

" 'O God, I been a-askin' ye, an' askin' ye, for all this long time, to make my massa an' missis better, an' you don't do it, an' what *can* be the reason? Why, maybe you *can't.* Well, I shouldn't wonder ef you couldn't. Well, now, I tell you, I'll make a bargain with you. Ef you'll help me to git away from my massa an' missis, I'll agree to be good; but ef you don't help me, I really don't think

I can be. Now,' says I, 'I want to git away; but the trouble's jest here: ef I try to git away in the night, I can't see; an' ef I try to git away in the daytime, they'll see me, an' be after me.'

"Then the Lord said to me, 'Git up two or three hours afore daylight, an' start off.'

"An' says I, 'Thank 'ee, Lord! that's a good thought.'

"So up I got, about three o'clock in the mornin', an' I started an' traveled pretty fast, till, when the sun rose, I was clear away from our place an' our folks, an' out o' sight. An' then I begun to think I didn't know nothin' where to go. So I kneeled down, and says I,—

" 'Well, Lord, you've started me out, an' now please to show me where to go.'

"Then the Lord made a house appear to me, an' He said to me that I was to walk on till I saw that house, an' then go in an' ask the people to take me. An' I traveled all day, an' didn't come to the house till late at night; but when I saw it, sure enough, I went in, an' I told the folks that the Lord sent me; an' they was Quakers, an' real kind they was to me. They jes' took me in, an' did for me as kind as ef I'd been one of 'em; an' after they'd giv me supper, they took me into a room where there was a great, tall, white bed; an' they told me to sleep there. Well, honey, I was kind o' skeered when they left me alone with that great white bed; 'cause I never had been in a bed in my life. It never came into my mind they could mean me to sleep in it. An' so I jes' camped down under it on the floor, an' then I slep' pretty well. In the mornin', when they came in, they asked me ef I hadn't been asleep; an' I said, 'Yes, I never slep' better.' An' they said, 'Why, you haven't been in the bed!' An' says I, 'Laws, you didn't think o' sech a thing as my sleepin' in dat ar *bed,* did you? I never heerd o' sech a thing in my life.'

"Well, ye see, honey, I stayed an' lived with 'em. An' now jes' look here: instead o' keepin' my promise an' bein' good, as I told the Lord I would, jest as soon as everything got a-goin' easy, *I forgot all about God.*

"Pretty well don't need no help; an' I gin up prayin'. I lived there two or three years, an' then the slaves in New York were all set free, an' ole massa came to our house to make a visit, an' he asked me ef I didn't want to go back an' see the folks on the ole place. An' I told him I did. So he said, ef I'd jes' git into the wagon with him, he'd carry me over. Well, jest as I was goin' out to git into the wagon, I *met God!* an' says I, 'O God, I didn't know as you was so great!' An' I turned right round an' come into the house, an' set down in my room; for 't was God all around me. I could feel it burnin', burnin', burnin' all around me, an' goin' through me; an' I saw I was so wicked, it seemed as ef it would burn me up. An' I said, "'Oh, somebody, somebody, stand between God an' me, for it burns me!' Then, honey, when I said so, I felt as it were somthin' like an *amberill* [umbrella] that came between me an' the light, an' I felt it was *somebody,*—somebody that stood between me an' God; an' it felt cool, like a shade; an' says I, 'Who's this that stands between me an' God? Is it old Cato?' He was a pious old preacher; but then I seemed to see Cato in the light, an' he was all polluted an' vile, like me; an' I said, 'Is it old Sally?' an' then I saw her, an' she seemed jes' so. An' then says I, *'Who* is this?' An' then, honey, for a while it was like the sun shinin' in a pail o' water, when it moves up an' down; for I begun to feel 't was somebody that loved me; an' I tried to know him. An' I said, 'I know you! I know you! I know you!'— an' then I said, 'I don't know you! I don't know you! I don't know you!' An' when I said, 'I know you, I know you,' the light came; an' when I said, 'I don't know you, I don't know you,' it went, jes' like the sun in a pail o' water. An' finally somthin' spoke out in me an' said, *'This is Jesus!'* an' I spoke out with all my might, an' says I, *'This is Jesus!* Glory be to God!' An' then the whole world grew bright, an' the trees they waved an' waved in glory, an' every little bit o' stone on the ground shone like glass; an' I shouted an' said, 'Praise, praise, praise to the Lord!' An' I begun to feel sech a love in my soul as I never felt before,—love to all creatures. An' then, all of a sudden, it stopped, an' I said, 'Dar's de white folks, that have abused you an' beat you an' abused your people,—think o' them!' But then there came another rush of love through my soul, an' I cried out loud, 'Lord, Lord, I can love *even de white folks!*'"

Glossary	From "Sojourner Truth: The Libyan Sibyl"
a-bitin'	biting
abolitionist	in favor of abolishing (ending) slavery in the United States
abused	used wrongly; hurt by treating badly; mistreated
agency	active force; action; power
an'	and
be	am
'bused	abused; mistreated badly
celebrated	famous, much spoken of; well known
composed	tranquil, calm
condescending	dealing with others in a proud way
conversant	familiar or acquainted with
convulsed	shaken with laughter
critturs	creatures; human beings
dar's	there's
dignity	stateliness; proper pride; self-respect
drollery	quaint humor
ef	if
eminent	famous, outstanding, noteworthy
full-blooded	vigorous, lusty; genuine, authentic
gin up	gave up
git	get
glistening	shining or sparkling with light
groans	deep sounds of pain or distress
hardships	difficulties; hard circumstances of life
heerd	heard
hither an' yon	here and there; everywhere
hushed	quieted, silenced
impersonation	representation, embodiment
indulgent	kind or lenient
jes'	just
jolliest	very full of high spirits and good humor
learned	showing much learning; well educated, well informed
Libyan Sibyl	the name of a statue of a beautiful African woman (inspired by Sojourner Truth) by the sculptor William Wetmore Story
Madras	large, bright-colored silk or cotton cloth, usually striped
massa	master
missis	mistress
moans	low sounds or sorrow or pain
nohow	in any way
ole	old

'peard	it appeared, seemed
phraseology	way of speaking or writing; diction
polluted	unclean, dirty; impure, corrupt
preacher	a person who preaches; clergyman
Quakers	members of Society of Friends, a Christian sect that rejects war
radical	extreme; favoring extreme change
reckon	suppose; think
reverie	dreamy thinking or imagining; daydreaming
rush	intense feeling
self-possessed	confident; in control of one's feelings and actions
sech	such
shade	a shadow; secluded place giving protection from the sun
singular	unique, the only one of its kind; strange
skeered	scared; afraid
solemn	serious, grave
spare	thin, lean
specimen	example
sphere	range of action, knowledge, experience, influence
spiritualistic	of the spirit or the soul, not the body
subtle	delicately skillful or clever
swelling	increasing in size, force, intensity
threshin'-floor	floor where grain is beaten from its husk
torrid zone	the area between the Tropic of Cancer and Tropic of Capricorn
turban	headdress of cloth wrapped in folds about the head
twa'nt	it wasn't
undercurrent	hidden opinion, tendency
vile	morally evil, wicked, sinful
wicked	morally bad or wrong; acting with evil intent
ye	you

Discussion

1. According to Stowe, what kind of person was Sojourner Truth?
2. How religious was Sojourner when she was a child?
3. When did Sojourner first turn to God?
4. Describe how Sojourner felt when she met God. What did she see?
5. Have you had a powerful religious experience? If so, can you describe it?

Style and Language

1. Circle the words that describe Harriet Beecher Stowe's writing style in this selection.

| formal | personal | romantic |
| informal | impersonal | realistic |

2. Complete the sentence with the appropriate words: The tone of Stowe's writing is

_____, _____, and _____.

authoritative	factual	positive
tentative	idealistic	negative

3. Stowe creates a vivid picture of Sojourner Truth by using colorful adjectives and adverbs and many detailed descriptions. Underline these descriptive words and phrases.

4. Stowe uses figurative language in the following sentence on pages 94–95: "She [Sojourner] stood among them, calm and erect, as one of her own native palm-trees waving alone in the desert." Identify the type of figure of speech and explain the meaning of the sentence.

Writing Assignments

1. Write an essay describing a powerful and impressive person whom you have met. Use precise details and colorful adjectives and adverbs to make your description vivid.

2. Have you ever had an intense religious experience? If so, write an essay explaining how you felt, what happened to you, and how this experience has changed your life.

3. After analyzing the steps that Sojourner goes through in her experience of meeting God, write an essay explaining her process of religious conversion.

Group Work

Working with a partner or in a small group, read this excerpt from Stowe's "Sojourner Truth: The Libyan Sibyl," in which Sojourner gives her opinion on women's rights. What do you think about her advice and her opinion about men? Write a brief summary of Sojourner's point of view. Then discuss what rights women have won in the United States and around the world since 1863, when Stowe wrote "Sojourner Truth." Consider the following aspects of women's rights: education, voting, marriage, divorce, abortion, work outside the home, ownership of property, and role in politics and government.

"Sojourner, what do you think of Women's Rights?"

"Well, honey, I's ben to der meetings, an' harked a good deal. Dey wanted me fur to speak. So I got up. Says I, 'Sisters, I ain't clear what you'd be after. Ef women want any rights more'n dey's got, why don't dey jes' *take 'em,* an' not be talkin' about it?' Some on 'em came round me, an' asked why I didn't wear bloomers [loose trousers]. An' I told 'em I had bloomers enough when I was in bondage. You see," she said, "dey used to weave what dey called nigger-cloth, an' each one of us got jes' sech a strip, an' had to wear it width-wise. Them that was short got along pretty well, but as for me"—She gave an indescribably droll glance at her long limbs and then at us, and added, "Tell *you,* I had enough of bloomers in them days."

Sojourner then proceeded to give her views of the relative capacity of the sexes, in her own way.

"S'pose a man's mind holds a quart, an' a woman's don't hold but a pint; ef her pint is *full,* it's as good as his quart."

W. E. B. Du Bois   From *The Souls of Black Folk*

"One ever feels his twoness,—an American, a Negro; two souls, two thoughts, two unreconciled strivings; two warring ideals in one dark body, whose dogged strength alone keeps it from being torn asunder."
W. E. B. Du Bois, *The Souls of Black Folk,* 1903

"One of the great books written in this country since the Civil War is the work of a colored man, *The Souls of Black Folk,* by W. E. B. Du Bois."
James Weldon Johnson, preface to *The Book of American Negro Poetry,* 1921

"At the turn of the century W. E. B. Dubois started his distinguished career with *The Souls of Black Folk,* which is still one of the best interpretations of Negro life and aspirations."
Sterling A. Brown, *The Massachusetts Review,* 1966

William Edward Burghardt Du Bois (1868–1963) was born in Massachusetts of mulatto, French Huguenot, Dutch, and African ancestry. He was a graduate of Fisk (an African American university) and received a Ph.D. in sociology from Harvard.

Du Bois was a scientist, a sociologist and a writer who spent his life trying to solve the problem of race in America. As he says in *The Souls of Black Folk:* "The problem of the twentieth century is the problem of the color line. . . . It was a phase of this problem that caused the Civil War. . . . the question of Negro slavery was the real cause of the conflict." His solution was to help African Americans achieve autonomy and gain self-realization so they could rise above the poverty and degradation caused by years of slavery.

The Souls of Black Folk (1903) is a beautifully written collection of essays that is considered a literary masterpiece today. It has been published in about thirty editions since 1903 and remains a classic expression of the desires and dreams "of the spirtual world" of black people. Du Bois also wrote fiction and poetry besides his essays and scholarly studies. His book *The Philadelphia Negro: A Social Study* (1899) is one of the first sociological studies of the African American.

Du Bois was a founder of the NAACP (National Association for the Advancement of Colored People) in 1908, and he was a major figure in the Harlem Renaissance of the 1920s. In 1915, in the journal *The Crisis,* he wrote concerning African American culture: "We should resurrect forgotten ancient Negro art and history, and we should set the black man before the world as both a creative artist and a strong subject for artistic treatment."

Du Bois was an early suporter of African American power, self-help and education. He believed blacks should use self-defense when attacked by whites and carry guns if necessary, and thus he was criticized for advocating violence in his writings. At the age of ninety-five, Du Bois left the United States and moved to Ghana to end his life in Africa.

Other works by Du Bois include *The Suppression of the Slave Trade, The Negro, John Brown,* and *The Gift of Black Folk.*

Preview

Skimming: Skim the reading to gain a general impression.
1. Read the title and first sentence of the chapter.
2. Skim the chapter to get an idea of its form and length.

Questioning: Answer the following questions and discuss your answers in class.
1. Would you like to be a teacher?
2. Have you ever been treated unfairly because of discrimination?

Scanning: Scan to answer the following questions to get an idea of the content and style.
1. When did the school that Du Bois taught in open?
2. Why did Du Bois like to stay with the Dowells?
3. For how many summers did Du Bois live in this world?

From *The Souls of Black Folk*   1903
W. E. B. Du Bois

Of the Meaning of Progress

Once upon a time I taught school in the hills of Tennessee, where the broad dark vale of the Missis-sippi begins to roll and crumple to greet the Alleghanies. I was a Fisk student then, and all Fisk men thought that Tennessee—beyond the Veil—was theirs alone, and in vacation time they sallied forth in lusty bands to meet the county school-commissioners. Young and happy, I too went, and I shall not soon forget that summer, seventeen years ago.

First, there was a Teachers' Institute at the county-seat; and there distinguished guests of the superintendent taught the teachers fractions and spelling and other mysteries,—white teachers in the morning, Negroes at night. A picnic now and then, and a supper, and the rough world was softened by laughter and song. I remember how—But I wander.

There came a day when all the teachers left the Institute and began the hunt for schools. I learn from hearsay (for my mother was mortally afraid of firearms) that the hunting of ducks and bears and men is wonderfully interesting, but I am sure that the man who has never hunted a country school has something to learn of the pleasures of the chase. I see now the white, hot roads lazily rise and fall and wind before me under the burning July sun; I feel the deep weariness of heart and limb as ten, eight, six miles stretch relentlessly ahead; I feel my heart sink heavily as I hear again and again, "Got a teacher? Yes." So I walked on and on—horses were too expensive until I had wandered beyond railways, beyond stage lines, to a land of "varmints" and rattlesnakes, where the coming of a stranger was an event, and men lived and died in the shadow of one blue hill.

Sprinkled over hill and dale lay cabins and farmhouses, shut out from the world by the forests and the rolling hills toward the east. There I found at last a little school. Josie told me of it; she was a thin, homely girl of twenty, with a dark-brown face and thick, hard hair. I had crossed the stream at Watertown, and rested under the great willows; then I had gone to the little cabin in the lot where Josie was resting on her way to town. The gaunt farmer made me welcome, and Josie, hearing my errand, told me anxiously that they wanted a school over the hill; that but once since the war had a teacher been there; that she herself longed to learn,—and thus she ran on, talking fast and loud, with much earnestness and energy.

Next morning I crossed the tall round hill, lingered to look at the blue and yellow mountains stretching toward the Carolinas, then plunged into the wood, and came out at Josie's home. It was a dull frame cottage with four rooms, perched just below the brow of the hill, amid peach-trees. The father was a quiet, simple soul calmly ignorant, with no touch of vulgarity. The mother was differ-ent,—strong, bustling, and energetic, with a quick restless tongue, and an ambition to live "like folks." There was a crowd of children. Two boys had gone away. There remained two growing girls; a shy midget of eight; John, tall, awkward, and eighteen; Jim, younger, quicker, and better looking; and two babies of indefinite age. Then there was Josie herself. She seemed to be the centre of the family: always busy at service, or at home, or berrypicking; a little nervous and inclined to scold, like her mother, yet faithful too, like her father. She had about her a certain fineness, the shadow of an unconscious moral heroism that would willingly give all of life to make life broader, deeper, and fuller for her and hers. I saw much of this family afterwards, and grew to love them for their honest efforts to be decent and comfortable, and for their knowledge of their own ignorance. There was with them no affectation. The mother would scold the father for being so "easy"; Josie would roundly berate the boys for carelessness; and all knew that it was a hard thing to dig a living out of a rocky side-hill.

I secured the school. I remember the day I rode horseback out to the commissioner's house with a pleasant young white fellow who wanted the white school. The road ran down the bed of a stream; the sun laughed and the water jingled, and we rode on. "Come in," said the commissioner,— "come in. Have a seat. Yes, that certificate will do. Stay to dinner. What do you want a month?" "Oh," thought I, "this is lucky"; but even then fell the awful shadow of the Veil, for they ate first, then I—alone.

The schoolhouse was a log hut, where Colonel Wheeler used to shelter his corn. It sat in a lot behind a rail fence and thorn bushes, near the sweetest of springs. There was an entrance where a door once was, and within, a massive rickety fireplace; great chinks between the logs served as windows. Furniture was scarce. A pale blackboard crouched in the corner. My desk was made of three boards, reinforced at critical points, and my chair, borrowed from the landlady, had to be returned every night. Seats for the children—these puzzled me much. I was haunted by a New England vision of neat little desks and chairs, but, alas! the reality was rough plank benches without backs, and at times without legs. They had the one virtue of making naps dangerous—possibly fatal, for the floor was not to be trusted.

It was a hot morning late in July when the school opened. I trembled when I heard the patter of little feet down the dusty road, and saw the growing row of dark solemn faces and bright eager eyes facing me. First came Josie and her brothers and sisters. The longing to know, to be a student in the great school at Nashville, hovered like a star above this child-woman amid her work and worry, and she studied doggedly. There were the Dowells from their farm over toward Alexandria,—Fanny, with her smooth black face and wondering eyes; Martha, brown and dull; the pretty girl-wife of a brother, and the younger brood.

There were the Burkes,—two brown and yellow lads, and a tiny haughty-eyed girl. Fat Reuben's little chubby girl came, with golden face and old-gold hair, faithful and solemn. 'Thenie was on hand early,—a jolly, ugly, good-hearted girl, who slyly dipped snuff and looked after her little bow-legged brother. When her mother could spare her, 'Tildy came,—a midnight beauty, with starry eyes and tapering limbs; and her brother, correspondingly homely. And then the big boys,—the hulking Lawrences; the lazy Neills, unfathered sons of mother and daughter; Hickman, with a stoop in his shoulders; and the rest.

There they sat, nearly thirty of them, on the rough benches, their faces shading from a pale cream to a deep brown, the little feet bare and swinging, the eyes full of expectation, with here and there a twinkle of mischief, and the hands grasping Webster's blueblack spelling-book. I loved my school, and the fine faith the children had in the wisdom of their teacher was truly marvellous. We read and spelled together, wrote a little, picked flowers, sang, and listened to stories of the world beyond the hill. At times the school would dwindle away, and I would start out. I would visit Mun Eddings, who lived in two very dirty rooms, and ask why little Lugene, whose flaming face seemed ever ablaze with the dark-red hair uncombed, was absent all last week, or why I missed so often the

African American family

inimitable rags of Mack and Ed. Then the father, who worked Colonel Wheeler's farm on shares, would tell me how the crops needed the boys; and the thin, slovenly mother, whose face was pretty when washed, assured me that Lugene must mind the baby. "But we'll start them again next week." When the Lawrences stopped, I knew that the doubts of the old folks about book-learning had conquered again, and so, toiling up the hill, and getting as far into the cabin as possible, I put Cicero "pro Archia Poeta" into the simplest English with local applications, and usually convinced them— for a week or so.

On Friday nights I often went home with some of the children,—sometimes to Doc Burke's farm. He was a great, loud, thin Black ever working, and trying to buy the seventy-five acres of hill and dale where he lived; but people said that he would surely fail, and the "white folks would get it all." His wife was a magnificent Amazon, with saffron face and shining hair, uncorseted and bare-footed, and the children were strong and beautiful. They lived in a one-and-a-half-room cabin in the hollow of the farm, near the spring. The front room was full of great fat white beds, scrupulously neat; and there were bad chromos on the walls, and a tired centre-table. In the tiny back kitchen I was often invited to "take out and help" myself to fried chicken and wheat biscuit, "meat" and corn pone, string-beans and berries. At first I used to be a little alarmed at the approach of bedtime in the one lone bedroom, but embarrassment was very deftly avoided. First, all the children nodded and slept, and were stowed away in one great pile of goose feathers; next, the mother and the father discreetly slipped away to the kitchen while I went to bed; then, blowing out the dim light, they retired in the dark. In the morning all were up and away before I thought of awaking. Across the road, where fat Reuben lived, they all went outdoors while the teacher retired, because they did not boast the luxury of a kitchen.

I liked to stay with the Dowells, for they had four rooms and plenty of good country fare. Uncle Bird had a small, rough farm, all woods and hills, miles from the big road; but he was full of tales,—

he preached now and then,—and with his children, berries, horses, and wheat he was happy and prosperous. Often, to keep the peace, I must go where life was less lovely; for instance, 'Tildy's mother was incorrigibly dirty, Reuben's larder was limited seriously, and herds of untamed insects wandered over the Eddingses' beds. Best of all I loved to go to Josie's, and sit on the porch, eating peaches, while the mother bustled and talked: how Josie had bought the sewing-machine; how Josie worked at service in winter, but that four dollars a month was "mighty little" wages; how Josie longed to go away to school, but that it "looked like" they never could get far enough ahead to let her; how the crops failed and the well was yet unfinished; and, finally, how "mean" some of the white folks were.

For two summers I lived in this little world; it was dull and humdrum. The girls looked at the hill in wistful longing, and the boys fretted and haunted Alexandria. Alexandria was "town,"—a straggling, lazy village of houses, churches, and shops, and an aristocracy of Toms, Dicks, and Captains. Cuddled on the hill to the north was the village of the colored folks, who lived in three- or four-room unpainted cottages, some neat and homelike, and some dirty. The dwellings were scattered rather aimlessly, but they centred about the twin temples of the hamlet, the Methodist, and the Hard-Shell Baptist churches. These, in turn, leaned gingerly on a sad-colored schoolhouse. Hither my little world wended its crooked way on Sunday to meet other worlds, and gossip, and wonder, and make the weekly sacrfice with frenzied priest at the altar of the "old-time religion." Then the soft melody and mighty cadences of Negro song fluttered and thundered.

I have called my tiny community a world, and so its isolation made it; and yet there was among us but a half-awakened common consciousness, sprung from common joy and grief, at burial, birth, or wedding; from a common hardship in poverty, poor land, and low wages; and, above all, from the sight of the Veil that hung between us and Opportunity. All this caused us to think some thoughts together; but these, when ripe for speech, were spoken in various languages. Those whose eyes twenty-five and more years before had seen "the glory of the coming of the Lord," saw in every present hindrance or help a dark fatalism bound to bring all things right in His own good time. The mass of those to whom slavery was a dim recollection of childhood found the world a puzzling thing: it asked little of them, and they answered with little, and yet it ridiculed their offering. Such a paradox they could not understand, and therefore sank into listless indifference, or shiftlessness, or reckless bravado. There were, however, some—such as Josie, Jim, and Ben—to whom War, Hell, and Slavery were but childhood tales, whose young appetites had been whetted to an edge by school and story and half-awakened thought. Ill could they be content, born without and beyond the World. And their weak wings beat against their barriers,—barriers of caste, of youth, of life; at last, in dangerous moments, against everything that opposed even a whim.

Glossary	From *The Souls of Black Folk*
ablaze	gleaming
affectation	artificial behavior, meant to impress others
aimlessly	without purpose or aim
Amazon	a large, strong masculine woman
amid	among
applications	practicality; relevance
barriers	anything that holds apart, separates, or hinders; obstacles
berate	to scold severely
bow-legged	having legs with an outward curvature
bravado	pretended courage where there is really none

brood	all the children in a family
bustled	hurried busily
bustling	hurrying with much fuss and bother
cadences	the harmonic endings
caste	any exclusive and restrictive social class or group
chinks	narrow openings; cracks
chromos	color prints; chromolithographs
Cicero	Roman statesman, orator, philosopher (106–43 B.C.)
corn pone	a kind of corn bread (chiefly Southern)
crouched	stooped or bent low
crumple	to fall or break down; collapse
cuddled	nestled; lay close and snug
dale	a valley
deftly	skillfully
dipped	put (snuff) on the gums with a stick
discreetly	carefully, keeping silent
doggedly	persistently; without giving in readily
dwindle	to keep on becoming smaller; shrink
earnestness	seriousness; intensity
"easy"	not strict or severe; lenient
fare	food
fatalism	acceptance of every event as inevitable
firearms	weapons from which a shot is fired; rifles or pistols
frenzied	in a wild or frantic state
gaunt	thin and bony; looking grim
gingerly	in a very careful or cautious way
gossip	idle talk and rumor about others
haughty-eyed	showing great pride in oneself and scorn for others
haunted	visited often or continuously
hearsay	rumor; something one has heard but does not know to be true
hindrance	obstacle
homely	unattractive; simple or plain
hovered	stayed suspended or fluttered in the air
hulking	large, heavy, and often clumsy
humdrum	dull, boring, monotonous
hunt	a search
hut	a little house or cabin of the plainest kind
ill	scarcely; with difficulty
inclined	having a tendency
incorrigibly	can't be corrected or improved; set in bad habits
inimitable	that cannot be matched
jingled	made a succession of light, ringing sounds
larder	place where food supplies are kept
listless	having no interest in what is going on
living	livelihood; the means of sustaining life
log	a section of the trunk or of a large branch of a tree

lone	sole; only
longed	wished earnestly; felt a strong yearning
longing	strong desire; yearning
lusty	strong; hearty; full of vigor
midget	a very small person
mighty	very
mortally	extremely; intensely
on shares	with each person concerned taking a share of the profit or loss
paradox	a situation that has contradictory or inconsistent qualities
patter	a series of quick, light taps
perched	placed on, set on
plunged	moved rapidly
"pro Archia Poeta"	For Ancient Poetry; On Behalf of Ancient Poetry (Greek)
reckless	careless; irresponsible
reinforced	strengthened; made stronger
relentlessly	persistently; increasingly severe
retired	went to bed
rickety	shaky; liable to fall down or break because weak
ridiculed	made something the object of scornful laughter
saffron	orange-yellow in color
sallied	rushed out or went out suddenly
scold	to find fault angrily
secured	obtained; got hold or possession of
shiftlessness	without the will or ability to acomplish anything
slovenly	careless in appearance; untidy
snuff	a preparation of powdered tobacco
solemn	serious; deeply earnest
sprung	arisen
stoop	the position of bending the body forward
stowed	hidden or packed in an orderly way
straggling	being scattered over a wide area
tapering	gradually decreasing in width
toiling	advancing with painful effort or difficulty
twinkle	a quick flash of amusement in the eye
uncorseted	not dressed in a corset (close-fitting undergarment)
untamed	not tamed; wild
vale	valley
varmints	animals regarded as troublesome or objectionable
veil	piece of cloth used as a separating screen or curtain; barrier
vulgarity	the quality of being unrefined, coarse, vulgar
well	a hole sunk in the earth to get underground water
wended	went on; proceeded
whetted	stimulated
whim	a sudden fancy; passing notion
willows	trees and shrubs of the willow family
wishful	longing pensively

Discussion

1. What does the word "veil" mean to Du Bois?
2. How did Du Bois find a teaching job in Tennessee?
3. What experience made Du Bois see "the awful shadow of the Veil"?
4. Describe the schoolhouse where Du Bois taught.
5. Why was it hard for Du Bois to make his students attend school regularly?
6. What common experiences did the people in his community share?
7. Could you live and work in a poor rural community such as the one Du Bois describes?

Style and Language

1. How would you describe Du Bois's writing style in the following passage?

    I secured the school. I remember the day I rode horseback out to the commissioner's house with a pleasant young white fellow who wanted the white school. The road ran down the bed of a stream; the sun laughed and the water jingled, and we rode on. "Come in," said the commissioner,—"come in. Have a seat. Yes, that certificate will do. Stay to dinner. What do you want a month?" "Oh," thought I, "this is lucky"; but even then fell the awful shadow of the Veil, for they ate first, then I— alone.

2. Circle the words that best describe Du Bois's tone in "Of the Meaning of Progress."
    objective   very optimistic   critical
    subjective   rather pessimistic   tolerant
    Give examples from the text that support your choices.

3. Why does Du Bois begin this chapter with the words "once upon a time"?

4. Du Bois uses many metaphors and personifications in his writing. Find several examples of this figurative language and explain the comparisons.

5. In "Of the Meaning of Progress," Du Bois sometimes writes with ironic humor to soften his serious tone. Underline the phrases that are ironic and discuss their meaning.

Writing Assignments

1. "Of the Meaning of Progress" describes Du Bois's first teaching job in a poor rural community in Tennessee. Write an essay explaining the meaning of the title. What type of progress occurs in this chapter? Why does Du Bois say: "I shall not soon forget that summer seventeen years ago"?

2. What characteristics or qualities are necessary in order for a person to be an excellent teacher? Write an essay in which you enumerate and describe three of these essential qualities or characteristics.

3. Langston Hughes (1902–67) was considered the poet laureate of black America. Hughes published his first poem, "The Negro Speaks of Rivers," when he was only nineteen, and he dedicated it to Du Bois. After reading "The Negro Speaks of Rivers," write an interpretation of the poem.

The Negro Speaks of Rivers   1921
Langston Hughes   (to W. E. B. Du Bois)

I've known rivers:
I've known rivers ancient as the world and older than the
  flow of human blood in human veins.

My soul has grown deep like the rivers.

I bathed in the Euphrates when dawns were young.
I built my hut near the Congo and it lulled me to sleep.
I looked upon the Nile and raised the pyramids above it.
I heard the singing of the Mississippi when Abe Lincoln
  went down to New Orleans, and I've seen its muddy
  bosom turn all golden in the sunset.

I've known rivers:
Ancient, dusky rivers.

My soul has grown deep like the rivers.

Group Work

Frederick Douglass (1818–95) was a famous abolitionist speaker, journalist, and social critic who also wrote a slave narrative after he gained his freedom. This autobiography, which is a classic in African American literature, was a bestseller when it was published in 1845. Working with a partner or in a small group, read these selections from *Narrative of the Life of Frederick Douglass,* in which Douglass describes how he taught himself to read and write. Underline the sentences that seem most important. Then, based on these excerpts, write a letter from Douglass to Mr. and Mrs. Auld, in which he thanks them for giving him the motivation to learn to read and write. Share your letter with the class.

From *Narrative of the Life of Frederick Douglass*   1845
Frederick Douglass

From Chapter 6

Very soon after I went to live with Mr. and Mrs. Auld, she very kindly commenced to teach me the A, B, C. After I had learned this, she assisted me in learning to spell words of three or four letters. Just at this point of my progress, Mr. Auld found out what was going on, and at once forbade Mrs. Auld to instruct me further, telling her, among other things, that it was unlawful, as well as unsafe, to teach a slave to read. To use his own words, further, he said, "If you give a nigger an inch, he will take an ell. A nigger should know nothing but to obey his master—to do as he is told to do. Learning would *spoil* the best nigger in the world. Now," said he, "if you teach that nigger (speaking of myself) how to read, there would be no keeping him. It would forever unfit him to be a slave. He would at once become unmanageable, and of no value to his master. As to himself, it could do him no good, but a great deal of harm. It would make him discontented and unhappy." These words sank deep into my heart, stirred up sentiments within that lay slumbering, and called into existence an entirely new train of thought. It was a new and special revelation, explaining dark and mysterious things, with which my youthful understanding had struggled, but struggled in vain. I now understood what had been to me a most perplexing difficulty—to wit, the white man's power to enslave the black man. It was a grand achievement, and I prized it highly. From that moment, I understood the pathway from slavery to freedom. It was just what I wanted, and I got it at a time when I the least expected it. Whilst I was saddened by the thought of losing the aid of my kind mistress, I was gladdened by the invaluable instruction which, by the merest accident, I had gained from my master. Though conscious of the difficulty of learning without a teacher, I set out with high hope, and a fixed purpose, at whatever cost of trouble, to learn how to read. The very decided manner with which he spoke, and strove to impress his wife with the evil consequences of giving me instruction, served to convince me that he was deeply sensible of the truths he was uttering. It gave me the best assurance that I might rely with the utmost confidence on the results which, he said, would flow from teaching me to read. What he most dreaded, that I most desired. What he most loved, that I most hated. That which to him was a great evil, to be carefully shunned, was to me a great good, to be diligently sought; and the argument which he so warmly urged, against my learning to read, only served to inspire me with a desire and determination to learn. In learning to read, I owe almost as much to the bitter opposition of my master, as to the kindly aid of my mistress. I acknowledge the benefit of both.

From Chapter 7

I went one day down on the wharf of Mr. Waters; and seeing two Irishmen unloading a scow of stone, I went, unasked, and helped them. When we had finished, one of them came to me and asked me if I were a slave. I told him I was. He asked, "Are ye a slave for life?" I told him that I was. The good Irishman seemed to be deeply affected by the statement. He said to the other that it was a pity so fine a little fellow as myself should be a slave for life. He said it was a shame to hold me. They both advised me to run away to the north; that I should find friends there, and that I should be free. I pretended not to be interested in what they said, and treated them as if I did not understand them; for I feared they might be treacherous. White men have been known to encourage slaves to escape, and then, to get the reward, catch them and return them to their masters. I was afraid that these seemingly good men might use me so; but I nevertheless remembered their advice, and from that time I resolved to run away. I looked forward to a time at which it would be safe for me to escape. I was too young to think of doing so immediately; besides, I wished to learn how to write, as I might have occasion to write my own pass. I consoled myself with the hope that I should one day find a good chance. Meanwhile, I would learn to write.

The idea as to how I might learn to write was suggested to me by being in Durgin and Bailey's ship-yard, and frequently seeing the ship carpenters, after hewing, and getting a piece of timber ready for use, write on the timber the name of that part of the ships for which it was intended. When a piece of timber was intended for the larboard side, it would be marked thus—"L." When a piece was for the starboard side, it would be marked thus—"S." A piece for the larboard side forward, would be marked thus—"L.F." When a piece was for starboard side forward, it would be marked thus—"S.F." For larboard aft, it would be marked thus—"L.A." For starboard aft, it would be marked thus—"S.A." I soon learned the names of these letters, and for what they were intended when placed upon a piece of timber in the ship-yard. I immediately commenced copying them, and in a short time was able to make the four letters named. After that, when I met with any boy who I knew could write, I would tell him I could write as well as he. The next word would be, "I don't believe you. Let me see you try it." I would then make the letters which I had been so fortunate as to learn, and ask him to beat that. In this way I got a good many lessons in writing, which it is quite possible I should never have gotten in any other way. During this time, my copy-book was the board fence, brick wall, and pavement; my pen and ink was a lump of chalk. With these, I learned mainly how to write. I then commenced and continued copying the Italics in Webster's Spelling Book, until I could make them all without looking on the book. By this time, my little Master Thomas had gone to school, and learned how to write, and had written over a number of copy-books. These had been brought home, and shown to some of our near neighbors, and then laid aside. My mistress used to go to class meeting at the Wilk Street meetinghouse every Monday afternoon, and leave me to take care of the house. When left thus, I used to spend the time in writing in the spaces left in Master Thomas's copy-book, copying what he had written. I continued to do this until I could write a hand very similar to that of Master Thomas. Thus, after a long, tedious effort for years, I finally succeeded in learning how to write.

Glossary   From *Narrative of the Life of Frederick Douglass*

a hand	handwriting
acknowledge	to admit to be true, confess
diligently	carefully, with hard work
ell	former English measure of length equal to 45 inches
hewing	cutting or chopping with an ax
nigger	used during author's time for *negro,* but considered highly offensive today
pass	authorization to come or go freely
perplexing	puzzling, confusing
resolved	decided
scow	a large boat
shunned	avoided
slumbering	sleeping
strove	tried very hard
tedious	tiresome, wearisome
treacherous	untrustworthy, traitorous

Chapter Synthesis

Discuss the desire for freedom as presented in Thoreau's *Walden,* Jacobs's *Incidents in the Life of a Slave Girl,* Stowe's "Sojourner Truth: The Libyan Sibyl" and Du Bois's *The Souls of Black Folk.* What does freedom mean in each of these selections? How could it be attained? Thesis: Although the search for freedom is a common theme in nineteenth-century American prose, freedom has different meanings to each author.

Chapter 4

Nineteenth- and Early-Twentieth-Century American Poetry: Romanticism

"The greatest poet brings the spirit of any or all events and passions and scenes and persons . . . to bear on your individual character as you hear or read."
Walt Whitman, preface to *Leaves of Grass,* 1855

"If I read a book and it makes my whole body so cold no fire can ever warm me, I know that is poetry. If I feel physically as if the top of my head were taken off, I know that is poetry. These are the only ways I know it. Is there any other way?"
Emily Dickinson, quoted by T. W. Higginson, *Atlantic Monthly,* 1891

I, too, dislike it:
   Reading it, however, with a perfect contempt for it, one
      discovers in
   it, after all, a place for the genuine.
Marianne Moore, *Poetry,* 1935

"A good poem packs so much meaning into so small a space that its impact on the mind of the reader is like an explosion."
Elizabeth Janeway, "Fiction's Place in a World Awry," *Opinions and Perspectives,* 1955

In nineteenth-century American literature, romanticism grew out of the Puritan faith of the early settlers, which was characterized by spiritualism and personal devotion. In addition to these religious influences, the American values of patriotism, democracy, liberty, equality, self-reliance, and individualism helped create the Romantic movement.

The American Romantic poets of the second half of the nineteenth century idealized the heart rather than the head, the particular rather than the general, the individual rather than the universal. Strongly influenced by the English Romanticists William Wordsworth and Samuel Coleridge, they believed in feelings and emotions, the creative imagination, and the wonders of nature. Thus, their themes were often the mysticism of nature and the power of the common person. Most of all, the American Romantic poets, just as the English, used their poetry to express their personal experiences. To the Romantics, poetry was primarily self-expression, a revelation of their inner life as well as their relationship with the external world.

Beginning about 1850 and continuing into the twentieth century, the styles and forms of American poetry became less structured and more diverse. Old-fashioned poetic diction was usually avoided, and most poets wrote as Wordsworth had suggested, in the real language of common people. The prime example of this natural style is Walt Whitman, who originated a new type of poetry, free verse, which has no rhyme or regular meter. At the same time, many nineteenth- and early-twentieth-century American poets continued to write with rhyme and meter, as seen in the poetry of Emily Dickinson, Henry Wadsworth Longfellow, and Countee Cullen.

Emily Dickinson   **"Could I but Ride Indefinite"**
                            "Because I Could Not Stop for Death"
                            "There Is No Frigate Like a Book"

"The impression of a wholly new and original poetic genius was as distinct on my mind at the first reading of these four poems as it is now, after thirty years of further knowledge."
T. W. Higginson, *Atlantic Monthly,* 1891

"She almost always grasped whatever she sought, but with some fracture of grammar and dictionary on the way. Often, too, she was obscure, and sometimes inscrutable."
T. W. Higginson, *Atlantic Monthly,* 1891

"Emily Dickinson was the best mind to appear among Western poets in nearly four centuries."
Harold Bloom, *The Western Canon*, 1994

Emily Dickinson (1830–86) was born in Amherst, Massachusetts, where she lived in her family home all her life. She did not marry, dressed only in white, and eventually became a recluse, never leaving the house. She dedicated her life to poetry, writing poems every day, and at the time of her death, had written seventeen hundred and seventy-five poems. As she said in one of her poems: "This is my letter to the world, that never wrote to me." Except for seven poems published anonymously, Dickinson's poetry was unpublished during her lifetime, and she died unknown. After her death, her sister Lavinia discovered her poems in a locked box in her bedroom. Because of her sister's efforts, her poetry was first published in 1890.

Today Emily Dickinson is considered one of the greatest nineteenth-century American poets and perhaps the greatest woman poet. Her poetry is written in an extremely condensed and intense style that contains beautiful images and originality of intellect. It appears easy to understand yet is characterized by ambiguity and mystery. In fact, Dickinson seems to have created a special language of her own that embodies her emotional and intellectual vision of life.

Dickinson's common themes include love, nature, poetry, death, and immortality. However, these abstract ideas are presented with a simplicity and clarity resulting from her use of imagery taken from everyday life and physical nature. Although she was not religious in the traditional sense, many of her poems concern her relationship with God and have a spiritual quality that is similar to the poetry of John Donne and the seventeenth-century English metaphysical poets.

Preview

Skimming: Skim the reading to gain a general impression.
1. Read the title and first two lines of each poem.
2. Skim the poem to get an idea of its form and length.

Questioning: Answer the following questions and discuss your answers in class.
1. What does the word *freedom* mean to you?
2. What is your conception of death? Do you believe in immortality?
3. How much do you enjoy reading? What are your favorite books?

Scanning: Scan to answer the following questions to get an idea of the content and style.
1. "Could I but Ride Indefinite": What does Dickinson want to be?
2. "Because I Could Not Stop for Death": Who stops to pick up Dickinson?
3. "There Is No Frigate Like a Book": Where does a book take us?

Could I but Ride Indefinite   **1862**
Emily Dickinson

Could I but ride indefinite,
      As doth the meadow-bee,
And visit only where I liked,
      And no man visit me,

And flirt all day with buttercups,
      And marry whom I may,
And dwell a little everywhere,
      Or better, run away

With no police to follow,
      Or chase me if I do,
Till I should jump peninsulas
      To get away from you,—

I said, but just to be a bee
      Upon a raft of air,
And row in nowhere all day long,
      And anchor off the bar,—
What liberty! So captives deem
      Who tight in dungeons are.

Because I Could Not Stop for Death   **1863**
Emily Dickinson

Because I could not stop for Death,
He kindly stopped for me;
The carriage held but just ourselves
And Immortality.

We slowly drove, he knew no haste,
And I had put away
My labor, and my leisure too,
For his civility.

We passed the school where children played
Their lessons scarcely done;
We passed the fields of gazing grain,
We passed the setting sun.

We paused before a house that seemed
A swelling of the ground;
The roof was scarcely visible,
The cornice but a mound.

Since then 'tis centuries; but each
Feels shorter than the day
I first surmised the horses' heads
Were toward eternity.

There Is No Frigate Like a Book   1873
Emily Dickinson

There is no frigate like a book
    To take us lands away,
Nor any coursers like a page
    Of prancing poetry.

This traverse may the poorest take
    Without oppress of toll;
How frugal is the chariot
    That bears a human soul!

Glossary	"Could I but Ride Indefinite"
anchor	to lower an anchor (iron weight) overboard to keep from moving
bar	sand bar, shoal of sand along a shore
buttercups	yellow flowers common in meadows
captives	prisoners
deem	to think, believe, or judge
doth	does
dungeons	dark underground cells, vaults, or prisons
dwell	to live, make one's home
flirt	to play at love
indefinite	without any limit or end
peninsulas	land area almost entirely surrounded by water
raft	boat or structure for floating on water

Glossary	"Because I Could Not Stop for Death"
but	only
civility	politeness
cornice	horizontal molding along the top of a building
eternity	endless time after death; eternal existence
gazing	looking long and attentively
immortality	the state of living forever; never dying
mound	heap of earth built over a grave
surmised	guessed, inferred
'tis	it is

Glossary	"There Is No Frigate Like a Book"
bears	carries, transports
chariot	light, four-wheeled carriage
coursers	graceful, spirited, swift horses
frigate	fast, medium-sized sailing warship
frugal	thrifty, not wasteful, economical
oppress	distress, problem

prancing	moving gaily or arrogantly, like a lively horse
toll	tax or charge for permission to pass over a bridge or highway
traverse	crossing, passing through, passage across

Discussion

1. Underline the verbs in "Could I but Ride Indefinite." What kinds of verbs are they?
2. In "Could I but Ride Indefinite," what different types of freedom does Dickinson want? Have you ever felt a similar desire?
3. In the last two lines of "Because I Could Not Stop for Death," Dickinson writes: "the horses' heads were toward eternity." What does this mean? What type of conclusion does this image provide?
4. What is unusual about Dickinson's description of death?
5. In "There Is No Frigate Like a Book," how is reading a book like going on a journey?
6. How do you like Dickinson's poems? What is the most memorable aspect of her poetry?
7. Write your personal definition of poetry, and share it with the class.

Style and Language

1. Complete this sentence with the words below: Emily Dickinson's style can be characterized

as _____, _____, and _____ _____.

personal	informal	tightly structured
impersonal	formal	loosely structured

2. Circle the words that describe the tone of Dickinson's poetry.

objective	serious	calm	conversational
subjective	humorous	dramatic	melancholy

3. Dickinson's poetic language contains
   a. complex descriptions.
   b. personifications.
   c. alliteration.
   d. similes and metaphors.
   Give specific examples of this language.

4. The rhyme scheme in Dickinson's poems is
   a. aabb aabb.
   b. abab abab.
   c. abcb abcb.
   d. abcd abcd.

5. Reread the last stanza of "Could I but Ride Indefinite." What is your interpretation of the meaning of the last two lines of that stanza?
   "What Liberty! So captives deem / Who tight in dungeons are."

Writing Assignments

1. Write an essay analyzing Dickinson's desire for liberty in "Could I but Ride Indefinite." What types of liberty does she want?

2. Many of Dickinson's poems concern death. Read the poem "I Heard a Fly Buzz When I Died." Then write an essay in which you compare and contrast it with "Because I Could Not Stop for Death" (page 113). Discuss Dickinson's description of death in each poem.

    I Heard a Fly Buzz When I Died   1862
    Emily Dickinson

    I heard a fly buzz when I died;
    The stillness round my form
    Was like the stillness in the air
    Between the heaves of storm.

    The eyes beside had wrung them dry
    And breaths were gathering sure
    For that last onset, when the king
    Be witnessed in his power.

    I willed my keepsakes, signed away
    What portion of me I
    Could make assignable—and then
    There interposed a fly,

    With blue, uncertain, stumbling buzz,
    Between the light and me;
    And then the windows failed, and then
    I could not see to see.

3. Dickinson usually wrote her poems in the simple 4-3 ballad form rhythm (iambic trimeter and tetrameter). Write a short poem in the same meter and rhyme scheme that Dickinson used. Keep your language simple, and include images to convey and clarify your meaning.

Group Work

In 1862 the essayist Thomas Wentworth Higginson wrote to Dickinson asking what she liked to read. Dickinson replied: "For Poets, I have Keats, and Mr. and Mrs. Browning." Of these nineteenth-century English poets, Dickinson especially admired Elizabeth Barrett Browning (1806–61), the wife of the poet Robert Browning. In fact, Dickinson wrote a poem about how Mrs. Browning's poetry changed her life.

Working with a partner or in a small group, read Dickinson's poem "Wild Nights!" and Barrett Browning's *Sonnets from the Portuguese* VI. Then compare and contrast these two poems. In your analysis, consider the four characteristics of poetry: (1) rhythm (meter); (2) rhyme; (3) compression (short form of expression); and (4) imagery (figures of speech). Include a one-sentence statement of the main idea of each poem.

Wild Nights! Wild Nights!   1861
Emily Dickinson

Wild nights! Wild nights!
Were I with thee,
Wild nights should be
Our luxury!

Futile the winds
To a heart in port,—
Done with the compass,
Done with the chart.

Rowing in Eden!
Ah! the sea!
Might I but moor[1]
To-night in thee!

Sonnets from the Portuguese VI   1850
Elizabeth Barrett Browning

Go from me. Yet I feel that I shall stand
    Henceforward in thy shadow. Nevermore
    Alone upon the threshold of my door
Of individual life I shall command
The uses of my soul, nor lift my hand
    Serenely in the sunshine as before,
    Without the sense of that which I forbore—
Thy touch upon the palm. The widest land
Doom takes to part us, leaves thy heart in mine
With pulses that beat double. What I do
And what I dream include thee, as the wine
    Must taste of its own grapes. And when I sue[2]
God for myself, He hears that name of thine,
    And sees within my eyes the tears of two.

Walt Whitman   **"On Journeys through the States"**
"Once I Pass'd through a Populous City"
"Facing West from California's Shores"
"O Captain! My Captain!"

"You speak of Mr. Whitman—I never read his Book—but was told that he was disgraceful."
Emily Dickinson, letter to T. W. Higginson, April 25, 1862

"O strong-winged soul with prophetic lips hot with the bloodbeats of song."
Algernon Charles Swinburne, *To Walt Whitman in America,* 1871

"Mr. Emerson once did the world great mischief by praising him."
J. G. Holland, *Everyday Topics,* 1876

"A large shaggy dog, just unchained, scouring the beaches of the world and baying at the moon."
R. L. Stevenson, *Familiar Studies of Men and Books,* 1882

"His *Leaves of Grass* is a sort of dictionary of the English language, and in it is the name of every-thing in creation set down with great reverence but without any particular connection."
Willa Cather, *Nebraska State Journal,* January 19, 1896

Walt Whitman (1819–92) was born in Long Island, New York. Although he only finished elementary school, he became a printer and a journalist. In 1855, Whitman published his poetry in *Leaves of Grass,* his greatest work, which was revised and published in nine editions during his lifetime. During the Civil War (1861–65), Whitman was a war correspondent and government clerk, and he

---

1. to secure a boat with anchors
2. pray to

Walt Whitman

visited the wounded in hospitals. He wrote about these experiences in *Drum-Taps* (1865) and *Memoranda during the War* (1875).

Ralph Waldo Emerson praised *Leaves of Grass,* but Whitman achieved little recognition in America during his lifetime. After English poets helped promote his poetry, he became increasingly well-known abroad and influential as a spokesperson for democracy and freedom. In 1871, Algernon Charles Swinburne wrote a poem, from England, "To Walt Whitman in America," asking for Whitman to "send but a song oversea for us / Heart of their hearts who are free, / Heart of their singer, to be for us / More than our singing can be."

Leaves of Grass today is considered one of the greatest works of American literature. It is Whitman's tribute to America and reflects the nationalism and patriotism of the mid-nineteenth century. Very proud of his young country, Whitman was a lover of liberty and democracy, which he expresses in his writing. His poetry is self-confessional ("Song of Myself") and highly personal, while at the same time containing philosophical themes of death, love, and religious faith. Influenced by Romanticism, he saw nature as a symbol of the spiritual world and God as a part of every individual. Most important to Whitman were his beliefs in the common people and the good in human nature.

Whitman created a new poetic style in the United States with his use of free verse, which has become the most common form of poetry in English. In most of his poems, there is no conventional rhyme or meter, but flowing, rhythmic lines of thought and ever-changing imagery that result in a feeling of expansive movement. Whitman's poetry, of all nineteenth-century poetry, is closest to that of the modern age, and many modern poets, such as Ezra Pound, have acknowledged their debt to Whitman.

   Whitman's most famous poems include "Song of Myself," "Crossing Brooklyn Ferry," and "Out of the Cradle Endlessly Rocking." He also wrote "When Lilacs Last in the Dooryard Bloom'd" and his popular "O Captain! My Captain!" from "Memories of President Lincoln," written in memory of President Abraham Lincoln, who was assassinated in 1865 in Washington, D.C.

Preview

Skimming: Skim the reading to gain a general impression.
1. Read the title and first two lines of each poem.
2. Skim each poem to get an idea of its form and length.

Questioning: Answer the following questions and discuss your answers in class.
1. Where have you traveled in the United States?
2. Can you remember a special person you met on your travels? Who was that person?
3. Would you like to take a trip around the world?
4. What political leaders have been killed (assassinated) in your country or in other countries?

Scanning: Scan to answer the following questions to get an idea of the content and style.
1. "On Journeys through the States": Where is Whitman sailing?
2. "Once I Pass'd through a Populous City": Who does Whitman remember?
3. "Facing West from California's Shores": What is Whitman seeking?
4. "O Captain! My Captain!": What has happened to the Captain?

On Journeys through the States   1860
Walt Whitman

On journeys through the States we start,
(Ay through the world, urged by these songs,
Sailing henceforth to every land, to every sea,)
We willing learners of all, teachers of all, and lovers of all.

We have watch'd the seasons dispensing themselves and passing on,
And have said, Why should not a man or woman do as much as the
      seasons, and effuse as much?

We dwell a while in every city and town,
We pass through Kanada, the North-east, the vast valley of the
      Mississippi, and the Southern States,
We confer on equal terms with each of the States,
We make trial of ourselves and invite men and women to hear,
We say to ourselves, Remember, fear not, be candid, promulge the
      body and the soul,
Dwell a while and pass on, be copious, temperate, chaste, magnetic,
And what you effuse may then return as the seasons return,
And may be just as much as the seasons.

Once I Pass'd through a Populous City   1860
Walt Whitman

Once I pass'd through a populous city imprinting my brain for future
  use with its shows, architecture, customs, traditions,
Yet now of all that city I remember only a woman I casually met
  there who detain'd me for love of me,
Day by day and night by night we were together —all else has long
  been forgotten by me,
I remember I say only that woman who passionately clung to me,
Again we wander, we love, we separate again,
Again she holds me by the hand, I must not go,
I see her close beside me with silent lips sad and tremulous.

Facing West from California's Shores   1860
Walt Whitman

Facing west from California's shores,
Inquiring, tireless, seeking what is yet unfound,
I, a child, very old, over waves, towards the house of maternity,
  the land of migrations, look afar,
Look off the shores of my Western sea, the circle almost circled;
For starting westward from Hindustan, from the vales of Kashmere,
From Asia, from the north, from the God, the sage, and the hero,
From the south, from the flowery peninsulas and the spice islands,
Long having wander'd since, round the earth having wander'd,
Now I face home again, very pleas'd and joyous,
(But where is what I started for so long ago?
And why is it yet unfound?)

O Captain! My Captain!   1865–66
Walt Whitman

O Captain! my Captain! our fearful trip is done,
The ship has weather'd every rack, the prize we sought is won,
The port is near, the bells I hear, the people all exulting,
While follow eyes the steady keel, the vessel grim and daring;
  But O heart! heart! heart!
   O the bleeding drops of red,
    Where on the deck my Captain lies,
     Fallen cold and dead.

O Captain! my Captain! rise up and hear the bells;
Rise up—for you the flag is flung—for you the bugle trills,
For you bouquets and ribbon'd wreaths—for you the shores
  a-crowding,

For you they call, the swaying mass, their eager faces turning;
    Here Captain! dear father!
      This arm beneath your head!
        It is some dream that on the deck,
          You've fallen cold and dead.

My Captain does not answer, his lips are pale and still,
My father does not feel my arm, he has no pulse nor will.
The ship is anchor'd safe and sound, its voyage closed and done,
From fearful trip the victor ship comes in with object won;
    Exult O shores, and ring O bells!
      But I with mournful tread,
        Walk the deck my Captain lies,
          Fallen cold and dead.

Glossary   "On Journeys through the States"

candid	very honest or frank
chaste	virtuous, pure, decent or modest in behavior
confer	to talk, meet for discussion
copious	very plentiful; full of information
dispensing	giving out
dwell	to live, make one's home
effuse	to pour out, spread out freely
henceforth	from this time on, subsequently
magnetic	powerfully attractive
promulge	to promulgate; to make known, to make widespread
temperate	moderate in actions and speech; self-restrained
urged	driven or pressed forward; impelled

Glossary   "Once I Pass'd through a Populous City"

clung	held on to by embracing, entwining
detain'd	detained, kept from going on, held back
imprinting	impressing, implanting firmly on the mind
tremulous	trembling; fearful

Glossary   "Facing West from California's Shores"

afar	at or to a distance
Hindustan	region in northern India
Kashmere	Kashmir; region in southern Asia between Tibet and Afghanistan
maternity	motherhood
migrations	moving from place to place; leaving one's country to settle in another

peninsulas	land areas almost entirely surrounded by water
sage	very wise, elderly man
seeking	looking for, searching for
Spice islands	former name of Moluccas, islands in Indonesia
tireless	untiring, not becoming tired
yet	still, even now, thus far

Glossary   "O Captain! My Captain!"

anchor'd	anchored; kept from drifting away, by an anchor
bouquets	bunches of cut flowers
bugle	brass wind instrument like a trumpet, used for military calls
exult	to rejoice greatly, to be jubilant
exulting	rejoicing greatly or jubilantly
flung	thrown with force, hurled
grim	fierce, relentless, resolute
keel	piece extending the length of the bottom of a ship, supporting frame
mass	large number of persons; the common people
pulse	regular beating in the arteries, caused by the contraction of the heart
rack	great mental or physical torment; storm or upheaval
sought	tried to get or find, pursued
still	without sound, quiet, silent
swaying	swinging or moving from side to side
tread	step, footstep
trills	sounds, sings, plays with a trill
vessel	ship
weather'd	weathered; survived, passed through safely
will	power of making a reasoned choice or controlling one's actions

Discussion

1. In "On Journeys through the States," what is the meaning of the phrase "We willing learners of all, teachers of all, and lovers of all"? What is the mood of the poem?
2. How would you interpret the last two lines in "Facing West from California's Shores"? What is the dominant mood of the poem?
3. What recurring words, images, and themes appear in these selections from Whitman's poetry?
4. Why does Whitman refer to President Abraham Lincoln as both "my captain" and "dear father" in "O Captain! My Captain!"?
5. Are there any lines in these poems that you do not understand? Which ones?
6. Do you find Whitman's poetic style appealing? Explain your response.

Style and Language

1. Complete the sentence with the words below: Whitman's style in "O Captain! My

   Captain!" is _____, _____, and _____, but in the other

   three poems, his style is _____, _____, and _____.

formal	modern	dramatic
informal	traditional	conversational

   Explain your choices by reading aloud sections from the appropriate poems.

2. Circle the words that best describe Whitman's tone in these poems.

emotional	satirical	romantic	subjective
critical	serious	realistic	objective

3. Whitman's language is characterized by
   a. enumeration (listing).
   b. rhythmic phrases.
   c. literary allusions.
   d. humorous satire.
   Support your choices with specific examples from the poems.

4. In "Facing West from California's Shores," Whitman describes himself as "a child, very old."
   Explain what he means by this apparent paradox (contradiction).

5. In "O Captain! My Captain!" what metaphors and symbols does Whitman use?

6. A refrain is a repeated line or group of lines in a poem, usually at the end of a stanza.
   Identify the refrain in "O Captain! My Captain!" and explain the effect it creates.

Writing Assignments

1. In an essay, contrast Whitman's conventional style in "O Captain! My Captain!" with the free
   verse style of his other poems. Discuss his use of the repeated words, the rhyme scheme (aabb
   cded) and the regular rhythm in "O Captain! My Captain!"

2. Write a poem in free verse (no rhyme or regular rhythm) about a journey you have taken.

3. Ezra Pound (1885–1972) was an extraordinary American poet who helped create modern
   verse. Read this poem that Pound wrote about Whitman, and write a one-paragraph interpretation of it.

A Pact   1916
Ezra Pound

I made a pact with you, Walt Whitman—
I have detested you long enough.
I come to you as a grown child
Who has had a pig-headed father;
I am old enough now to make friends.
It was you that broke new wood,
Now is a time for carving.
We have one sap and one root—
Let there be commerce between us.

Group Work

Working with a partner or in a small group, read "A Supermarket in California" by the twentieth-century American poet Allen Ginsberg (1926–97). A true nonconformist, Ginsberg was a member of the "Beat Generation," writers who dropped out of middle-class society in the 1950s. This poem, written one hundred years after *Leaves of Grass,* is in free verse (no regular rhythm or rhyme) and shows the influence of Whitman on Ginsberg.

Discuss your interpretations of the poem and whether you like it. Possible ideas to consider when discussing the meaning of the poem are: Why is Ginsberg thinking about Whitman? How is his poem similar to Whitman's poetry? Is there any humor in the poem? Underline the words and phrases that seem important, and develop a one-sentence statement of the main idea. Then write your main idea statement on the board and compare it with what the other groups have written.

A Supermarket in California   1955
Allen Ginsberg

What thoughts I have of you tonight, Walt Whitman, for I walked down the sidestreets under the trees with a headache self-conscious looking at the full moon.

In my hungry fatigue, and shopping for images, I went into the neon fruit supermarket, dreaming of your enumerations!

What peaches and what penumbras! Whole families shopping at night! Aisles full of husbands! Wives in the avocados, babies in the tomatoes!—and you, Garcia Lorca, what were you doing down by the watermelons?

I saw you, Walt Whitman, childless, lonely old grubber, poking among the meats in the refrigerator and eyeing the grocery boys.

I heard you asking questions of each: Who killed the pork chops? What price bananas? Are you my Angel?

I wandered in and out of the brilliant stacks of cans following you, and followed in my imagination by the store detective.

We strode down the open corridors together in our solitary fancy tasting artichokes, possessing every frozen delicacy, and never passing the cashier.

Where are we going, Walt Whitman? The doors close in an hour. Which way does your beard point tonight?

(I touch your book and dream of our odyssey in the supermarket and feel absurd.)

Will we walk all night through solitary streets? The trees add shade to shade, lights out in the houses, we'll both be lonely.

Will we stroll dreaming of the lost America of love past blue automobiles in driveways, home to our silent cottage?

Ah, dear father, graybeard, lonely old courage-teacher, what America did you have when Charon quit poling his ferry and you got out on a smoking bank and stood watching the boat disappear on the black waters of Lethe?

Glossary	"A Supermarket in California"
absurd	ridiculous
artichokes	plants with leafy flower that may be eaten as a vegetable
Charon	a figure in Greek myth who ferries (takes) the dead over the river Styx
fatigue	great tiredness
ferry	a boat that crosses a river carrying people and things
Garcia Lorca	Spanish writer (1899–1936), killed by Spanish dictator Franco
grubber	a person who searches for something, such as food
Lethe	a river in Hades (Hell) whose waters cause drinkers to forget
odyssey	a journey or long wandering
penumbras	shadows
poling	pushing a boat with a pole

Henry Wadsworth Longfellow   "Paul Revere's Ride"

"As the blood of all nations is mingling with our own, so will their thoughts and feelings finally mingle in our literature. We shall draw from the Germans tenderness; from the Spaniards, passion; from the French, vivacity; to mingle more and more with our English solid sense."
Henry Wadsworth Longfellow, *Kavanagh,* 1849

"I noticed an unusual interest among the attendants and servants. . . . I have since inquired among them, and am surprised and pleased to find that many of his poems are familiar to them. No other distinguished person has come here that has excited so peculiar an interest. Such poets wear a crown that is imperishable."
Queen Victoria, comment on Longfellow's visit to Windsor Castle, July 4, 1868

"Longfellow for rich color, graceful forms and incidents—all that makes life beautiful and love refined."
Walt Whitman, *Specimen Days,* April 16, 1881

"Longfellow, gentle as he is, maintains beneath his gentleness a fair share of that unyielding perception of reality which belongs to good poetry wherever and whenever written."
Howard Nemerov, introduction to *Longfellow,* 1959

Henry Wadsworth Longfellow

Henry Wadsworth Longfellow (1807–82) was from Maine. He was a learned college professor at Harvard who soon became an extremely popular poet; he was one of the most widely read poets in the English language during the nineteenth century. Schoolchildren used to study his poems and memorize them in order to recite them in class. Many of these poems retell the history and legends of the American colonial age. They include "The Village Blacksmith," "Paul Revere's Ride," and three long narrative poems, *Evangeline, The Song of Hiawatha,* and *The Courtship of Miles Standish.*

Because of Longfellow's desire to create a national literature, much of his poetry is built on American themes from Puritan times. However, Longfellow also wrote poetry based on his extensive knowledge of the literature and history of Europe. Some of his best poems are his simple sonnets on the English poets: "Chaucer," "Milton," "Shakespeare," and "Keats." In fact, Longfellow was one of the greatest sonnet writers of the nineteenth century.

A teacher and a moralist, Longfellow conceived of his poems as lessons in ethical values, often drawn from stories of the past. His poems are gently rhythmic in style, accessible in meaning, and have a musical elegance. They are generally romantic and idealistic in perspective, combine the European and American cultures, and contain universal truths. As Longfellow wrote in *Kavanagh:* "All that is best in the great poets of all countries is not what is national in them, but what is universal."

"Paul Revere's Ride" is part of a collection of narrative poems called *Tales of a Wayside Inn,* which Longfellow modeled on Chaucer's *Canterbury Tales.* The stories in poem form are told by a group of friends meeting at a country inn outside of Boston. "Paul Revere's Ride" is the story of the night before the first battle of the American Revolution in Lexington and Concord, Massachusetts, in 1775.

Preview

Skimming: Skim the reading to gain a general impression.
1. Read the title and first two lines of the poem.
2. Skim the poem to get an idea of its form and length.

Questioning: Answer the following questions and discuss your answers in class.
1. Have you studied about the American Revolution in 1775?
2. Was there a war of independence in your country? Was there a national hero of the war?

Scanning: Scan to answer the following questions to get an idea of the content and style.
1. What signal did Paul Revere tell his friend to send?
2. What happened to the British Regulars (soldiers)?

Paul Revere's Ride   1863
Henry Wadsworth Longfellow

Listen, my children, and you shall hear
Of the midnight ride of Paul Revere,
On the eighteenth of April, in Seventy-five;
Hardly a man is now alive
Who remembers that famous day and year.

He said to his friend, "If the British march
By land or sea from the town to-night,
Hang a lantern aloft in the belfry arch
Of the North Church tower as a signal light,—
One, if by land, and two, if by sea;
And I on the opposite shore will be,
Ready to ride and spread the alarm
Through every Middlesex village and farm,
For the country folk to be up and to arm."

Then he said, "Good night!" and with muffled oar
Silently rowed to the Charlestown shore,
Just as the moon rose over the bay,
Where swinging wide at her moorings lay
The Somerset, British man-of-war;
A phantom ship with each mast and spar
Across the moon like a prison bar,
And a huge black hulk, that was magnified
By its own reflection in the tide.

Meanwhile, his friend, through alley and street,
Wanders and watches with eager ears,
Till in the silence around him he hears
The muster of men at the barrack door,
The sound of arms, and the tramp of feet,
And the measured tread of the grenadiers,

Marching down to their boats on the shore.
Then he climbed the tower of the Old North Church,
By the wooden stairs, with stealthy tread,
To the belfry-chamber overhead,
And startled the pigeons from their perch
On the sombre rafters, that round him made
Masses and moving shapes of shade,—
By the trembling ladder, steep and tall,
To the highest window in the wall,
Where he paused to listen and look down
A moment on the roofs of the town,
And the moonlight flowing over all.

Beneath, in the churchyard, lay the dead,
In their night-encampment on the hill,
Wrapped in silence so deep and still
That he could hear, like a sentinel's tread,
The watchful night-wind, as it went
Creeping along from tent to tent,
And seeming to whisper, "All is well!"
A moment only he feels the spell
Of the place and the hour, and secret dread
Of the lonely belfry and the dead;
For suddenly all his thoughts are bent
On a shadowy something far away,
Where the river widens to meet the bay,—
A line of black that bends and floats
On the rising tide, like a bridge of boats.

Meanwhile, impatient to mount and ride,
Booted and spurred, with a heavy stride
On the opposite shore walked Paul Revere.
Now he patted his horse's side,
Now gazed at the landscape far and near,
Then, impetuous, stamped the earth,
And turned and tightened his saddle-girth;
But mostly he watched with eager search
The belfry-tower of the Old North Church,
As it rose above the graves on the hill,
Lonely and spectral and sombre and still.
And lo! as he looks, on the belfry's height
A glimmer, and then a gleam of light!
He springs to the saddle, the bridle he turns,
But lingers and gazes, till full on his sight
A second lamp in the belfry burns!

A hurry of hoofs in a village street,
A shape in the moonlight, a bulk in the dark,

And beneath, from the pebbles, in passing, a spark
Struck out by a steed flying fearless and fleet:
That was all! And yet, through the gloom and the light,
The fate of a nation was riding that night;
And the spark struck out by that steed, in his flight,
Kindled the land into flame with its heat.

He has left the village and mounted the steep,
And beneath him, tranquil and broad and deep,
Is the Mystic, meeting the ocean tides;
And under the alders that skirt its edge,
Now soft on the sand, now loud on the ledge,
Is heard the tramp of his steed as he rides.

It was twelve by the village clock,
When he crossed the bridge into Medford town.
He heard the crowing of the cock,
And the barking of the farmer's dog,
And felt the damp of the river fog,
That rises after the sun goes down.

It was one by the village clock,
When he galloped into Lexington.
He saw the gilded weathercock
Swim in the moonlight as he passed,
And the meeting-house windows, blank and bare,
Gaze at him with a spectral glare,
As if they already stood aghast
At the bloody work they would look upon.

It was two by the village clock,
When he came to the bridge in Concord town.
He heard the bleating of the flock,
And the twitter of birds among the trees,
And felt the breath of the morning breeze
Blowing over the meadows brown.
And one was safe and asleep in his bed
Who at the bridge would be first to fall,
Who that day would be lying dead,
Pierced by a British musket-ball.

You know the rest. In the books you have read,
How the British Regulars fired and fled,—
How the farmers gave them ball for ball,
From behind each fence and farm-yard wall,
Chasing the red-coats down the lane,
Then crossing the fields to emerge again
Under the trees at the turn of the road,
And only pausing to fire and load.

So through the night rode Paul Revere;
And so through the night went his cry of alarm
To every Middlesex village and farm,—
A cry of defiance and not of fear,
A voice in the darkness, a knock at the door,
And a word that shall echo forevermore!
For, borne on the night-wind of the Past,
Through all our history, to the last,
In the hour of darkness and peril and need,
The people will waken and listen to hear
The hurrying hoof-beats of that steed,
And the midnight message of Paul Revere.

Glossary	"Paul Revere's Ride"
aghast	feeling great horror or dismay; terrified, horrified
alders	trees of the birch family
aloft	far above the ground; in the air
arm	to equip with weapons; to prepare for war
arms	weapons, instruments used in fighting
barrack	building for housing soldiers
belfry	part of a tower or steeple that holds the bells
bent	inclined toward, set in a course
bleating	cry of sheep, goats or calves
borne	carried, transported
defiance	challenge; open, bold resistance to opposition
emerge	to come forth into view, become visible
fled	ran away or escaped from danger
fleet	fast, swift, rapid
gleam	flash or beam of light
glimmer	faint, flickering light
grenadiers	infantry soldiers who carry and throw grenades
hulk	body of a ship
impetuous	acting suddenly, impulsively
kindled	ignited, set on fire; aroused or excited
lantern	transparent case for a light, protecting it from wind and weather
lingers	continues to stay, delays leaving
mast	tall structure rising vertically from the deck of a ship, to support the sails
moorings	place where a ship is held in place by cables or anchors
mount	to get up on the back of a horse
muffled	wrapped or covered to prevent sound
musket-ball	bullet shot from a musket (a long-barreled firearm)
muster	gathering together or assembling of troops
perch	resting place or position
peril	danger; exposure to harm or injury

phantom	something feared or dreaded
red-coats	British soldiers with red coats, during the American Revolution
sentinel	person set to guard a group; sentry
skirt	to form the border or edge of
sombre	dark and gloomy
spar	any pole supporting a sail of a ship
spark	glowing bit of matter thrown off by a fire; tiny beginning
spectral	having the nature of a specter or phantom; ghostly
spell	magical power or influence, fascination
stealthy	secret, sly
steed	high-spirited riding horse
tide	rise and fall of the surface of oceans and seas, caused by the attraction of the moon and sun
tramp	sound of heavy steps, of people marching
tranquil	calm, peaceful, serene; quiet or motionless
twitter	light, sharp vocal sound of birds; chirping
weathercock	weather vane that swings in the wind to show the direction from which the wind is blowing

Discussion

1. Read the first three sections of the poem aloud as a class. Do you hear a regular rhyme scheme? Do you feel a regular rhythmic beat? How many beats are in each line?
2. What makes "Paul Revere's Ride" a popular poem?
3. What is the dominant mood of the poem?
4. How does Longfellow create the feeling of dramatic tension?
5. What adjectives does Longfellow use to describe Paul Revere?
6. What other poems do you know that retell historical events? Can you recite a poem that you learned in school?

Style and Language

1. Circle the words that describe the techniques Longfellow uses to create his style in this poem.
   repetitive questions   very formal sentences   dramatic contrasts
   rhyme and alliteration   realistic dialogues   musical rhythms
   Give quotations from the poem that are examples of these techniques.

2. Choose the sentence that best describes the tone of the poem.
   a. The tone of "Paul Revere's Ride" can be described as humorous and negative.
   b. The tone of "Paul Revere's Ride" can be described as serious and positive.

3. Longfellow's language in this poem contains
   a. metaphors.
   b. religious symbols.
   c. similes.
   d. ironic humor.
   Give quotations from the poem that are examples of this language.

4. What meter is the poem written in?
   a. Iambic trimeter
   b. Iambic tetrameter
   c. Iambic pentameter
   d. Iambic hexameter

5. Identify the figure of speech in the following sentence and explain its meaning: "The fate of a nation was riding that night" (line 78).

Writing Assignments

1. Longfellow's poem begins: "Listen, my children, and you shall *hear*." Underline all the words in the poem that relate to the sense of hearing, and then write an essay analyzing Longfellow's emphasis on sounds in "Paul Revere's Ride."

2. Longfellow uses personification (giving human qualities to inanimate objects) in several places in this poem. Explain the uses of personification in lines 46–48, 78, 95–96, 97–100. What effect does Longfellow create through personification?

3. Write a poem about a famous historical figure from your country. In your poem, describe his or her accomplishments.

Group Work

Working with a partner or in a small group, read Longfellow's poem "Haroun Al Raschid," which is about the Abbasis Caliph (Muslim ruler) who ruled in Iraq from 786 to 809. Then compare and contrast it with "Ozymandias of Egypt" by the English Romantic poet Percy Bysshe Shelley. These poems both focus on ancient kings of monumental ambition. Discuss the form, content, and style of these poems. Which poem has a stronger impact and why? Write a brief summary of your discussion, and include a one-sentence statement of the main idea of each poem.

Haroun Al Raschid   1863
Henry Wadsworth Longfellow

One day, Haroun Al Raschid read
A book wherein the poet said:—

"Where are the kings, and where the rest
Of those who once the world possessed?

"They're gone with all their pomp and show,
They're gone the way that thou shalt go.

"O thou who choosest for thy share
The world, and what the world calls fair,

"Take all that it can give or lend,
But know that death is at the end!"

Haroun Al Raschid bowed his head:
Tears fell upon the page he read.

Ozymandias of Egypt   1817
Percy Bysshe Shelley

I met a traveller from an antique land
Who said: Two vast and trunkless legs of stone
Stand in the desert. Near them, on the sand,
Half sunk, a shattered visage lies, whose frown,
And wrinkled lip, and sneer of cold command,
Tell that its sculptor well those passions read
Which yet survive, stamped on these lifeless things,
The hand that mocked them and the heart that fed:
And on the pedestal these words appear:
"My name is Ozymandias, king of kings:
Look on my works, ye Mighty, and despair!"
Nothing beside remains. Round the decay
Of that colossal wreck, boundless and bare
The lone and level sands stretch far away.

Glossary	"Ozymandias of Egypt"
antique	ancient, old
boundless	without end, unlimited; vast
colossal	huge, gigantic, enormous
decay	wasting away, deterioration
fed	nourished

Percy Bysshe Shelley

lone	isolated and unfrequented
Mighty	rulers of the world
mocked	imitated
Ozymandias	Greek name for the Egyptian Pharaoh Ramses II
pedestal	base or support of a statue
shattered	broken into pieces or fragments
sneer	facial expression of scorn or contempt
stamped	imprinted, impressed, marked
trunkless	without the upper part of the body (the trunk)
vast	very large in size
visage	face
works	acts, deeds
wreck	ruin
wrinkled	curled to express displeasure; creased by frowning or aging
ye	you

Countee Cullen   From "Heritage"

"I believe that the richest contribution the Negro poet can make to the American literature of the future will be the fusion into it of his own individual artistic gifts."
James Weldon Johnson, preface to *The Book of American Negro Poetry,* 1921

"Because life in the black American community, as in every American community, is characterized by diversity, divisions, and conflicts, there can be no single approach to Negro life, the black experience, or the literature and culture created by Afro-Americans."
Abraham Chapman, introduction to *Black Voices,* 1968

"More than any other presence of the time, including Langston Hughes, Cullen defined his age, and in that sense dominated it as much as a man of Cullen's temperament could dominate anything. Alas, what he defined was not the triumphs of being black and not even its anguish but the conundrum of blackness."
Gerald Early, introduction to *My Soul's High Song: The Collected Writings of Countee Cullen,* 1991

Whether Countee Cullen (1903–46) was born in Louisville, Kentucky, or in New York City has not been determined. An orphan, he was raised in New York City by the Reverend and Mrs. Frederick Cullen, foster parents who later adopted him. He was a Phi Beta Kappa graduate of New York University, after which he received an M.A. from Harvard. Cullen's great poetic gifts were recognized when his first book of poetry, *Color,* was published in 1925, while he was still an undergraduate. A teacher, editor, and writer, Cullen produced several volumes of poetry, a novel, and a play, *St. Louis Woman,* which became a Broadway musical.

   Cullen is one of the major figures of the Harlem Renaissance, an exciting period that arose in the 1920s when African American writers achieved a new expressive power and creativity. Writers of the Harlem Renaissance include James Weldon Johnson, Claude McKay, Jean Toomer, Langston Hughes, Arna Bontemps, Sterling Brown, and Zora Neale Hurston. According to James Weldon Johnson, the Harlem Renaissance involved "an effort to get away from 'race problem' poetry, an attempt to break through racial barriers that hedge in even art in the United States, a desire to be simply poets."[1]   Although Cullen did not accept racial limitations to his poetry, his best poems focus on the black experience. As he says in "Yet Do I Marvel," one of his most famous poems : "Yet do I marvel at this curious thing: / To make a poet black, and bid him sing!"

Cullen's poetry is classical in form and romantic in theme. The Romantic poets John Keats, Percy Bysshe Shelley, and Edna St. Vincent Millay exerted a profound influence on his writing. His style is lyrical, and he uses conventional English patterns such as the sonnet to contain his richly imaginative and intellectual ideas. Somewhat pessimistic in tone, Cullen's poetry rises to a level of universal beauty that is worthy of his predecessor Keats. In "To John Keats, Poet, at Springtime," Cullen writes: "And you and I, shall we lie still, John Keats, / while Beauty summons us?"

Cullen published all of his major poems by the age of twenty-six, including "Heritage," which is considered to be his masterpiece. Later, he turned to writing novels, translations, drama, song lyrics, and children's books and became a teacher in the New York City public schools.

Preview

Skimming: Skim the reading to gain a general impression.
1. Read the title and first line of the poem.
2. Skim the poem to get an idea of its form and length.

Questioning: Answer the following questions and discuss your answers in class.
Do you live in the land of your ancestors? If not, would you like to go back to visit that land?

Scanning: Scan to answer the following question to get an idea of the content and style.
1. For how many centuries has Cullen been removed (away) from Africa?
2. What sound does the poet want to hear?

From "Heritage"   1925
Countee Cullen

What is Africa to me:
Copper sun or scarlet sea,
Jungle star or jungle track,
Strong bronzed men, or regal black
Women from whose loins I sprang
When the birds of Eden sang?
One three centuries removed
From the scenes his fathers loved,
Spicy grove, cinnamon tree,
What is Africa to me?

So I lie, who all day long
Want no sound except the song
Sung by wild barbaric birds
Goading massive jungle herds,
Juggernauts of flesh that pass
Trampling tall defiant grass
Where young forest lovers lie,

---

1.   Preface to *The Book of American Negro Poetry,* revised ed. (New York: Harcourt Brace Jovanovich, 1931).

Plighting troth beneath the sky.
So I lie, who always hear,
Though I cram against my ear
Both my thumbs, and keep them there,
Great drums throbbing through the air.
So I lie, whose fount of pride,
Dear distress, and joy allied,
Is my somber flesh and skin,
With the dark blood dammed within
Like great pulsing tides of wine
That, I fear, must burst the fine
Channels of the chafing net
Where they surge and foam and fret.

Africa? A book one thumbs
Listlessly, till slumber comes.
Unremembered are her bats
Circling through the night, her cats
Crouching in the river reeds,
Stalking gentle flesh that feeds
By the river brink; no more
Does the bugle-throated roar
Cry that monarch claws have leapt
From the scabbards where they slept.
Silver snakes that once a year
Doff the lovely coats you wear,
Seek no covert in your fear
Lest a mortal eye should see;
What's your nakedness to me?
Here no leprous flowers rear
Fierce corollas in the air;
Here no bodies sleek and wet,
Dripping mingled rain and sweat,
Tread the savage measures of
Jungle boys and girls in love.
What is last year's snow to me,
Last year's anything? The tree
Budding yearly must forget
How its past arose or set—
Bough and blossom, flower, fruit,
Even what shy bird with mute
Wonder at her travail there,
Meekly labored in its hair.
One three centuries removed
From the scenes his fathers loved,
Spicy grove, cinnamon tree,
What is Africa to me?

Glossary   From "Heritage"

barbaric	uncivilized, primitive, unrestrained
brink	edge, bank
bronzed	reddish-brown color
chafing	rubbing
copper	reddish-brown; copper-colored
corollas	petals or inner leaves of a flower
covert	shelter, protected place, hiding place
cram	to force, press
dammed	confined, kept back
doff	to remove, discard
Eden	garden where Adam and Eve lived; paradise
fount	source
fret	to become rough or disturbed
goading	pushing into action
juggernauts	terrible, irresistible forces; sacred idols on carts (India)
leprous	like the disease of leprosy
lest	that, for fear that
listlessly	without interest, as a result of weariness or dejection
loins	part of the body that gives birth; reproductive organs
meekly	patiently, gently
monarch	royal
mute	silent, voiceless
plighting troth	promising marriage
pulsing	regular beating, vibrating
regal	royal, splendid, magnificent
scabbards	sheaths for swords and daggers
sprang	emerged suddenly
stalking	pursuing an enemy secretly
surge	to swell violently; to rise and fall
thumbs	turns with the thumb
travail	very hard work

Discussion

1. What does the word *heritage* mean to you? What is your heritage?
2. What does Cullen miss about Africa?
3. How does Cullen feel about his "somber flesh and skin"?
4. Explain why Cullen asks these questions: What is Africa to me? What's your nakedness to me? What is last year's snow to me, last year's anything?
5. What is the main idea or theme of "Heritage"?
6. What do you find beautiful or memorable about this poem?

Style and Language

1. Cullen uses a variety of techniques to create his style in the opening of "Heritage": allusion, color words, enumeration, metaphor, parallelism, and questions. Identify each of these techniques in the following lines:

   > What is Africa to me:
   > Copper sun or scarlet sea,
   > Jungle star or jungle track,
   > Strong bronzed men, or regal black
   > Women from whose loins I sprang
   > When the birds of Eden sang?

2. Circle the words that best describe the tone of "Heritage."

subjective	melancholy	unemotional
objective	cheerful	emotional

3. The intensity and power of "Heritage" are created through Cullen's use of
   a. paradox.
   b. repetition.
   c. questions.
   d. religious symbolism.
   Give quotations from the poem that support your choices.

4. Explain what is being compared and how these figures of speech clarify Cullen's theme:
   simile: "dark blood dammed within / like great pulsing tides of wine" (lines 26–27)
   metaphor: "Africa? A book one thumbs / listlessly, til slumber comes" (lines 31–32)
   personifications: tides of wine "surge and foam and fret " (line 30); the "tree / budding yearly must forget / How its past arose or set " (lines 54–55)

5. "Heritage" is traditional in form: it has four regular stresses per line and rhymed couplets. Would it be as powerful or beautiful if it were in free verse? Rewrite the first eighteen lines of "Heritage" in a free verse style (no rhyme or regular rhythm), adding more words if necessary, and read your lines to the class.

Writing Assignments

1. Cullen uses beautiful imagery to intensify the emotional power of his poem. Write an essay analyzing the type of imagery he uses and the senses to which it appeals (sight, hearing, taste, touch, or smell).

2. Write a poem asking the question "What is _____ to me?" Use the name of your native country, and model the rhyme scheme and rhythm on Cullen's poem.

3. "Heritage" contains a great deal of alliteration. Underline all the alliterative sounds, and write a one-paragraph explanation of how these sounds enhance Cullen's meaning.

Group Work

Working with a partner or in a small group, read these poems by the African American poets Claude McKay (1891–1948) and Langston Hughes (1902–67), who were contemporaries of Countee Cullen. Then compare and contrast "Outcast" and "Afro-American Fragment" with Cullen's "Heritage." In your analysis, discuss the following questions:

- Do the poems have the same rhythm or rhyme?
- Are there any identical or similar words?
- Is the mood the same?
- Which poem seems the most traditional?
- Which seems the most convincing?

Write a summary of your discussion, and include a one-sentence statement of the main idea of each poem.

Outcast   1922
Claude McKay

For the dim regions whence my fathers came
My spirit, bondaged[1] by the body, longs.
Words felt, but never heard, my lips would frame;
My soul would sing forgotten jungle songs.
I would go back to darkness and to peace,
But the great western world holds me in fee,[2]
And I may never hope for full release
While to its alien gods I bend my knee.
Something in me is lost, forever lost,
Some vital thing has gone out of my heart,
And I must walk the way of life a ghost
Among the sons of earth, a thing apart.

For I was born, far from my native clime,[3]
Under the white man's menace, out of time.

Afro-American Fragment   1930
Langston Hughes

So long,
So far away
Is Africa.
Not even memories alive
Save those that history books create,
Save those that songs
Beat back into the blood—
Beat out of blood with words sad-sung
In strange un-Negro tongue—
So long,
So far away
Is Africa.

Subdued and time-lost
Are the drums—and yet
Through some vast mist of race
There comes this song
I do not understand,
This song of atavistic[4] land,
Of bitter yearnings lost
Without a place—
So long,
So far away
Is Africa's
Dark face.

---

1. enslaved
2. ownership
3. climate
4. tribal or archaic

Chapter Synthesis

Write a synthesis in which you compare and contrast the poetry of Emily Dickinson, Walt Whitman, Henry Wadsworth Longfellow, and Countee Cullen. Which poet seems to be the most nontraditional (modern)? Justify your opinion with specific quotations and examples from their poems. Consider the form, content, and style of their poetry. Thesis: Although Dickinson, Whitman, Longfellow, and Cullen all created unique and beautiful poetry, Whitman is the most nontraditional in his form, style, and content.

Chapter 5

Nineteenth- and Early-Twentieth-Century American Prose: The Novel

"Every novel is a debtor to Homer."
Ralph Waldo Emerson, *Representative Men,* 1850

"How far off from life and manners and motives the novel still is! Life lies about us dumb; the day as we know it has not yet found a tongue."
Ralph Waldo Emerson, *Society and Solitude,* 1870

"My task which I am trying to achieve is, by the power of the written word to make you hear, to make you feel—it is, before all, to make you see. That—and no more, and it is everything."
Joseph Conrad, *New Review,* December 1897

"Art deals with what we see; it must first contribute full-handed that ingredient; it plucks its material, otherwise expressed, in the garden of life."
Henry James, preface to *The Ambassadors,* 1907

"Each sentence must have at its heart, a little spark of fire, and this, whatever the risk, the novelist must pluck with his own hands from the blaze."
Virginia Woolf, *The Common Reader,* 1925

Since 1880, the novel has been the major American literary prose form, and the origins of the modern novel can be found in the novels of the nineteenth century. From the early frontier adventure tales of James Fenimore Cooper (1820s–1840s) to the complex moral and social relationships of Henry James (1870s–1904), the novel continued to develop in an ever more realistic direction.

As Henry James says in *The Art of Fiction* (1884): "The only reason for the existence of a novel is that it does attempt to represent life. A novel is in its broadest definition a personal, a direct impression of life: that, to begin with, constitutes its value, which is greater or lesser according to the intensity of the impression." The nineteenth-century novelists were interested in representing life as they lived and knew it. They wrote about the emotions and experiences of average men and women, with particular focus on the development of plot, the exploration of character, and the creation of natural settings.

According to Walter Allen in *The English Novel,* there is no "evolution in the form of the novel that can be equated with improvement. There is nothing in the development of art analogous with material progress. Art does not get better and better. Its manifestations merely change, and Richardson is as perfect in his way as Henry James in his." [1]

In fact, the novel has continued to change; the innovations in content, style, and form have increased, and there is emphasis on revealing the inner lives of the characters. At the same time, novelists have become more sophisticated in their control of point of view, one of the most important structural factors. Henry James's early novels are told from the perspective of the omniscient author (third-person narrator), who acts as a kind of mediator between the reader and the novel, but his later novels, while using the limited third-person narrator, present complex, multiple points of view. Ishmael in Herman Melville's *Moby Dick* and Mark Twain's Huck Finn tell their own stories (first-person narrative). Eventually, the first-person narrative led to the development of the stream-of-consciousness method of the twentieth century, which is seen in the novels of Virginia Woolf and James Joyce.

Henry James   From *Washington Square*

"Henry James went to France and read Turgenev. W. D. Howells stayed at home and read Henry James."
George Moore, *Confessions of a Young Man,* 1888

"Henry James writes fiction as if it were a painful duty."
Oscar Wilde, *The Decay of Lying,* 1891

"You are never startled, never surprised, never thrilled or never enraptured; always delighted by that masterly prose that is as correct, as classical, as calm and as subtle as the music of Mozart."
Willa Cather, "Henry James," *Courier,* November 16, 1895

"He has created a genre of his own. He has the distinction that makes the scientist a servant; he has contributed something to the sum, the common stock."
W. C. Brownell, *American Prose Masters,* 1909

"He wrote social comedy—light, witty, brilliant, full of the comic strokes of moral superiority and slashed with the darker strokes of straight perception, showing, now and then, the bare cross-grain of inner disturbance: the springs of action that run counter to all the interests of the self."
R. P. Blackmur, introduction to *Washington Square and The Europeans,* 1959

---

1.   Walter Allen, *The English Novel* (New York: E.P. Dutton and Co., 1958) p. XXIII.

Henry James (1843–1916) was born in New York City. His father was a theologian, and his brother was the philosopher and psychologist William James. Educated abroad and at Harvard Law School, James chose to devote himself to writing fiction. He moved to Europe in 1875, and lived for twenty years in London, where he wrote stories and novels centering on the themes of the expatriate and the international experience. Because he was an American living in England, he wrote with sensitivity about the contrasts between the young American and the older European cultures. The characters in his novels, who are frequently traveling abroad, exemplify American innocence and European sophistication.

James is considered one of the greatest novelists of all time. A member of the realistic school of writing, James presents the moral and psychological truths that underlie human behavior. Throughout his literary career, he subtly analyzed the ambiguities and uncertainties of social manners and relationships. His advice to writers was to "be one of those on whom nothing is lost," and this intensity of feeling is a characteristic of his work.

His novels are finely crafted and perfect in form. His prose style is somewhat complicated because of the intellectual complexities it conveys. Nevertheless, his stories are fascinating portrayals of the inner lives of his characters, who are faced with difficult ethical choices in rather tragic situations. James's novels, which usually have an international setting, deal with the basic question of good and evil. To James, evil is one person's attempt to control the destiny of another person, and good is the ability to achieve personal integrity and to live life with awareness, "to see all you can."

James's central contribution to the genre of the novel is his limitation of the third-person narrative point of view, in which the reader sees and understands a story through the eyes of one or a few characters. In his later works, by developing these characters with whom the reader can identify and experience the drama, he enlarged and refined the realistic method and determined the future course of the novel.

Major works by James include *The American, The Portrait of a Lady, The Wings of the Dove, The Ambassadors,* and *The Golden Bowl.* He also wrote a series of prefaces to his novels called *The Art of the Novel,* stories ("The Turn of the Screw"), and short novels (*Daisy Miller, The Europeans, Washington Square*). In chapter XXIV of *Washington Square,* Dr. Sloper, who strongly disapproves of his daughter Catherine's engagement to Morris Townsend, takes her abroad, hoping that she will forget him and break her engagement.

Preview

Skimming: Skim the reading to gain a general impression.
1. Read the title and first sentence of the chapter.
2. Skim the chapter to get an idea of its form and length.

Questioning: Answer the following question and discuss your answers in class.
1. Do parents in the United States give their children too much freedom?
2. Would you marry someone even if your parents disapproved of him or her?

Scanning: Scan to answer the following questions to get an idea of the content and style.
1. Where were Catherine and her father at the end of the summer?
2. What does Catherine mean (intend) to do about Morris Townsend?

From *Washington Square*   1881
Henry James

Chapter XXIV

The Doctor, during the first six months he was abroad, never spoke to his daughter of their little difference, partly on system, and partly because he had a great many other things to think about. It was idle to attempt to ascertain the state of her affections without direct inquiry, because if she had not had an expressive manner among the familiar influences of home, she failed to gather animation from the mountains of Switzerland or the monuments of Italy. She was always her father's docile and reasonable associate—going through their sightseeing in deferential silence, never complaining of fatigue, always ready to start at the hour he had appointed overnight, making no foolish criticisms, and indulging in no refinements of appreciation. "She is about as intelligent as the bundle of shawls," the Doctor said, her main superiority being that, while the bundle of shawls sometimes got lost, or tumbled out of the carriage, Catherine was always at her post, and had a firm and ample seat. But her father had expected this, and he was not constrained to set down her intellectual limitations as a tourist to sentimental depression; she had completely divested herself of the characteristics of a victim, and during the whole time that they were abroad she never uttered an audible sigh. He supposed she was in correspondence with Morris Townsend, but he held his peace about it, for he never saw the young man's letters, and Catherine's own missives were always given to the courier to post. She heard from her lover with considerable regularity, but his letters came enclosed in Mrs. Penniman's; so that, whenever the Doctor handed her a packet addressed in his sister's hand, he was an involuntary instrument of the passion he condemned. Catherine made this reflection, and six months earlier she would have felt bound to give him warning; but now she deemed herself absolved. There was a sore spot in her heart that his own words had made when once she spoke to him as she thought honor prompted; she would try and please him as far as she could, but she would never speak that way again. She read her lover's letters in secret.

One day, at the end of the summer, the two travellers found themselves in a lonely valley of the Alps. They were crossing one of the passes, and on the long ascent they had got out of the carriage and had wandered much in advance. After awhile the Doctor described a foot-path which, leading through a transverse valley, would bring them out, as he justly supposed, at a much higher point of the ascent. They followed this devious way, and finally lost the path; the valley proved very wild and rough, and their walk became rather a scramble. They were good walkers, however, and they took their adventure easily; from time to time they stopped, that Catherine might rest; and then she sat upon a stone and looked about her at the hard-featured rocks and the glowing sky. It was late in the afternoon, in the last of August; night was coming on, and as they had reached a great elevation, the air was cold and sharp. In the west there was a great suffusion of cold red light, which made the sides of the little valley look only the more rugged and dusky. During one of their pauses her father left her and wandered away to some high place, at a distance, to get a view. He was out of sight; she sat there alone in the stillness, which was just touched by the vague murmur somewhere of a mountain brook. She thought of Morris Townsend, and the place was so desolate and lonely that he seemed very far away. Her father remained absent a long time; she began to wonder what had become of him. But at last he reappeared, coming toward her in the clear twilight, and she got up to go on. He made no motion to proceed, however, but came close to her, as if he had something to say. He stopped in front of her, and stood looking at her with eyes that had kept the light of the flushing snow-summits on which they had just been fixed. Then abruptly, in a low tone, he asked her an unexpected question,

"Have you given him up?"

The question was unexpected, but Catherine was only superficially unprepared.

"No, father," she answered.

He looked at her again for some moments without speaking.

"Does he write to you?" he asked.

"Yes, about twice a month."

The Doctor looked up and down the valley, swinging his stick; then he said to her, in the same low tone,

"I am very angry."

She wondered what he meant—whether he wished to frighten her. If he did, the place was well chosen: this hard, melancholy dell, abandoned by the summer light, made her feel her loneliness. She looked around her, and her heart grew cold; for a moment her fear was great. But she could think of nothing to say, save to murmur gently, "I am sorry."

"You try my patience," her father went on, "and you ought to know what I am. I am not a very good man. Though I am very smooth externally, at bottom I am very passionate; and I assure you I can be very hard."

She could not think why he told her these things. Had he brought her there on purpose, and was it part of a plan? What was the plan? Catherine asked herself. Was it to startle her suddenly into a retraction—to take an advantage of her by dread? Dread of what? The place was ugly and lonely, but the place could do her no harm. There was a kind of still intensity about her father which made him dangerous, but Catherine hardly went so far as to say to herself that it might be part of his plan to fasten his hand—the neat, fine, supple hand of a distinguished physician—in her throat. Nevertheless, she receded a step. "I am sure you can be anything you please," she said; and it was her simple belief.

"I am very angry," he replied, more sharply.

"Why has it taken you so suddenly?"

"It has not taken me suddenly. I have been raging inwardly for the last six months. But just now this seemed a good place to flare out. It's so quiet, and we are alone."

"Yes, it's very quiet," said Catherine, vaguely looking about her. "Won't you come back to the carriage?"

"In a moment. Do you mean that in all this time you have not yielded an inch?"

"I would if I could, father; but I can't."

The Doctor looked round him too. "Should you like to be left in such a place as this, to starve?"

"What do you mean?" cried the girl.

"That will be your fate—that's how he will leave you."

He would not touch her, but he had touched Morris. The warmth came back to her heart. "That is not true, father," she broke out, "and you ought not to say it. It is not right, and it's not true."

He shook his head slowly. "No, it's not right, because you won't believe it. But it *is* true. Come back to the carriage."

He turned away, and she followed him; he went faster, and was presently much in advance. But from time to time he stopped, without turning round, to let her keep up with him, and she made her way forward with difficulty, her heart beating with the excitement of having for the first time spoken to him in violence. By this time it had grown almost dark, and she ended by losing sight of him. But she kept her course, and after a little, the valley making a sudden turn, she gained the road, where the carriage stood waiting. In it sat her father, rigid and silent; in silence, too, she took her place beside him.

It seemed to her, later, in looking back upon all this, that for days afterward not a word had been exchanged between them. The scene had been a strange one, but it had not permanently affected her feeling toward her father, for it was natural, after all, that he should occasionally make a scene of some kind, and he had let her alone for six months. The strangest part of it was that he had said he was not a good man; Catherine wondered a good deal what he had meant by that. The statement failed to appeal to her credence, and it was not grateful to any resentment that she entertained. Even in the utmost bitterness that she might feel, it would give her no satisfaction to think him less complete. Such a saying as that was a part of his great subtlety—men so clever as he might say anything and mean anything; and as to his being hard, that surely, in a man, was a virtue.

He let her alone for six months more—six months during which she accommodated herself without a protest to the extension of their tour. But he spoke again at the end of this time: it was at the very last, the night before they embarked for New York, in the hotel at Liverpool. They had been dining together in a great, dim, musty sitting-room; and then the cloth had been removed, and the Doctor walked slowly up and down. Catherine at last took her candle to go to bed, but her father motioned her stay.

"What do you mean to do when you get home?" he asked, while she stood there with her candle in her hand.

"Do you mean about Mr. Townsend?"

"About Mr. Townsend."

"We shall probably marry."

The Doctor took several turns again while she waited.

"Do you hear from him as much as ever?"

"Yes, twice a month," said Catherine, promptly.

"And does he always talk about marriage?"

"Oh yes; that is, he talks about other things too, but he always says something about that."

"I am glad to hear he varies his subjects; his letters might otherwise be monotonous."

"He writes beautifully," said Catherine, who was very glad of a chance to say it.

"They always write beautifully. However, in a given case that doesn't diminish the merit. So, as soon as you arrive, you are going off with him?"

This seemed a rather gross way of putting it, and something that there was of dignity in Catherine resented it.

"I cannot tell you till we arrive," she said.

"That's reasonable enough," her father answered. "That's all I ask of you—that you *do* tell me, that you give me definite notice. When a poor man is to lose his only child, he likes to have an inkling of it beforehand."

"Oh, father! you will not lose me," Catherine said, spilling her candle wax.

"Three days before will do," he went on, "if you are in a position to be positive then. He ought to be very thankful to me, do you know. I have done a mighty good thing for him in taking you abroad; your value is twice as great, with all the knowledge and taste that you have acquired. A year ago, you were perhaps a little limited— a little rustic; but now you have seen everything, and appreciated everything, and you will be a most entertaining companion. We have fattened the sheep for him before he kills it." Catherine turned away, and stood staring at the blank door. "Go to bed," said her father; "and as we don't go aboard till noon, you may sleep late. We shall probably have a most uncomfortable voyage."

Glossary	From *Washington Square*
absolved	pronounced free from guilt or blame
accommodated	adjusted, adapted
animation	vivacity; brisk, lively quality
ascertain	to find out with certainty
audible	loud enough to be heard
credence	belief, especially in the reports or testimony of another
deemed	thought or believed
deferential	very respectful
dell	a small, secluded valley or glen, usually a wooded one
descried	caught sight of
desolate	uninhabited, deserted
devious	not in a straight path; winding
diminish	to reduce in degree or importance
divested	deprived, rid
docile	easy to manage or discipline
embarked	went aboard a ship
fatigue	physical or mental exhaustion
flare out	to burst out suddenly in anger or violence
gross	lacking in refinement, insensitive
indulging	yielding to or satisfying (a desire)
inkling	vague idea, slight indication
involuntary	unintentional, not done of one's own free will
missives	letters or written messages
monotonous	having little or no variation or variety
musty	having a stale, moldy smell
notice	warning, announcement, or information
receded	moved back or away
retraction	withdrawal, as of a statement, promise, or charge
rigid	not moving, firmly fixed
rustic	lacking refinement, elegance, polish, or sophistication
shawls	square cloths worn as a covering for the head or shoulders
still	quiet or silent
subtlety	the quality of being clever or ingenious, sly or crafty, indirect
suffusion	an overspreading so as to fill with a glow, color, or fluid
supple	able to bend and move easily
transverse	situated or placed across
try	to subject to annoyance
utmost	greatest

Discussion

1. Summarize what takes place in chapter XXIV of *Washington Square*.
2. Where does James use description of the landscape to emphasize the characters' emotions?
3. Describe the personalities of Dr. Sloper and Catherine.

4. Explain the meaning of the doctor's metaphorical statement to Catherine about her trip abroad: "We have fattened the sheep for him before he kills it." Who is "the sheep"? Who is "him"? How will he kill it?

5. Which character do you have the most sympathy for or identify with? Why?

6. Will Catherine marry Morris Townsend? Why or why not? How would you end the story?

Style and Language

1. How would you describe James's writing style in the following sentences?
   There was a kind of still intensity about her father which made him dangerous, but Catherine hardly went so far as to say to herself that it might be part of his plan to fasten his hand—the neat, fine, supple hand of a distinguished physician—in her throat. Nevertheless, she receded a step. "I am sure you can be anything you please," she said; and it was her simple belief.

2. Select the sentence that best expresses your opinion.
   a. The tone in *Washington Square* is dramatic, highly emotional, and subjective.
   b. The tone in *Washington Square* is balanced, rather calm, and objective.

3. James's language is characterized by
   a. modern idiomatic expressions.
   b. complex words and sentence structure.
   c. realistic dialogue.
   d. humorous anecdotes.

4. Choose the best paraphrase of the following statement by Catherine's father: ". . . and I assure you that I can be very hard" (p. 145).
   a. I am an inflexible and strong person.
   b. I am a difficult person to understand.

5. The novel is told from the point of view of
   a. Morris Townsend.
   b. Catherine.
   c. the doctor.
   d. the third-person narrator (omniscient author).

6. James uses a simile to express the doctor's opinion of his daughter's intelligence: "She is about as intelligent as the bundle of shawls." What does this sentence reveal about the personality of the doctor?
   a. The doctor is a kind and gentle person.
   b. The doctor is a cold and critical person.
   c. The doctor is a clever and witty person.
   d. The doctor is an artistic and sensitive person.

Writing Assignments

1. Have you ever had a major difference of opinion with a family member on an important issue? Did you give in or did you maintain your position? Describe the disagreement and the outcome in a short essay.

2. Write a summary of the action that takes place in chapter XXIV of *Washington Square*.

3. In *Washington Square* (chapter XXIV) Catherine and her father have opposite opinions about Catherine's future. Write an essay analyzing their conflict and explaining which character you most identify with. Justify your position with specific reasons and quotations from the text.

Group Work

In some countries such as India and China, arranged marriages, in which parents choose husbands or wives for their children, are still customary. Divorce statistics show that these arranged marriages are as successful as nonarranged marriages. Working with a partner or in a small group, discuss the marriage customs in your country. Then read the following statements and decide which one represents your opinion. Share your opinion with the other members of your group, and justify your point of view with specific reasons. Write a brief summary of your discussion.
   1. Parents should choose their children's husbands or wives.
   2. Parents should approve of their children's choices for husbands or wives.
   3. Parents should not interfere at all in their children's decisions about marriage.

Mark Twain (Samuel Clemens)   From *The Adventures of Huckleberry Finn*

"I think he mainly misses fire; I think his life misses fire: he might have been something; he comes near to being something: but he never arrives."
Walt Whitman, *To Horace Traubel in Camden*, c. 1890

"I would rather sail on the raft down the Missouri again with 'Huck' Finn and Jim than go down the Nile in December or see Venice from a gondola in May."
Willa Cather, *Home Monthly,* May 1897

"He never wrote a line that a father could not read to a daughter."
W. H. Taft, statement to the press on Clemens's death, 1910

"There are some books that refuse to be written. They stand their ground year after year and will not be persuaded. It isn't because the book is not there and worth being written—it is only because the right form for the story does not present itself. There is only one right form for a story and if you fail to find that form the story will not tell itself."
Mark Twain (Samuel Clemens), *The Autobiography of Mark Twain,* 1917

"*Huckleberry Finn* is more telling an indictment of slavery than more patently antislavery novels are. . . .The characterization of Jim, superstitious but shrewd, kindly, self-sacrificial, but determined to be free—not contented in slavery—all of these are vividly rendered."
Sterling A. Brown, *Massachusetts Review,* 1966

Mark Twain (1835–1910), the pseudonym for Samuel Langhorne Clemens, was born in Missouri. He received only a grade school education, but he was a man of many and varied accomplishments: riverboat pilot, gold miner, journalist, printer, publisher, and author of both humorous and serious fiction.

Twain first became known as a humorist after he published *The Celebrated Jumping Frog of Calaveras County, and Other Sketches* (1867) and *Innocents Abroad* (1869). He also wrote *Roughing It,* about his life as a miner in Nevada, *The Prince and the Pauper,* a story for children, and *A Connecticut Yankee in King Arthur's Court,* a satire on American society.

Twain is best known as an American regional author who writes about the simple folk of the old South. His most popular works are *The Adventures of Tom Sawyer,* a narrative about the pleasures and pains of childhood, and *The Adventures of Huckleberry Finn* (the sequel). In these books, Twain describes the life of the frontier in the Mississippi Valley and makes fun of the conventions of society and the hypocrisy of people. His use of language is innovative because his characters speak in authentic dialects, adding to the realism of his novels.

Huckleberry Finn is a more serious and pessimistic book in which Twain recreates the complex moral issues of slavery in the relationship between Huck and the runaway slave Jim. His major theme is the autonomy of the individual. The basic structure of the novel is the journey Huck and Jim take on a raft down the Mississippi River. The novel contrasts the freedom and happiness of the river with the slavery and violence of the shore. The Mississippi River is a symbol of the freedom, spirit, and power of the natural world that Twain evokes so beautifully.

Twain's enormous contribution to American literature can be summarized by the statements made by two well-known writers. In *My Mark Twain* (1910), William Dean Howells said: "Clemens was sole, incomparable, the Lincoln of our literature." In 1935, Ernest Hemingway wrote in *Green Hills of Africa:* "All modern American literature comes from one book by Mark Twain called *Huckleberry Finn.*"

Preview

Skimming: Skim the reading to gain a general impression.
1. Read the title and first sentence of each chapter.
2. Skim each chapter to get an idea of its form and length.

Questioning: Answer the following question and discuss your answers in class.
Do you know who Huckleberry Finn and Tom Sawyer are? If so, describe them.

Scanning: Scan to answer the following questions to get an idea of the content and style.
1. Chapter I: Who took Huck into her house to try to civilize him?
2. Chapter IX: Who did Huck and Jim find in the floating house?
3. Chapter X: Where did the snake bite Jim?

From *The Adventures of Huckleberry Finn*   **1884**
Mark Twain (Samuel Clemens)

EXPLANATORY

In this book a number of dialects are used, to wit: the Missouri Negro dialect; the extremist form of the backwoods Southwestern dialect; the ordinary "Pike County" dialect; and four modified varieties of this last. The shadings have not been done in a haphazard fashion, or by guesswork; but painstakingly, and with the trustworthy guidance and support of personal familiarity with these several forms of speech.

I make this explanation for the reason that without it many readers would suppose that all these characters were trying to talk alike and not succeeding.

THE AUTHOR

NOTICE

Persons attempting to find a motive in this narrative will be prosecuted; persons attempting to find a moral in it will be banished; persons attempting to find a plot in it will be shot.

BY ORDER OF THE AUTHOR,
Per G. G., Chief of Ordnance.

Chapter I   Civilizing Huck—Miss Watson—Tom Sawyer Waits

You don't know about me without you have read a book by the name of *The Adventures of Tom Sawyer;* but that ain't no matter. That book was made by Mr. Mark Twain, and he told the truth, mainly. There was things which he stretched, but mainly he told the truth. That is nothing. I never seen anybody but lied one time or another, without it was Aunt Polly, or the widow, or maybe Mary. Aunt Polly—Tom's Aunt Polly, she is—and Mary, and the Widow Douglas is all told about in that book, which is mostly a true book, with some stretchers, as I said before.

Now the way that the book winds up is this: Tom and me found the money that the robbers hid in the cave, and it made us rich. We got six thousand dollars apiece—all gold. It was an awful sight of money when it was piled up. Well, Judge Thatcher he took it and put it out at interest, and it fetched us a dollar a day apiece all the year round—more than a body could tell what to do with. The Widow Douglas she took me for her son, and allowed she would sivilize me; but it was rough living in the house all the time, considering how dismal regular and decent the widow was in all her ways; and so when I couldn't stand it no longer I lit out. I got into my old rags and my sugar hogshead again, and was free and satisfied. But Tom Sawyer he hunted me up and said he was going to start a band of robbers, and I might join if I would go back to the widow and be respectable. So I went back.

The widow she cried over me, and called me a poor lost lamb, and she called me a lot of other names, too, but she never meant no harm by it. She put me in them new clothes again, and I couldn't do nothing but sweat and sweat, and feel all cramped up. Well, then, the old thing commenced again. The widow rung a bell for supper, and you had to come to time. When you got to the table you couldn't go right to eating, but you had to wait for the widow to tuck down her head and grumble a little over the victuals, though there warn't really anything the matter with them—that is, nothing only everything was cooked by itself. In a barrel of odds and ends it is different; things get mixed up, and the juice kind of swaps around, and the things go better.

After supper she got out her book and learned me about Moses and the Bulrushers, and I was in a sweat to find out all about him; but by and by she let it out that Moses had been dead a considerable long time; so then I didn't care no more about him, because I don't take no stock in dead people.

Pretty soon I wanted to smoke, and asked the widow to let me. But she wouldn't. She said it was a mean practice and wasn't clean, and I must try to not do it any more. That is just the way with some people. They get down on a thing when they don't know nothing about it. Here she was a-bothering about Moses, which was no kin to her, and no use to anybody, being gone, you see, yet finding a power of fault with me for doing a thing that had some good in it. And she took snuff, too; of course that was all right, because she done it herself.

Her sister, Miss Watson, a tolerable slim old maid, with goggles on, had just come to live with her, and took a set at me now with a spelling book. She worked me middling hard for about an hour, and then the widow made her ease up. I couldn't stood it much longer. Then for an hour it was deadly dull, and I was fidgety. Miss Watson would say, "Don't put your feet up there, Huckleberry"; and "Don't scrunch up like that, Huckleberry—set up straight"; and pretty soon she would say, "Don't gap and stretch like that, Huckleberry—why don't you try to behave?" Then she told me all about the bad place, and I said I wished I was there. She got mad then, but I didn't mean no harm. All I wanted was to go somewheres; all I wanted was a change, I warn't particular. She said it was wicked to say what I said; said she wouldn't say it for the whole world; *she* was going to live so as to go to the good place. Well, I couldn't see no advantage in going where she was going, so I made up my mind I wouldn't try for it. But I never said so, because it would only make trouble, and wouldn't do no good.

Now she had got a start, and she went on and told me all about the good place. She said all a body would have to do there was to go around all day long with a harp and sing, forever and ever. So I didn't think much of it. But I never said so. I asked her if she reckoned Tom Sawyer would go there, and she said not by a considerable sight. I was glad about that, because I wanted him and me to be together.

Miss Watson she kept pecking at me, and it got tiresome and lonesome. By and by they fetched the niggers in and had prayers, and then everybody was off to bed. I went up to my room with a piece of candle, and put it on the table. Then I set down in a chair by the window and tried to think of something cheerful, but it warn't no use. I felt so lonesome I most wished I was dead. The stars were shining, and the leaves rustled in the woods ever so mournful; and I heard an owl, away off, who-whooing about somebody that was dead, and a whippowill and a dog crying about somebody that was going to die; and the wind was trying to whisper something to me, and I couldn't make out what it was, and so it made the cold shivers run over me. Then away out in the woods I heard that kind of a sound that a ghost makes when it wants to tell about something that's on its mind and can't make itself understood, and so can't rest easy in its grave, and has to go about that way every night grieving. I got so downhearted and scared I did wish I had some company. Pretty soon a spider went crawling up my shoulder, and I flipped it off and it lit in the candle; and before I could budge it was all shriveled up. I didn't need anybody to tell me that that was an awful bad sign and would fetch me some bad luck, so I was scared and most shook the clothes off of me. I got up and turned around in my tracks three times and crossed my breast every time; and then I tied up a little lock of my hair with a thread to keep witches away. But I hadn't no confidence. You do that when you've lost a horseshoe that you've found, instead of nailing it up over the door, but I hadn't ever heard anybody say it was any way to keep off bad luck when you'd killed a spider.

I set down again, a-shaking all over, and got out my pipe for a smoke; for the house was all as still as death now, and so the widow wouldn't know. Well, after a long time I heard the clock away off in the town go boom—boom—boom—twelve licks; and all still again—stiller than ever. Pretty soon I heard a twig snap down in the dark amongst the trees—something was a-stirring. I set still and listened. Directly I could just barely hear a *"me-yow! me-yow!"* down there. That was good! Says I, *"me-yow! me-yow!"* as soft as I could, and then I put out the light and scrambled out of the window on to the shed. Then I slipped down to the ground and crawled in among the trees, and sure enough, there was Tom Sawyer waiting for me.

Chapter IX   The Cave—The Floating House

I wanted to go and look at a place right about the middle of the island that I'd found when I was exploring; so we started and soon got to it, because the island was only three miles long and a quarter of a mile wide.

This place was a tolerable long, steep hill or ridge about forty foot high. We had a rough time getting to the top, the sides was so steep and the bushes so thick. We tramped and clumb around all over it, and by and by found a good big cavern in the rock, most up to the top on the side towards Illinois. The cavern was as big as two or three rooms bunched together, and Jim could stand up straight in it. It was cool in there. Jim was for putting our traps in there right away, but I said we didn't want to be climbing up and down there all the time.

Jim said if we had the canoe hid in a good place, and had all the traps in the cavern, we could rush there if anybody was to come to the island, and they would never find us without dogs. And, besides, he said them little birds had said it was going to rain, and did I want the things to get wet?

So we went back and got the canoe, and paddled up abreast the cavern, and lugged all the traps up there. Then we hunted up a place close by to hide the canoe in, amongst the thick willows. We took some fish off of the lines and set them again, and begun to get ready for dinner.

The door of the cavern was big enough to roll a hogshead in, and on one side of the door the floor stuck out a little bit, and was flat and a good place to build a fire on. So we built it there and cooked dinner.

We spread the blankets inside for a carpet, and eat our dinner in there. We put all the other things handy at the back of the cavern. Pretty soon it darkened up, and begun to thunder and lighten; so the birds was right about it. Directly it begun to rain, and it rained like all fury, too, and I never see the wind blow so. It was one of these regular summer storms. It would get so dark that it looked all blue-black outside, and lovely; and the rain would thrash along by so thick that the trees off a little ways looked dim and spider-webby; and here would come a blast of wind that would bend the trees down and turn up the pale underside of the leaves; and then a perfect ripper of a gust would follow along and set the branches to tossing their arms as if they was just wild; and next, when it was just about the bluest and blackest—*fst!* it was as bright as glory, and you'd have a little glimpse of treetops a-plunging about away off yonder in the storm, hundreds of yards further than you could see before; dark as sin again in a second, and now you'd hear the thunder let go with an awful crash, and then go rumbling, grumbling, tumbling, down the sky towards the under side of the world, like rolling empty barrels downstairs—where it's long stairs and they bounce a good deal, you know.

"Jim, this is nice," I says. "I wouldn't want to be nowhere else but here. Pass me along another hunk of fish and some hot cornbread."

"Well, you wouldn't 'a' ben here 'f it hadn't 'a' ben for Jim. You'd 'a' ben down dah in de woods widout any dinner, an gittin' mos' drownded, too; dat you would, honey. Chickens knows when it's gwyne to rain, en so do de birds, chile."

The river went on raising and raising for ten or twelve days, till at last it was over the banks. The water was three or four foot deep on the island in the low places and on the Illinois bottom. On that side it was a good many miles wide, but on the Missouri side it was the same old distance across—a half a mile—because the Missouri shore was just a wall of high bluffs.

Daytimes we paddled all over the island in the canoe. It was mighty cool and shady in the deep woods, even if the sun was blazing outside. We went winding in and out amongst the trees, and sometimes the vines hung so thick we had to back away and go some other way. Well, on every old broken-down tree you could see rabbits and snakes and such things; and when the island had been overflowed a day or two they got so tame, on account of being hungry, that you could paddle right up and put your hand on them if you wanted to; but not the snakes and turtles—they would slide off in the water. The ridge our cavern was in was full of them. We could 'a' had pets enough if we'd wanted them.

One night we catched a little section of a lumber raft—nice pine planks. It was twelve foot wide and about fifteen or sixteen foot long, and the top stood above water six or seven inches—a solid, level floor. We could see saw logs go by in the daylight sometimes, but we let them go; we didn't show ourselves in daylight.

Another night when we was up at the head of the island, just before daylight, here comes a frame house down, on the west side. She was a two-story, and tilted over considerable. We paddled out and got aboard—clumb in at an upstairs window. But it was too dark to see yet, so we made the canoe fast and set in her to wait for daylight.

The light begun to come before we got to the foot of the island. Then we looked in at the window. We could make out a bed, and a table, and two old chairs, and lots of things around about on the floor, and there was clothes hanging against the wall. There was something laying on the floor in the far corner that looked like a man. So Jim says:

"Hello, you!"

But it didn't budge. So I hollered again, and then Jim says:

"De man ain't asleep—he's dead. You hold still—I'll go en see."

He went, and bent down and looked, and says:

"It's a dead man. Yes, indeedy; naked, too. He's ben shot in de back. I reck'n he's ben dead two er three days. Come in, Huck, but doan' look at his face—it's too gashly."

I didn't look at him at all. Jim throwed some old rags over him, but he needn't done it; I didn't want to see him. There was heaps of old greasy cards scattered around over the floor, and old whisky bottles, and a couple of masks made out of black cloth; and all over the walls was the ignorantest kind of words and pictures made with charcoal. There was two old dirty calico dresses, and a sunbonnet, and some women's underclothes hanging against the wall, and some men's clothing, too. We put the lot into the canoe—it might come good. There was a boy's old speckled straw hat on the floor; I took that, too. And there was a bottle that had milk in it, and it had a rag stopper for a baby to suck. We would 'a' took the bottle, but it was broke. There was a seedy old chest, and an old hair trunk with the hinges broke. They stood open, but there warn't nothing left in them that was any account. The way things was scattered about we reckoned the people left in a hurry, and warn't fixed so as to carry off most of their stuff.

We got an old tin lantern, and a butcher knife without any handle, and a bran-new Barlow knife worth two bits in any store, and a lot of tallow candles, and a tin candlestick, and a gourd, and a tin cup, and a ratty old bedquilt off the bed, and a reticule with needles and pins and beeswax and buttons and thread and all such truck in it, and a hatchet and some nails, and a fish line as thick as my little finger with some monstrous hooks on it, and a roll of buckskin, and a leather dog collar, and a horseshoe, and some vials of medicine that didn't have no label on them; and just as we was leaving I found a tolerable good currycomb, and Jim he found a ratty old fiddle bow, and a wooden leg. The straps was broke off of it, but, barring that, it was a good enough leg, though it was too long for me and not long enough for Jim, and we couldn't find the other one, though we hunted all around.

And so, take it all around, we made a good haul. When we was ready to shove off we was a quarter of a mile below the island, and it was pretty broad day; so I made Jim lay down in the canoe and cover up with a quilt, because if he set up people could tell he was a nigger a good ways off. I paddled over to the Illinois shore, and drifted down most a half a mile doing it. I crept up the dead water under the bank, and hadn't no accidents and didn't see nobody. We got home all safe.

Chapter X   The Find—Old Hank Bunker—In Disguise

After breakfast I wanted to talk about the dead man and guess out how he come to be killed, but Jim didn't want to. He said it would fetch bad luck; and besides, he said, he might come and ha'nt us; he said a man that warn't buried was more likely to go a-ha'nting around than one that was planted and comfortable. That sounded pretty reasonable, so I didn't say no more; but I couldn't keep from studying over it and wishing I knowed who shot the man, and what they done it for.

We rummaged the clothes we'd got, and found eight dollars in silver sewed up in the lining of an old blanket overcoat. Jim said he reckoned the people in that house stole the coat, because if they'd 'a' knowed the money was there they wouldn't 'a' left it. I said I reckoned they killed him, too; but Jim didn't want to talk about that. I says:

"Now you think it's bad luck; but what did you say when I fetched in the snakeskin that I found on the top of the ridge day before yesterday? You said it was the worst bad luck in the world to touch a snakeskin with my hands. Well, here's your bad luck! We've raked in all this truck and eight dollars besides. I wish we could have some bad luck like this every day, Jim."

"Never you mind, honey, never you mind. Don't you git too peart. It's a-comin'. Mind I tell you, it's a-comin'."

It did come, too. It was a Tuesday that we had that talk. Well, after dinner Friday we was laying around in the grass at the upper end of the ridge, and got out of tobacco. I went to the cavern to get some, and found a rattlesnake in there. I killed him, and curled him up on the foot of Jim's blanket, ever so natural, thinking there'd be some fun when Jim found him there. Well, by night I forgot all about the snake, and when Jim flung himself down on the blanket while I struck a light the snake's mate was there, and bit him.

He jumped up yelling, and the first thing the light showed was the varmint curled up and ready for another spring. I laid him out in a second with a stick, and Jim grabbed pap's whisky-jug and begun to pour it down.

He was barefooted, and the snake bit him right on the heel. That all comes of my being such a fool as to not remember that wherever you leave a dead snake its mate always comes there and curls around it. Jim told me to chop off the snake's head and throw it away, and then skin the body and roast a piece of it. I done it, and he eat it and said it would help cure him. He made me take off the rattles and tie them around his wrist, too. He said that that would help. Then I slid out quiet and throwed the snakes clear away amongst the bushes; for I warn't going to let Jim find out it was all my fault, not if I could help it.

Jim sucked and sucked at the jug, and now and then he got out of his head and pitched around and yelled; but every time he come to himself he went to sucking at the jug again. His foot swelled up pretty big, and so did his leg; but by and by the drunk begun to come, and so I judged he was all right; but I'd druther been bit with a snake than pap's whisky.

Jim was laid up for four days and nights. Then the swelling was all gone and he was around again. I made up my mind I wouldn't ever take a-holt of a snakeskin again with my hands, now that I see what had come of it. Jim said he reckoned I would believe him next time. And he said that handling a snakeskin was such awful bad luck that maybe we hadn't got to the end of it yet. He said he druther see the new moon over his left shoulder as much as a thousand times than take up a snakeskin in his hand. Well, I was getting to feel that way myself, though I've always reckoned that looking at the new moon over your left shoulder is one of the carelessest and foolishest things a body can do. Old Hank Bunker done it once, and bragged about it; and in less than two years he got drunk and fell off of the shot tower, and spread himself out so that he was just a kind of a layer, as you may say; and they slid him edgeways between two barn doors for a coffin, and buried him so, so they say, but I didn't see it. Pap told me. But anyway, it all come of looking at the moon that way, like a fool.

Well, the days went along, and the river went down between its banks again; and about the first thing we done was to bait one of the big hooks with a skinned rabbit and set it and catch a catfish that was as big as a man, being six foot two inches long, and weighed over two hundred pounds. We couldn't handle him, of course; he would 'a' flung us into Illinois. We just set there and watched him rip and tear around till he drownded. We found a brass button in his stomach and a round ball, and lots of rubbage. We split the ball open with a hatchet, and there was a spool in it. Jim said he'd had it there a long time, to coat it over so and make a ball of it. It was as big a fish as was ever catched in the Mississippi, I reckon. Jim said he hadn't ever seen a bigger one. He would 'a' been worth a good deal over at the village. They peddle out such a fish as that by the pound in the markethouse there; everybody buys some of him; his meat's as white as snow and makes a good fry.

Next morning I said it was getting slow and dull, and I wanted to get a stirring-up some way. I said I reckoned I would slip over the river and find out what was going on. Jim liked that notion; but he said I must go in the dark and look sharp. Then he studied it over and said, couldn't I put on some of them old things and dress up like a girl? That was a good notion, too. So we shortened up one of the calico gowns, and I turned up my trouser legs to my knees and got into it. Jim hitched it behind with the hooks, and it was a fair fit. I put on the sunbonnet and tied it under my chin, and then for a body to look in and see my face was like looking down a joint of stovepipe. Jim said nobody would know me, even in the daytime, hardly. I practised around all day to get the hang of the things, and by and by I could do pretty well in them, only Jim said I didn't walk like a girl; and he said I must quit pulling up my gown to get at my britches pocket. I took notice, and done better.

I started up the Illinois shore in the canoe just after dark.

I started across to the town from a little below the ferry landing, and the drift of the current fetched me in at the bottom of the town. I tied up and started along the bank. There was a light burning in a little shanty that hadn't been lived in for a long time, and I wondered who had took up quarters there. I slipped up and peeped in at the window. There was a woman about forty year old in there knitting by a candle that was on a pine table. I didn't know her face; she was a stranger, for you couldn't start a face in that town that I didn't know. Now this was lucky, because I was weakening; I was getting afraid I had come; people might know my voice and find me out. But if this woman had been in such a little town two days she could tell me all I wanted to know; so I knocked at the door, and made up my mind I wouldn't forget I was a girl.

Glossary   From *The Adventures of Huckleberry Finn*

ain't	is not; does not
bluffs	high, steep, broad-faced banks or cliffs
budge	to move even a little
canoe	narrow, light boat with sides meeting in a sharp edge at each end
cavern	cave
chile	child
clumb	climbed
currycomb	comb for cleaning a horse's coat
druther	rather
fast	firmly fastened
fetched	brought, got
fidgety	nervous, uneasy

gashly	ghastly, terrible
goggles	large spectacles
gwyne	going
ha'nt	haunt
haul	load or quantity transported
hogshead	large barrel or cask holding from 63 to 140 gallons
kin	relatives, family
laid up	disabled, confined to bed or the sickroom
lantern	transparent case for a light to protect it from wind and weather
make out	to see with some difficulty
middling	fairly, moderately
niggers	used during author's time for *negroes,* but considered highly offensive today
notion	general idea, vague thought
paddled	propelled (a canoe) by means of a paddle or paddles
peart	cheerful
pecking at	bothering
peeped in	looked through a small opening or from a place of hiding
raft	flat structure of logs fastened together and floated on water
rags	old, worn clothes
reckoned	thought, considered
reticule	woman's small handbag
scrambled	climbed or crawled hurriedly
shanty	small, shabby dwelling, shack, hut
sharp	showing or having a keen awareness, attentive, vigilant
snuffpowdered	tobacco taken into the nose by sniffing
still	not moving, quiet
stirring-up	state of excitement
stock	to have faith in, give credence to, or attribute real significance to
stretched	strained in application to questionable or unreasonable limits
swelled up	became larger at a particular point
take a-holt	take ahold, seize, grasp
thrash	to make move violently or wildly
tilted	slanted, sloped
tolerable	fairly good, passable
truck	small articles of little value
varmint	person or animal regarded as troublesome or objectionable
victuals	food or other provisions
warn't	wasn't
winds up	concludes, comes to an end

Discussion

1. What is Huck's reaction to the Widow Douglas's desire to "sivilize" him?
2. What social and moral values do the widow Douglas and Miss Watson represent?
3. What social and moral values does Huck represent?

4. Jim and Huck believe in superstitions and folk wisdom. Give examples of their beliefs.

5. In what ways are Huck and Jim outsiders (not a part of society)?

6. How do you feel about Huck's values and goals in life? Can you identify with him?

Style and Language

1. Circle the words that describe Twain's style in *Huckleberry Finn*.

   formal   impersonal   realistic

   informal   personal   romantic

2. Give several examples of words, phrases, and sentences in chapter I that establish the humorous, conversational, and subjective tone of *Huckleberry Finn*.

3. Twain's language in *Huckleberry Finn* contains
   a. authentic dialects.
   b. figures of speech.
   c. romantic dialogues.
   d. detailed descriptions.
   Give quotations from the text that are examples of this language.

4. The story is told from the point of view of
   a. the omniscient author.
   b. Huckleberry Finn.
   c. Jim.
   d. Aunt Polly.

5. In *Huckleberry Finn* all Twain's characters speak in their local dialects (the vernacular). Thus, many sentences contain grammar errors and idiomatic vocabulary words. Explain the meaning of the first sentence of chapter I: "You don't know about me without you have read a book by the name of *The Adventures of Tom Sawyer;* but that ain't no matter." What does *without* mean? What does *ain't* mean? What does *no matter* mean? Now write a paraphrase in correct English of the entire first paragraph of chapter I.

Writing Assignments

1. Write an essay in which you discuss Twain's humorous tone in *Huckleberry Finn*. Give examples of his uses of irony and simple comedy and explain their humorous effects.

2. In chapter IX, paragraph 6, Twain describes a severe summer thunderstorm. Underline the descriptive words, and analyze his similes, metaphors, and personifications.

3. *Huckleberry Finn* is considered a realistic novel. Write an essay analyzing the writing techniques Twain uses to create the atmosphere of realism. Discuss his use of language (dialects) and his choice of Huck as the first-person narrator of this adventure story.

Group Work

In *The Autobiography of Mark Twain* (1917), Twain writes that the character of Huckleberry Finn was based on his childhood friend named Tom Blankenship. Working with a partner or in a small group, read this description and discuss whether it seems to fit Huck Finn. Then write a paraphrase of Twain's paragraph, changing the sentence structure and using synonyms to express Twain's ideas. Share your paraphrase with the class.

> In *Huckleberry Finn* I have drawn Tom Blankenship exactly as he was. He was ignorant, unwashed, insufficiently fed; but he had as good a heart as ever any boy had. His liberties were totally unrestricted. He was the only really independent person—boy or man—in the community, and by consequence he was tranquilly and continuously happy and was envied by all the rest of us. We liked him; we enjoyed his society. And as his society was forbidden us by our parents the prohibition trebled and quadrupled its value, and therefore we sought and got more of his society than of any other boy's.

Charles Chesnutt   From *The Marrow of Tradition*

"My books were written, from one point of view, a generation too soon. There was no such demand then as there is now for books by and about colored people. And I was writing against the trend of public opinion on the race question at that particular time."
Charles Chesnutt, July 3, 1928

"With his shorter sketches, Chesnutt may well rank with such American masters of the craft as Mark Twain and Bret Harte, with both of whom he shared an intensity of feeling for the rawness of an emergent America."
Earl Schenck Miers, introduction to *The Wife of His Youth and Other Stories*, 1968

"*The Marrow of Tradition* was the most comprehensively realistic picture of the black man's dilemma in the South yet to be published in American fiction."
Robert M. Farnsworth, introduction to *The Marrow of Tradition*, 1969

Charles Chesnutt (1858–1932) was born in Cleveland, Ohio, but he was raised in North Carolina, where his father owned a grocery store. Chesnutt became a public school teacher and principal before moving back to Cleveland to earn his living as a lawyer and businessman. His first writings were short stories in the black dialect. After the popular success of these humorous and ironic stories, Chesnutt turned to writing novels that dealt with the problems faced by light-skinned, middle-class African Americans living in cities in the North. These novels portray the effects of the Supreme Court's 1896 decision in favor of the South's "separate but equal" racial doctrine, a doctrine that resulted in solidifying the segregation of blacks and whites in schools, restaurants, theaters, and other public areas.

The Marrow of Tradition belongs to the late-nineteenth-century school of American realism. It is a strong novel of social purpose that depicts the impact of white supremacist politics on two North Carolina families, one white and one mixed race. Chesnutt writes in a sophisticated style with an emotional yet factual tone. The climax of the plot is a violent race riot (modeled on an actual riot, the Wilmington massacre of November 1898), but the novel's ending holds out hope for reconciliation of the races out of mutual need and respect. Even so, many readers of his age found Chesnutt's picture of racial injustice much too bitter.

Chesnutt was one of the first widely read African American writers to address the American color line problem in all its complexity. Although *The Marrow of Tradition* was not well liked by

Chesnutt's predominately white audience, his writing had a great influence on Americans of the late nineteenth and early twentieth century, who were struggling with the legacy of slavery and racial hatred. In fact, according to E. S. Miers, Chesnutt is "the first American Negro literary figure of enduring distinction" and one of several African Americans at the close of the nineteenth century whose books caused a social revolution in "Black America."

Other works by Chesnutt include *The Conjure Woman, The Wife of His Youth and Other Stories of the Color Line, The House Behind the Cedars,* and *The Colonel's Dream.*

In this excerpt, Dr. Miller, an African American, is searching for his wife and child because a race riot has begun in his town. The title of the chapter, "The Valley of the Shadow," is an allusion to the line from the 23rd Psalm of the Bible: Even though I walk through the valley of the shadow of death, I fear no evil; for thou art with me.

Preview

Skimming: Skim the reading to gain a general impression.
1. Read the title and first sentence of the chapter.
2. Skim the chapter to get an idea of its form and length.

Questioning: Answer the following questions and discuss your answers in class.
1. Does racial discrimination exist in your country?
2. Have you had any race riots in your country? When?

Scanning: Scan to answer the following questions to get an idea of the content and style.
1. For whom is Dr. Miller looking?
2. Whom does Dr. Miller find lying on the sidewalk?

From *The Marrow of Tradition*   1901
Charles Chesnutt

The Valley of the Shadow

Miller knocked at the door. There was no response. He went round to the rear of the house. The dog had slunk behind the woodpile. Miller knocked again, at the back door, and, receiving no reply, called aloud.

"Mrs. Butler! It is I, Dr. Miller. Is my wife here?"

The slats of a near-by blind opened cautiously.

"Is it really you, Dr. Miller?"

"Yes, Mrs. Butler. I am looking for my wife and child,—are they here?"

"No, sir; she became alarmed about you, soon after the shooting commenced, and I could not keep her. She left for home half an hour ago. It is coming on dusk, and she and the child are so near white that she did not expect to be molested."

"Which way did she go?"

"She meant to go by the main street. She thought it would be less dangerous than the back streets. I tried to get her to stay here, but she was frantic about you, and nothing I could say would keep her. Is the riot almost over, Dr. Miller? Do you think they will murder us all, and burn down our houses?"

"God knows," replied Miller, with a groan. "But I must find her, if I lose my own life in the attempt."

Surely, he thought, Janet would be safe. The white people of Wellington were not savages; or at least their temporary reversion to savagery would not go as far as to include violence to delicate women and children. Then there flashed into his mind Josh Green's story of his "silly" mother, who for twenty years had walked the earth as a child, as the result of one night's terror, and his heart sank within him.

Miller realized that his buggy, by attracting attention, had been a hindrance rather than a help in his progress across the city. In order to follow his wife, he must practically retrace his steps over the very route he had come. Night was falling. It would be easier to cross the town on foot. In the dusk his own color, slight in the daytime, would not attract attention, and by dodging in the shadows he might avoid those who might wish to intercept him. But he must reach Janet and the boy at any risk. He had not been willing to throw his life away hopelessly, but he would cheerfully have sacrificed it for those whom he loved.

He had gone but a short distance, and had not yet reached the centre of mob activity, when he intercepted a band of negro laborers from the cotton compress, with big Josh Green at their head.

"Hello, doctuh!" cried Josh, "does you wan' ter jine us?"

"I'm looking for my wife and child, Josh. They're somewhere in this den of murderers. Have any of you seen them?"

No one had seen them.

"You men are running a great risk," said Miller. "You are rushing on to certain death."

"Well, suh, maybe we is; but we're gwine ter die fightin'. Dey say de w'ite folks is gwine ter bu'n all de cullud schools an' chu'ches, an' kill all de niggers dey kin ketch. Dey're gwine ter bu'n yo' new hospittle, ef somebody don' stop 'em."

"Josh—men—you are throwing your lives away. It is a fever; it will wear off to-morrow, or to-night. They'll not burn the schoolhouses, nor the hospital —they are not such fools, for they benefit the community; and they'll only kill the colored people who resist them. Every one of you with a gun or a pistol carries his death warrant in his own hand. I'd rather see the hospital burn than have one of you lose his life. Resistance only makes the matter worse,—the odds against you are too long."

"Things can't be any wuss, doctuh," replied one of the crowd sturdily. "A gun is mo' dange'ous ter de man in front of it dan ter de man behin' it. Dey 're gwine ter kill us anyhow; an' we're tired,—we read de newspapers,—an' we're tired er bein' shot down like dogs, widout jedge er jury. We'd ruther die fightin' dan be stuck like pigs in a pen!"

"God help you!" said Miller. "As for me, I must find my wife and child."

"Good-by, doctuh," cried Josh, brandishing a huge knife. " 'Member 'bout de ole 'oman, ef you lives thoo dis. Don' fergit de headbo'd an' de footbo'd, an' a silver plate on de coffin, ef dere's money ernuff."

They went their way, and Miller hurried on. They might resist attack; he thought it extremely unlikely that they would begin it; but he knew perfectly well that the mere knowledge that some of the negroes contemplated resistance would only further inflame the infuriated whites. The colored men might win a momentary victory, though it was extremely doubtful; and they would as surely reap the harvest later on. The qualities which in a white man would win the applause of the world would in a negro be taken as the marks of savagery. So thoroughly diseased was public opinion in matters of race that the negro who died for the common rights of humanity might look for no need of admiration or glory. At such a time, in the white man's eyes, a negro's courage would be mere desperation; his love of liberty, a mere animal dislike of restraint. Every finer human instinct would be interpreted in terms of savagery. Or, if forced to admire, they would none the less repress.

They would applaud his courage while they stretched his neck, or carried off the fragments of his mangled body as souvenirs, in much the same way that savages preserve the scalps or eat the hearts of their enemies.

But concern for the fate of Josh and his friends occupied only a secondary place in Miller's mind for the moment. His wife and child were somewhere ahead of him. He pushed on. He had covered about a quarter of a mile more, and far down the street could see the signs of greater animation, when he came upon the body of a woman lying upon the sidewalk. In the dusk he had almost stumbled over it, and his heart came up in his mouth. A second glance revealed that it could not be his wife. It was a fearful portent, however, of what her fate might be. The "war" had reached the women and children. Yielding to a professional instinct, he stooped, and saw that the prostrate form was that of old Aunt Jane Letlow. She was not yet quite dead, and as Miller, with a tender touch, placed her head in a more comfortable position, her lips moved with a last lingering flicker of consciousness:—

"Comin', missis, comin'!"

Mammy Jane had gone to join the old mistress upon whose memory her heart was fixed; and yet not all her reverence for her old mistress, nor all her deference to the whites, nor all their friendship for her, had been able to save her from this raging devil of race hatred which momentarily possessed the town.

Perceiving that he could do no good, Miller hastened onward, sick at heart. Whenever he saw a party of white men approaching,—these brave reformers never went singly,—he sought concealment in the shadow of a tree or the shrubbery in some yard until they had passed. He had covered about two thirds of the distance homeward, when his eyes fell upon a group beneath a lamp-post, at sight of which he turned pale with horror, and rushed forward with a terrible cry.

Glossary   From *The Marrow of Tradition*

animation	liveliness
bu'n	burn
chu'ches	churches
coffin	the case or box in which a dead body is buried
commenced	began
contemplated	considered, thought about
cullud	colored (African Americans)
dange'ous	dangerous
de	the
deference	courteous respect; giving in to wishes of others
den	place for wild animals or thieves
desperation	recklessness resulting from despair
dey	they
doctuh	doctor
dodging	moving quickly
don'	don't
ernuff	enough
fixed	attached; set firmly
flicker	quick, light feeling
footbo'd	footboard of a bed or coffin
frantic	wild with worry
groan	deep sound expressing pain or distress

gwine	going
hastened	hurried; moved quickly
headbo'd	headboard of a bed or coffin
hindrance	obstacle
inflame	to arouse violence in; to excite with anger
infuriated	very angry, enraged, furious
intercept	to seize or stop on the way, before arrival
jedge	judge
jine	join
ketch	catch
kin	can
lingering	continuing to live although close to death
mangled	cut up or mutilated
meed	reward
'member	remember
mere	nothing more or less
missis	mistress
mo'	more
mob	disorderly and lawless crowd
molested	annoyed, harmed, troubled with intent to harm
momentary	lasting for only a moment; temporary
odds	advantage
ole 'oman	old woman (wife)
portent	omen; sign of unfortunate future event
prostrate	lying flat on the ground
reap the harvest	to gain the reward of action or conduct
repress	to keep down or hold back; restrain; control strictly
restraint	a loss of limitation of liberty; confinement
reverence	feeling of deep respect, love, awe
reversion	reversal; returning to a former state
ruther	rather
savagery	the condition of being wild, brutal, uncivilized
savages	fierce, brutal, uncivilized persons
scalps	skin on the top and back of a head, torn from heads of enemies
shrubbery	bushes
singly	alone; individually
slunk	moved in a quiet manner, from fear or guilt
sought	looked for; tried to find
sturdily	strongly, firmly, resolutely
suh	sir
ter	to
thoo	through
w'ite	white
wan'	want
widout	without
wuss	worse
yo'	your

Discussion

1. Summarize what takes place in "The Valley of the Shadow."
2. How does Dr. Miller view the white people of Wellington?
3. What do Josh Green and his men want to do? Why?
4. Why is Dr. Miller against the blacks' resistance? Do you agree or disagree with his ideas?
5. How do the white men view the blacks' courage and love of liberty?

Style and Language

1. True or false: Chesnutt's writing style is old fashioned and romantic.

2. True or false: The tone of "The Valley of the Shadow" is generally satirical, unemotional, and optimistic.

3. The story is told from the point of view of
   a. the third-person narrator.
   b. Dr. Miller.
   c. Mrs. Butler.
   d. Josh Green.

4. Chesnutt uses an analogy (comparison of unlike things or ideas) to convey his meaning about the race hatred in Wellington. Explain the meaning of this analogy (page 162):
   "They would applaud his courage while they stretched his neck, or carried off the fragments of his mangled body as souvenirs, in much the same way that savages preserve the scalps or eat the hearts of their enemies."

Writing Assignments

1. Chesnutt's characters speak in authentic dialect in *The Marrow of Tradition*. Without looking at the glossary, change the statements in dialect into correct Standard English.

2. Dr. Miller and Josh Green have opposite opinions about how to respond to the race riots in Wellington. Write an essay contrasting these points of view. You may use the following thesis: Although Dr. Miller and Josh Green are both African Americans, they do not agree about resistance to whites. Support your thesis with specific quotations from the text.

3. Does racial prejudice or discrimination exist in your country? If so, write an essay defining and describing this racial prejudice. Which groups are affected? Can the problems be resolved? Include specific examples to support your major points.

Group Work

Working with a partner or in a small group, read aloud the following poems by the African American poets Claude McKay (1891–1948), Langston Hughes (1902–67), and Arna Bontemps (1902–73), members of the Harlem Renaissance. Compare and contrast these poems with "The Valley of the Shadow." In what ways do these poems have the same theme as "The Valley of the Shadow"? Are there any identical words or phrases? Write a brief explanation of how the meaning of each poem relates to "The Valley of the Shadow."

If We Must Die   1922
Claude McKay

If we must die, let it not be like hogs
Hunted and penned in an inglorious spot,
While round us bark the mad and hungry dogs,
Making their mock at our accursed lot.
If we must die, O let us nobly die,
So that our precious blood may not be shed
In vain; then even the monsters we defy
Shall be constrained to honor us though dead!
O kinsmen! we must meet the common foe!
Though far outnumbered let us show us brave,
And for their thousand blows deal one deathblow!
What though before us lies the open grave?
Like men we'll face the murderous, cowardly pack,
Pressed to the wall, dying, but fighting back!

Warning   1931
Langston Hughes

Negroes,
Sweet and docile,
Meek, humble, and kind:
Beware the day
They change their mind!

Wind
In the cotton fields,
Gentle breeze:
Beware the hour
It uproots trees!

The Day-Breakers   1931
Arna Bontemps

We are not come to wage a strife
with swords upon this hill:
it is not wise to waste the life
against a stubborn will.

Yet would we die as some have done:
beating a way for the rising sun.

Willa Cather   From *My Antonia*

"Even where the affections are not strongly moved by any superior excellence, the companions of our childhood always possess a certain power over our minds which hardly any later friend can obtain."
Mary Shelley, *Frankenstein,* 1818

"The only way to have a friend is to be one."
Ralph Waldo Emerson, "Friendship," *Essays,* 1841

"Friends are generally of the same sex, for when men and women agree, it is only in their conclusions; their reasons are always different."
George Santayana, *The Life of Reason,* 1905–6

"The higher processes of art are all processes of simplification. The novelist must learn to write and then he must unlearn it."
Willa Cather, *Not under Forty,* 1936

Willa Cather (1873–1947) was born in Winchester, Virginia, the oldest of seven children. She moved with her family to Nebraska when she was nine. After graduating from the University of Nebraska, Cather worked as a journalist, editor, and teacher before becoming a full-time writer. Today Cather, who was instrumental in developing the modern novel, is recognized as one of the most outstanding writers of the twentieth century. Although she belongs to the modern age of literature, Cather's works reaffirm the traditional values of an earlier and simpler time.

Many of Cather's works are set in the Nebraska prairie and realistically describe the lives of the early pioneers who immigrated from Europe to find a more prosperous life in America. Her books explore the conflict between the older, gentler European culture and the newer, harsher American society. Sarah Orne Jewett, a short story writer from Maine, was a major influence on Cather and her writing style. Cather said: "One of the few really helpful words I ever heard from an older writer I had from Sarah Orne Jewett when she said to me: 'Of course one day you will write about your country. In the meantime, get all you can. One must know the world *so well* before one can know the parish.'"

In 1906, Cather moved to New York City, where she wrote her greatest works, the four novels set in Nebraska: *O Pioneers, The Song of the Lark, My Antonia,* and *Lucy Gayheart.* Her themes in these novels about the early pioneers are the wild beauty of the middlewestern prairie and the enduring bravery of the immigrants who attempted to conquer the land. Other well-known works are *A Lost Lady, The Professor's House, Death Comes to the Archbishop,* and *One of Ours,* for which she won the Pulitzer Prize.

Cather, who never married, centered many of her stories around strong, spirited heroines who overshadow the male characters. *My Antonia* is based on the childhood memories of Jim Burden and his description of the life of a courageous young woman from a Bohemian (Czech) immigrant family. Antonia overcomes extreme poverty and loneliness to achieve fulfillment living on the prairie land. Cather had her tombstone inscribed with a sentence from *My Antonia* that describes the mystical feeling of the country and the beauty of its landscape: "That is happiness; to be dissolved into something complete and great."

In chapter III, Jim Burden visits the widow Steavens to find out what happened to his childhood friend Antonia. In chapter IV, Antonia and Jim Burden are reunited after many years and pledge to remain friends although Jim is leaving the Nebraska prairie to go to law school in New York.

Preview

Skimming: Skim the reading to gain a general impression.
1. Read the title and first sentence of each chapter.
2. Skim the chapters to get an idea of their form and length.

Questioning: Answer the following question and discuss your answers in class.
Have you stayed in touch with any special friends from your childhood?

Scanning: Scan to answer the following questions to get an idea of the content and style.
1. Chapter III: How did Mrs. Steavens watch over Antonia?
2. Chapter IV: Where does Jim find Antonia?
3. Chapter IV: What does Jim promise Antonia when he leaves her?

From *My Antonia*　　1918
Willa Cather

The Pioneer Woman's Story

III

On the first or second day of August I got a horse and cart and set out for the high country, to visit the Widow Steavens. The wheat harvest was over, and here and there along the horizon I could see black puffs of smoke from the steam threshing-machines. The old pasture land was now being broken up into wheatfields and cornfields, the red grass was disappearing, and the whole face of the country was changing. There were wooden houses where the old sod dwellings used to be, and little orchards, and big red barns; all this meant happy children, contented women, and men who saw their lives coming to a fortunate issue. The windy springs and the blazing summers, one after another, had enriched and mellowed that flat tableland; all the human effort that had gone into it was coming back in long, sweeping lines of fertility. The changes seemed beautiful and harmonious to me; it was like watching the growth of a great man or of a great idea. I recognized every tree and sandbank and rugged draw. I found that I remembered the conformation of the land as one remembers the modelling of human faces.

When I drew up to our old windmill, the Widow Steavens came out to meet me. She was brown as an Indian woman, tall, and very strong. When I was little, her massive head had always seemed to me like a Roman senator's. I told her at once why I had come.

"You'll stay the night with us, Jimmy? I'll talk to you after supper. I can take more interest when my work is off my mind. You've no prejudice against hot biscuit for supper? Some have, these days."

While I was putting my horse away, I heard a rooster squawking. I looked at my watch and sighed; it was three o'clock, and I knew that I must eat him at six.

After supper Mrs. Steavens and I went upstairs to the old sitting-room, while her grave, silent brother remained in the basement to read his farm papers. All the windows were open. The white summer moon was shining outside, the windmill was pumping lazily in the light breeze. My hostess put the lamp on a stand in the corner, and turned it low because of the heat. She sat down in her favourite rocking-chair and settled a little stool comfortably under her tired feet. "I'm troubled with calluses, Jim; getting old," she sighed cheerfully. She crossed her hands in her lap and sat as if she were at a meeting of some kind.

"Now, it's about that dear Antonia you want to know? Well, you've come to the right person. I've watched her like she'd been my own daughter.

"When she came home to do her sewing that summer before she was to be married, she was over here about every day. They've never had a sewing-machine at the Shimerdas', and she made all her things here. I taught her hemstitching, and I helped her to cut and fit. She used to sit there at that machine by the window, pedalling the life out of it—she was so strong—and always singing them queer Bohemian songs, like she was the happiest thing in the world.

" 'Antonia,' I used to say, 'don't run that machine so fast. You won't hasten the day none that way.'

"Then she'd laugh and slow down for a little, but she'd soon forget and begin to pedal and sing again. I never saw a girl work harder to go to housekeeping right and well-prepared. Lovely table-linen the Harlings had given her, and Lena Lingard had sent her nice things from Lincoln. We hemstitched all the table-cloths and pillow-cases, and some of the sheets. Old Mrs. Shimerda knit yards and yards of lace for her underclothes. Tony told me just how she meant to have everything in her house. She'd even bought silver spoons and forks, and kept them in her trunk. She was always coaxing brother to go to the post-office. Her young man did write her real often, from the different towns along his run.

"The first thing that troubled her was when he wrote that his run had been changed, and they would likely have to live in Denver. 'I'm a country girl,' she said, 'and I doubt if I'll be able to manage so well for him in a city. I was counting on keeping chickens, and maybe a cow.' She soon cheered up, though.

"At last she got the letter telling her when to come. She was shaken by it; she broke the seal and read it in this room. I suspected then that she'd begun to get faint-hearted, waiting; though she'd never let me see it.

"Then there was a great time of packing. It was in March, if I remember rightly, and a terrible muddy, raw spell, with the roads bad for hauling her things to town. And here let me say, Ambrosch did the right thing. He went to Black Hawk and bought her a set of plated silver in a purple velvet box, good enough for her station. He gave her three hundred dollars in money; I saw the cheque. He'd collected her wages all those first years she worked out, and it was but right. I shook him by the hand in this room. 'You're behaving like a man, Ambrosch,' I said, 'and I'm glad to see it, son.'

"'Twas a cold, raw day he drove her and her three trunks into Black Hawk to take the night train for Denver—the boxes had been shipped before. He stopped the wagon here, and she ran in to tell me good-bye. She threw her arms around me and kissed me, and thanked me for all I'd done for her. She was so happy she was crying and laughing at the same time, and her red cheeks was all wet with rain.

" 'You're surely handsome enough for any man,' I said, looking her over.

"She laughed kind of flighty-like, and whispered, 'Good-bye, dear house!' and then ran out to the wagon. I expect she meant that for you and your grandmother, as much as for me, so I'm particular to tell you. This house had always been a refuge to her.

"Well, in a few days we had a letter saying she got to Denver safe, and he was there to meet her. They were to be married in a few days. He was trying to get his promotion before he married, she said. I didn't like that, but I said nothing. The next week Yulka got a postal card, saying she was 'well and happy.' After that we heard nothing. A month went by, and old Mrs. Shimerda began to get fretful. Ambrosch was as sulky with me as if I'd picked out the man and arranged the match.

"One night brother William came in and said that on his way back from the fields he had passed a livery team from town, driving fast out the west road. There was a trunk on the front seat with the driver, and another behind. In the back seat there was a woman all bundled up; but for all her veils, he thought 'twas Antonia Shimerda, or Antonia Donova, as her name ought now to be.

"The next morning I got brother to drive me over. I can walk still, but my feet ain't what they used to be, and I try to save myself. The lines outside the Shimerdas' house was full of washing, though it was the middle of the week. As we got nearer, I saw a sight that made my heart sink—all those underclothes we'd put so much work on, out there swinging in the wind. Yulka came bringing a dishpanful of wrung clothes, but she darted back into the house like she was loath to see us. When I went in, Antonia was standing over the tubs, just finishing up a big washing. Mrs. Shimerda was going about her work, talking and scolding to herself. She didn't so much as raise her eyes. Tony wiped her hand on her apron and held it out to me, looking at me steady but mournful. When I took her in my arms she drew away. 'Don't, Mrs. Steavens,' she says, 'you'll make me cry, and I don't want to.'

"I whispered and asked her to come out-of-doors with me. I knew she couldn't talk free before her mother. She went out with me, bareheaded, and we walked up toward the garden.

" 'I'm not married, Mrs. Steavens,' she says to me very quiet and natural-like, 'and I ought to be.'

" 'Oh, my child,' says I, 'what's happened to you? Don't be afraid to tell me!'

"She sat down on the draw-side, out of sight of the house. 'He's run away from me,' she said. 'I don't know if he ever meant to marry me.'

" 'You mean he's thrown up his job and quit the country?' says I.

" 'He didn't have any job. He'd been fired; blacklisted for knocking down fares. I didn't know. I thought he hadn't been treated right. He was sick when I got there. He'd just come out of the hospital. He lived with me till my money gave out, and afterward I found out he hadn't really been hunting work at all. Then he just didn't come back. One nice fellow at the station told me, when I kept going to look for him, to give it up. He said he was afraid Larry'd gone bad and wouldn't come back any more. I guess he's gone to Old Mexico. The conductors get rich down there, collecting half-fares off the natives and robbing the company. He was always talking about fellows who had got ahead that way.'

"I asked her, of course, why she didn't insist on a civil marriage at once—that would have given her some hold on him. She leaned her head on her hands, poor child, and said, 'I just don't know, Mrs. Steavens. I guess my patience was wore out, waiting so long. I thought if he saw how well I could do for him, he'd want to stay with me.'

"Jimmy, I sat right down on that bank beside her and made lament. I cried like a young thing. I couldn't help it. I was just about heart-broke. It was one of them lovely warm May days, and the wind was blowing and the colts jumping around in the pastures; but I felt bowed with despair. My Antonia, that had so much good in her, had come home disgraced. And that Lena Lingard, that was always a bad one, say what you will, had turned out so well, and was coming home here every summer in her silks and her satins, and doing so much for her mother. I give credit where credit is due, but you know well enough, Jim Burden, there is a great difference in the principles of those two girls. And here it was the good one that had come to grief! I was poor comfort to her. I marvelled at her calm. As we went back to the house, she stopped to feel of her clothes to see if they was drying well, and seemed to take pride in their whiteness—she said she'd been living in a brick block, where she didn't have proper conveniences to wash them.

"The next time I saw Antonia, she was out in the fields ploughing corn. All that spring and summer she did the work of a man on the farm; it seemed to be an understood thing. Ambrosch didn't get any other hand to help him. Poor Marek had got violent and been sent away to an institution a good while back. We never even saw any of Tony's pretty dresses. She didn't take them out of her trunks. She was quiet and steady. Folks respected her industry and tried to treat her as if nothing had happened. They talked, to be sure; but not like they would if she'd put on airs. She was so crushed and quiet that nobody seemed to want to humble her. She never went anywhere. All that summer she never once came to see me. At first I was hurt, but I got to feel that it was because this house reminded her of too much. I went over there when I could, but the times when she was in from the fields were the times when I was busiest here. She talked about the grain and the weather as if she'd never had another interest, and if I went over at night she always looked dead weary. She was afflicted with toothache; one tooth after another ulcerated, and she went about with her face swollen half the time. She wouldn't go to Black Hawk to a dentist for fear of meeting people she knew. Ambrosch had got over his good spell long ago, and was always surly. Once I told him he ought not to let Antonia work so hard and pull herself down. He said, 'If you put that in her head, you better stay home.' And after that I did.

"Antonia worked on through harvest and threshing, though she was too modest to go out threshing for the neighbours, like when she was young and free. I didn't see much of her until late that fall when she begun to herd Ambrosch's cattle in the open ground north of here, up toward the big dog-town. Sometimes she used to bring them over the west hill, there, and I would run to meet her and walk north a piece with her. She had thirty cattle in her bunch; it had been dry, and the pasture was short, or she wouldn't have brought them so far.

"It was a fine open fall, and she liked to be alone. While the steers grazed, she used to sit on them grassy banks along the draws and sun herself for hours. Sometimes I slipped up to visit with her, when she hadn't gone too far.

" 'It does seem like I ought to make lace, or knit like Lena used to,' she said one day, 'but if I start to work, I look around and forget to go on. It seems such a little while ago when Jim Burden and I was playing all over this country. Up here I can pick out the very places where my father used to stand. Sometimes I feel like I'm not going to live very long, so I'm just enjoying every day of this fall.'

"After the winter begun she wore a man's long overcoat and boots, and a man's felt hat with a wide brim. I used to watch her coming and going, and I could see that her steps were getting heavier. One day in December, the snow began to fall. Late in the afternoon I saw Antonia driving her cattle homeward across the hill. The snow was flying round her and she bent to face it, looking more lonesome-like to me than usual. 'Deary me,' I says to myself, 'the girl's stayed out too late. It'll be dark before she gets them cattle put into the corral.' I seemed to sense she'd been feeling too miserable to get up and drive them.

"That very night, it happened. She got her cattle home, turned them into the corral, and went into the house, into her room behind the kitchen, and shut the door. There, without calling to anybody, without a groan, she lay down on the bed and bore her child.

"I was lifting supper when old Mrs. Shimerda came running down the basement stairs, out of breath and screeching:

" 'Baby come, baby come!' she says. 'Ambrosch much like devil!'

"Brother William is surely a patient man. He was just ready to sit down to a hot supper after a long day in the fields. Without a word he rose and went down to the barn and hooked up his team. He got us over there as quick as it was humanly possible. I went right in, and began to do for Antonia; but she laid there with her eyes shut and took no account of me. The old woman got a tubful of warm water to wash the baby. I overlooked what she was doing and I said out loud: 'Mrs. Shimerda, don't you put that strong yellow soap near that baby. You'll blister its little skin.' I was indignant.

" 'Mrs. Steavens,' Antonia said from the bed, 'if you'll look in the top tray of my trunk, you'll see some fine soap.' That was the first word she spoke.

"After I'd dressed the baby, I took it out to show it to Ambrosch. He was muttering behind the stove and wouldn't look at it.

" 'You'd better put it out in the rain-barrel,' he says.

"Now, see here, Ambrosch,' says I, 'there's a law in this land, don't forget that. I stand here a witness that this baby has come into the world sound and strong, and I intend to keep an eye on what befalls it.' I pride myself I cowed him.

"Well, I expect you're not much interested in babies, but Antonia's got on fine. She loved it from the first as dearly as if she'd had a ring on her finger, and was never ashamed of it. It's a year and eight months old now, and no baby was ever better cared for. Antonia is a natural-born mother. I wish she could marry and raise a family, but I don't know as there's much chance now."

I slept that night in the room I used to have when I was a little boy, with the summer wind blowing in at the windows, bringing the smell of the ripe fields. I lay awake and watched the moonlight shining over the barn and the stacks and the pond, and the windmill making its old dark shadow against the blue sky.

IV

The next afternoon I walked over to the Shimerdas'. Yulka showed me the baby and told me that Antonia was shocking wheat on the southwest quarter. I went down across the fields, and Tony saw me from a long way off. She stood still by her shocks, leaning on her pitchfork, watching me as I came. We met like the people in the old song, in silence, if not in tears. Her warm hand clasped mine.

"I thought you'd come, Jim. I heard you were at Mrs. Steavens's last night. I've been looking for you all day."

She was thinner than I had ever seen her, and looked as Mrs. Steavens said, "worked down," but there was a new kind of strength in the gravity of her face, and her colour still gave her that look of deep-seated health and ardour. Still? Why, it flashed across me that though so much had happened in her life and in mine, she was barely twenty-four years old.

Antonia stuck her fork in the ground, and instinctively we walked toward that unploughed patch at the crossing of the roads as the fittest place to talk to each other. We sat down outside the sagging wire fence that shut Mr. Shimerda's plot off from the rest of the world. The tall red grass had never been cut there. It had died down in winter and come up again in the spring until it was as thick and shrubby as some tropical garden-grass. I found myself telling her everything: why I had decided to study law and to go into the law office of one of my mother's relatives in New York City; about Gaston Cleric's death from pneumonia last winter, and the difference it had made in my life. She wanted to know about my friends, and my way of living, and my dearest hopes.

"Of course it means you are going away from us for good," she said with a sigh. "But that don't mean I'll lose you. Look at my papa here; he's been dead all these years, and yet he is more real to me than almost anybody else. He never goes out of my life. I talk to him and consult him all the time. The older I grow, the better I know him and the more I understand him."

She asked me whether I had learned to like big cities. "I'd always be miserable in a city. I'd die of lonesomeness. I like to be where I know every stack and tree, and where all the ground is friendly. I want to live and die here. Father Kelly says everybody's put into this world for something, and I know what I've got to do. I'm going to see that my little girl has a better chance than ever I had. I'm going to take care of that girl, Jim."

I told her I knew she would. "Do you know, Antonia, since I've been away, I think of you more often than of anyone else in this part of the world. I'd have liked to have you for a sweetheart, or a wife, or my mother or my sister—anything that a woman can be to a man. The idea of you is a part of my mind; you influence my likes and dislikes, all my tastes, hundreds of times when I don't realize it. You really are a part of me."

She turned her bright, believing eyes to me, and the tears came up in them slowly. "How can it be like that, when you know so many people, and when I've disappointed you so? Ain't it wonderful, Jim, how much people can mean to each other? I'm so glad we had each other when we were little. I can't wait till my little girl's old enough to tell her about all the things we used to do. You'll always remember me when you think about old times, won't you? And I guess everybody thinks about old times, even the happiest people."

As we walked homeward across the fields, the sun dropped and lay like a great golden globe in the low west. While it hung there, the moon rose in the east, as big as a cart-wheel, pale silver and streaked with rose colour, thin as a bubble or a ghost-moon. For five, perhaps ten minutes, the two luminaries confronted each other across the level land, resting on opposite edges of the world.

In that singular light every little tree and shock of wheat, every sunflower stalk and clump of snow-on-the-mountain, drew itself up high and pointed; the very clods and furrows in the fields seemed to stand up sharply. I felt the old pull of the earth, the solemn magic that comes out of those fields at nightfall. I wished I could be a little boy again, and that my way could end there.

We reached the edge of the field, where our ways parted. I took her hands and held them against my breast, feeling once more how strong and warm and good they were, those brown hands, and remembering how many kind things they had done for me. I held them now a long while, over my heart. About us it was growing darker and darker, and I had to look hard to see her face, which I meant always to carry with me; the closest, realest face, under all the shadows of women's faces, at the very bottom of my memory.

"I'll come back," I said earnestly, through the soft, intrusive darkness.

"Perhaps you will"—I felt rather than saw her smile. "But even if you don't, you're here, like my father. So I won't be lonesome."

As I went back alone over that familiar road, I could almost believe that a boy and girl ran along beside me, as our shadows used to do, laughing and whispering to each other in the grass.

Glossary

From *My Antonia*

Chapter III

ain't	are not
befalls	happens
blacklisted	put on a list of persons who are refused employment
blister	to cause blisters to form
Bohemian	from Bohemia (Czechoslovakia)
bore	gave birth to
bowed	overwhelmed; crushed
brim	projecting edge of hat
calluses	hardened, thick places on skin
civil marriage	marriage performed by justice of the peace, not a clergyman
conformation	shape or outline; structure
corral	enclosure for holding animals
crushed	subdued; overwhelmed
draw	a gully or ravine that water drains into
faint-hearted	cowardly, timid, afraid
fares	money paid for transportation
flighty-like	silly or foolish
grazed	fed on growing grass
hasten	speed up, hurry
hauling	transporting by wagon
heart-broke	heart broken; overwhelmed with sorrow, disappointment
issue	result or consequence
loath	unwilling, reluctant
made lament	expressed deep sorrow
marvelled	wondered; was amazed

massive	large and imposing
match	an agreement to marry
mellowed	made softer, gentler, richer
modest	shy or reserved
muttering	complaining or grumbling to himself
pasture	ground suitable or grazing (feeding) animals
put on airs	acted arrogant or better than others
refuge	shelter or protection from danger
run	regular trip of a train
screeching	screaming; making a high-pitched sound
sod	made of earth
squawking	crying loudly and harshly
sulky	showing ill humor by sullen behavior
tableland	high, broad, level region; plateau
threshing-machines	machines for threshing (beating) grain
thrown up	given up; abandoned
took no accont	did not notice
ulcerated	became infected
wore out	worn out, exhausted; used up
wrung	squeezed or compressed to force out water

Chapter IV

ain't	is not
ardour	passion, emotional warmth; enthusiasm, eagerness
cart-wheel	a silver dollar; a large coin
clasped	held tightly, firmly
clods	lumps of earth, soil
clump	a mass, cluster
consult	to ask the advice of; to seek an opinion from
deep-seated	deep-rooted
earnestly	seriously and intensely; sincerely
fittest	most suitable, appropriate
furrows	narrow grooves made in the ground by a plough (plow)
globe	round, ball-shaped thing; sphere
gravity	seriousness, solemnity
instinctively	spontaneously; done by instinct
intrusive	intruding; forcing of itself upon others
luminaries	bodies that give off light, like the sun and the moon
pitchfork	large, long-handled fork used for lifting and tossing hay
plot	small area of ground used for burial
pneumonia	a disease with inflammation or infection of the lungs
quarter	one-fourth of the land
sagging	hanging down unevenly or loosely

shock	a heap or pile
shocking	gathering and piling wheat
shrubby	covered with plants and bushes
solemn	sacred; serious or grave; very impressive
stack	a pile of straw or hay
streaked	marked with streaks
unploughed	not cut and turned up with a plough

Discussion

1. What kind of person is Antonia? Does she fit the stereotypical idea of a woman?
2. What kind of man was Antonia engaged to?
3. How does she feel about her baby?
4. Describe the relationship between Jim and Antonia.
5. In what ways are the lives of Jim and Antonia different?
6. Do you think that Jim will come back to the farm someday?
7. Did you enjoy this selection from *My Antonia?* Would you like to read the entire story?

Style and Language

1. The writing style in *My Antonia* is simple, clear, and realistic. Underline sentences in the text that are examples of this simplicity and clarity of style, and read them aloud.

2. Complete the following sentence by choosing the best words. The tone in *My Antonia* is

   _____, _____, and _____.

   objective   pessimistic   humorous
   subjective   optimistic   serious

3. Cather's language is characterized by
   a. complex sentence structures.
   b. figures of speech.
   c. realistic dialogue.
   d. abstract philosophical ideas.
   Give quotations from the text that are examples of your choices.

4. The story is told from the point of view of
   a. Mrs. Steavens.
   b. Antonia.
   c. Jim Burden.
   d. the omniscient author.
   How does this point of view influence the telling of the story?

Writing Assignments

1. Write a letter to a close friend from your childhood. Describe what you have done and where you have lived since you last saw him or her, and explain your current activities and lifestyle.

2. Antonia says to Jim in chapter IV: "I guess everybody thinks about old times, even the happiest people." In an essay, discuss the "old times" that you think about.

3. Antonia says that even though her father is dead, he never goes out of her life. She talks to him and consults him. Is there such a person in your life? If so, write a poem or an essay about this person. Explain what makes this person so important to you.

Group Work

Working with a partner or in a small group, read the following poems by the twentieth-century African American writers Alice Walker (1944–) and Nikki Giovanni (1943–). Then compare and contrast these poems with chapter IV from "The Pioneer Woman's Story" in *My Antonia*. Discuss which poem is closer in meaning to the meaning of chapter IV and which poem you prefer. Then write a one-paragraph interpretation of each poem.

Beyond What   1970
Alice Walker

We reach for destinies beyond
what we have come to know
and in the romantic hush
of promises
perceive each
the other's life
as known mystery.
Shared. But inviolate.[1]
No melting. No squeezing
into One.
We swing our eyes around
as well as side to side
to see the world.

To choose, renounce,[2]
this, or that—
call it a council between equals
call it love.

A Poem of Friendship   1978
Nikki Giovanni

We are not lovers
because of the love
we make
but the love
we have

We are not friends
because of the laughs
we spend
but the tears
we save

I don't want to be near you
for the thoughts we share
but the words we never have
to speak
I will never miss you
because of what we do
but what we are
together

1. not violated or changed
2. to give up

Chapter Synthesis

The plots of novels often center on the exploration of personal relationships among the major characters. Analyze the personal relationships of the characters in the excerpts from James's *Washington Square,* Twain's *Huckleberry Finn,* Cather's *My Antonia,* and Chesnutt's *The Marrow of Tradition.* Which characters are involved? What are the dominant emotions? What are their conflicts? Thesis: In *Washington Square, Huckleberry Finn, My Antonia,* and *The Marrow of Tradition,* the action focuses on the personal relationship between two major characters.

Chapter 6

Twentieth-Century American Prose: Diversity

"There is no agony like bearing an untold story inside you."
Zora Neale Thurston, *Dust Tracks on the Road,* 1942

"Perversity is the muse of modern literature."
Susan Sontag, *Against Interpretation,* 1966

"The universe is made of stories, not of atoms."
Muriel Rukeyser, *The Speed of Darkness,* 1968

"I am visible—see this Indian face—yet I am invisible. But I exist, we exist. They'd like to think I have melted in the pot. But I haven't, we haven't."
Gloria Anzaldúa, *Borderlands/La Frontera: The New Mestiza,* 1987

"There is an eerie, sometimes pathetic, oftimes beautiful urge that prevails in Black American lore, lyrics and literature. The impulse, simply put, is to tell the story . . . to tell one's own story . . . as one has known it, and loved it, and even died it."
Maya Angelou, foreword to *Dust Tracks on the Road,* 1991

The late twentieth century in the United States could be considered the age of cultural diversity. This diversity is brilliantly reflected in the literature, which is increasingly multicultural, multiracial, and multiethnic. Because Americans have become fascinated by their family histories, their roots, their heritage, many writers are exploring the lives of their ancestors, whose stories they are telling. This exploration is evidenced by the flowering of literary works by Native Americans, African Americans, Asian Americans, Latin Americans, and many other cultural groups.

The earlier American authors (Hawthorne, Whitman, Thoreau) were concerned with establishing an "American literature," to distinguish it from the European tradition, and they worked successfully toward this end. Today's authors are more interested in developing a literature of personal discovery, and their styles are much too diverse to be categorized under one general heading. Writers may be neoclassicists, realists, romanticists, impressionists, symbolists, naturalists, surrealists, or magical realists. All this means that reading literature is more of a journey into the unknown than ever before, a journey to "somewhere I have never travelled," as the poet e. e. cummings wrote in 1931.

The last decades of this century have been rich in literature despite a society that spends much of its time watching television and movies. Literary styles and forms in the modern age, both poetry and prose, are as varied as the writers who are creating them, and content ranges from that of the classical and Romantic writers of the past to an emphasis on the reality of inner experience in the present. Whether the author is a "new American" whose family immigrated to the United States recently or an aboriginal inhabitant of North America, these creations of literary imagination give meaning to our own experiences.

What is perhaps most exciting about this period in literary history is that these works that celebrate cultural diversity have become part of mainstream American literature and culture. In this chapter your journey will come to a close with selections by a Native American writer whose ancestors arrived on the North American continent centuries ago, a Chinese American writer who describes what it was like to grow up as a first-generation American, and two authors of Anglo and Mexican heritage.

N. Scott Momaday   From *The Way to Rainy Mountain*

"They approach like foxes, fight like lions, and fly away like birds."
A Jesuit description of the Iroquois, c. 1600

"I believe the Indian to be in body and mind equal to the white man."
Thomas Jefferson, letter to F. J. Chastellux, 1785

"The only good Indians I ever saw were dead."
General W. T. Sherman, January 1869

"Indians think it is important to remember, while Americans believe it is important to forget."
Paula Gunn Allen, *The Sacred Hoop,* 1986

"As my eyes search the prairie
I feel the summer in the spring."
Chippewa Indian, *Spring Song*

Natachee Scott Momaday (Tsoai-talee) was born in 1934 in Oklahoma. He grew up on Indian reservations in the Southwest and was educated at the University of New Mexico and Stanford. He is a Kiowa Indian and has been writing for over thirty years about the Kiowa myths that his grandmother taught him when he was a child. Momaday is not only a writer of both poetry and prose but also an artist and a storyteller. In his novels, essays, and poems, he retells the Indian myths and legends while describing the Kiowa ways of life and traditions. His writing is a mixture of the ancient and the modern, a gentle and dignified recreation of Indian beliefs in the power of nature and the sacred spirit. Writing in a clear and graphic style with eloquence and beauty, Momaday uses

American Indian male

words as if he were painting a picture or making a sculpture. As he says in the preface to *In the Presence of the Sun: A Gathering of Shields:* "I have been called 'the man made of words,' a phrase that I myself coined some years ago in connection with a Kiowa folktale. It is an identity that pleases me. In a sense, a real sense, my life has been composed of words. Reading and writing, talking, telling stories, listening, remembering, and thinking (someone has said that thinking is talking to oneself) have been the cornerstones of my existence."

Momaday is professor of English at the University of Arizona. In 1969 he won the Pulitzer Prize for his novel *House Made of Dawn*. He also was awarded the Premio Letterario Internazionale "Mondello" by Italy. Other works by Momaday include *The Journey of Tai-me, The Gourd Dancer* (a book of poetry), and *The Ancient Child,* a novel.

The Way to Rainy Mountain is a retelling of the tribal history and literature of the Kiowa Indians, who were forced to give up their culture and their land and adapt to the White Man's way of life, as were the other Native Americans. In the prologue and introduction, Momaday explains why he wants to journey to Rainy Mountain, the home of his Kiowa ancestors.

Preview

Skimming: Skim the reading to gain a general impression.
1. Read the title and first sentence of the reading.
2. Skim the reading to get an idea of its form and length.

Questioning: Answer the following questions and discuss your answers in class.
1. What have you learned about the American Indians (Native Americans)?
2. Why did they lose their land? Where do many of them live today?

American Indian female

Scanning: Scan to answer the following questions to get an idea of the content and style.
1. What happened to the Plains culture of the Kiowas?
2. Why did Momaday return to Rainy Mountain?

From *The Way to Rainy Mountain*   1969
N. Scott Momaday

Prologue

Headwaters

> Noon in the intermountain plain:
> There is scant telling of the marsh—
> A log, hollow and weather-stained,
> An insect at the mouth, and moss—
> Yet waters rise against the roots,
> Stand brimming to the stalks. What moves?
> What moves on this archaic force
> Was wild and welling at the source.

The journey began one day long ago on the edge of the northern Plains. It was carried on over a course of many generations and many hundreds of miles. In the end there were many things to remember, to dwell upon and talk about.

"You know, everything had to begin. . . ." For the Kiowas the beginning was a struggle for existence in the bleak northern mountains. It was there, they say, that they entered the world through a hollow log. The end, too, was a struggle, and it was lost. The young Plains culture of the Kiowas withered and died like grass that is burned in the prairie wind. There came a day like destiny; in every direction, as far as the eye could see, carrion lay out in the land. The buffalo was the animal representation of the sun, the essential and sacrificial victim of the Sun Dance. When the wild herds were destroyed, so too was the will of the Kiowa people; there was nothing to sustain them in spirit. But these are idle recollections, the mean and ordinary agonies of human history. The interim was a time of great adventure and nobility and fulfillment.

Tai-me came to the Kiowas in a vision born of suffering and despair. "Take me with you," Tai-me said, "and I will give you whatever you want." And it was so. The great adventure of the Kiowas was a going forth into the heart of the continent. They began a long migration from the headwaters of the Yellowstone River eastward to the Black Hills and south to the Wichita Mountains. Along the way they acquired horses, the religion of the Plains, a love and possession of the open land. Their nomadic soul was set free. In alliance with the Comanches they held dominion in the southern Plains for a hundred years. In the course of that long migration they had come of age as a people. They had conceived a good idea of themselves; they had dared to imagine and determine who they were.

In one sense, then, the way to Rainy Mountain is preeminently the history of an idea, man's idea of himself, and it has old and essential being in language. The verbal tradition by which it has been preserved has suffered a deterioration in time. What remains is fragmentary: mythology, legend, lore, and hearsay—and of course the idea itself, as crucial and complete as it ever was. That is the miracle.

The journey herein recalled continues to be made anew each time the miracle comes to mind, for that is peculiarly the right and responsibility of the imagination. It is a whole journey, intricate with motion and meaning; and it is made with the whole memory, that experience of the mind which is legendary as well as historical, personal as well as cultural. And the journey is an evocation of three things in particular: a landscape that is incomparable, a time that is gone forever, and the human spirit, which endures. The imaginative experience and the historical express equally the traditions of man's reality. Finally, then, the journey recalled is among other things the revelation of one way in which these traditions are conceived, developed, and interfused in the human mind. There are on the way to Rainy Mountain many landmarks, many journeys in the one. From the beginning the migration of the Kiowas was an expression of the human spirit, and that expression is most truly made in terms of wonder and delight: "There were many people, and oh, it was beautiful. That was the beginning of the Sun Dance. It was all for Tai-me, you know, and it was a long time ago."

Introduction

A single knoll rises out of the plain in Oklahoma, north and west of the Wichita Range. For my people, the Kiowas, it is an old landmark, and they gave it the name Rainy Mountain. The hardest weather in the world is there. Winter brings blizzards, hot tornadic winds arise in the spring, and in summer the prairie is an anvil's edge. The grass turns brittle and brown, and it cracks beneath your feet. There are green belts along the rivers and creeks, linear groves of hickory and pecan, willow and witch hazel. At a distance in July or August the steaming foliage seems almost to writhe in fire. Great green and yellow grasshoppers are everywhere in the tall grass, popping up like corn to sting the flesh, and tortoises crawl about on the red earth, going nowhere in the plenty of time. Loneliness is an aspect of the land. All things in the plain are isolate; there is no confusion of objects in the eye, but one hill or one tree or one man. To look upon that landscape in the early morning, with the sun at your back, is to lose the sense of proportion. Your imagination comes to life, and this, you think, is where Creation was begun.

I returned to Rainy Mountain in July. My grandmother had died in the spring, and I wanted to be at her grave. She had lived to be very old and at last infirm. Her only living daughter was with her when she died, and I was told that in death her face was that of a child.

I like to think of her as a child. When she was born, the Kiowas were living the last great moment of their history. For more than a hundred years they had controlled the open range from the Smoky Hill River to the Red, from the headwaters of the Canadian to the fork of the Arkansas and Cimarron. In alliance with the Comanches, they had ruled the whole of the southern Plains. War was their sacred business, and they were among the finest horsemen the world has ever known. But warfare for the Kiowas was pre-eminently a matter of disposition rather than of survival, and they never understood the grim, unrelenting advance of the U.S. Cavalry. When at last, divided and ill-provisioned, they were driven onto the Staked Plains in the cold rains of autumn, they fell into panic. In Palo Duro Canyon they abandoned their crucial stores to pillage and had nothing then but their lives. In order to save themselves, they surrendered to the soldiers at Fort Sill and were imprisoned in the old stone corral that now stands as a military museum. My grandmother was spared the humiliation of those high gray walls by eight or ten years, but she must have known from birth the affliction of defeat, the dark brooding of old warriors.

Her name was Aho, and she belonged to the last culture to evolve in North America. Her forebears came down from the high country in western Montana nearly three centuries ago. They were a mountain people, a mysterious tribe of hunters whose language has never been positively classified in any major group. In the late seventeenth century they began a long migration to the south and east. It was a journey toward the dawn, and it led to a golden age. Along the way the Kiowas were befriended by the Crows, who gave them the culture and religion of the Plains. They acquired horses, and their ancient nomadic spirit was suddenly free of the ground. They acquired Tai-me, the sacred Sun Dance doll, from that moment the object and symbol of their worship, and so shared in the divinity of the sun. Not least, they acquired the sense of destiny, therefore courage and pride. When they entered upon the southern Plains they had been transformed. No longer were they slaves to the simple necessity of survival; they were a lordly and dangerous society of fighters and thieves, hunters and priests of the sun. According to their origin myth, they entered the world through a hollow log. From one point of view, their migration was the fruit of an old prophecy, for indeed they emerged from a sunless world.

Although my grandmother lived out her long life in the shadow of Rainy Mountain, the immense landscape of the continental interior lay like memory in her blood. She could tell of the Crows, whom she had never seen, and of the Black Hills, where she had never been. I wanted to see in reality what she had seen more perfectly in the mind's eye, and traveled fifteen hundred miles to my pilgrimage.

Glossary	From *The Way to Rainy Mountain*
affliction	pain, suffering caused by misfortune, loss
alliance	a union; close association for a common objective
anvil	iron or steel block on which metal objects are hammered
bleak	exposed to wind and cold; treeless and bare; not cheerful
blizzards	severe snowstorms
brittle	easily broken because hard, fragile
brooding	worrying, thinking about something in a troubled way
carrion	decaying flesh of dead body, regarded as food for animals

Comanches	North American Indians
conceived	brought to life; formed or developed in the mind
corral	enclosure for holding animals
Creation	God's creating of the world; the universe and everything in it
Crows	North American Indians
disposition	inclination, tendency; one's nature, temperament
divinity	divine power; quality of being godlike, holy
dwell	to keep the attention directed on
evocation	calling forth or summoning
evolve	to develop by gradual changes, unfold
forebears	ancestors
fruit	result, product of any action
generations	periods between birth of one generation and the next (thirty years)
grim	fierce, cruel, savage
hearsay	rumor, gossip
herein	in this matter; in this writing
humiliation	loss of pride or dignity
idle	having no value, useless
ill-provisioned	not properly provided with food for the future
infirm	weak, not strong physically
interfused	combined by mixing, blending
interim	period of time between, meantime
intricate	complex, hard to understand because of puzzling details
isolate	set apart, separate, alone
Kiowas	North American Indians in Colorado, Oklahoma, and western states
knoll	mound, small hill
linear	extended in a line
log	section of the trunk or large branch of a cut tree
lore	knowledge of a particular group, especially of its traditions
mean	low in quality, poor, inferior
migration	movement from one place to another
myth	traditional story or legend
nomadic	wandering constantly in search of food, having no permanent home
pillage	loss of property by violence
preeminently	dominantly above others
prophecy	prediction of the future under influence of divine guidance
proportion	relationship between parts or things
sacrificial	used in a sacrifice
sting	to prick or wound; to cause sharp, sudden pain
stores	supplies, especially of food, clothing, weapons
sustain	to keep in existence, maintain or prolong; to support
Tai-me	Sun Dance Doll of the Kiowas
tortoises	turtles that live on land
unrelenting	refusing to yield, inflexible; without mercy
withered	dried up, decayed, weakened
writhe	to twist or turn

Discussion

1. How old is your culture? Do you think it will continue, or could it disappear someday?
2. Who are the native (aboriginal) inhabitants of your country?
3. Does your culture have myths or legends about its origins? If so, what are they?
4. Why is it important to maintain cultural beliefs and pass them on to the next generation?
5. Write a two-sentence explanation of why Momaday wanted to return to Rainy Mountain, and share your explanation with the class.
6. What do you find most interesting about Momaday's writing? Which sentences are hard to understand? Read these sentences aloud and try to interpret them.

Style and Language

1.   List several adjectives that describe the style and tone of *The Way to Rainy Mountain.*
               Style   *Tone*

      _____   _____

      _____   _____

      _____   _____

      Give examples from the text to support your choices.

2. *The Way to Rainy Mountain* is told from the first-person narrator's point of view; however, in *The Remembered Earth* (p. 170), Momaday said he used "three distinct narrative voices in *The Way to Rainy Mountain*—the mythical, the historical, and the immediate." What do you think this means? Which voices do you hear in the prologue and the introduction?

3. Underline the figures of speech found in this reading and explain their meanings.

4. Momaday writes about his ancestors in a factual yet poetic manner. Underline the words and phrases that describe the Kiowas and their culture. What were their main characteristics?

Writing Assignments

1. Momaday's prose style is often close to poetry. Using paragraph 1 of the prologue and paragraph 2 of the introduction, arrange the sentences in the form of a poem. Many ways are possible.

2. In an essay, classify the various cultural or ethnic groups that live in your country. Who were the original inhabitants? Are they still there? Which group is the largest?   Are all groups granted citizenship and treated fairly, or is there discrimination against a minority?

3. Read Momaday's poem "Wreckage." Some of the themes that are found in the excerpt from *The Way to Rainy Mountain* are also found in this poem.   Rewrite this poem as prose in three or four sentences that explain Momaday's message simply. You should add words to clarify the meaning.

Wreckage   1992
N. Scott Momaday

Had my bones, like the sun,
been splintered on this canyon wall
and burned among these buckled plates,
this bright debris; had it been so,
I should not have lingered so long
among my losses. I should have come
loudly, like a warrior, to my time.

Group Work

Working with a partner or in a small group, read the following excerpt from the novel *Ceremony* by
the writer Leslie Marmon Silko (1948–). Silko is of mixed ancestry—Laguna Pueblo, Mexican, and
white. Discuss the major points in Silko's excerpt, and compare them with Momaday's description
of the Kiowa Indians' experience. Do you agree with Silko's sentence: "It is the people who belong
to the mountain"? What does this mean? Write an interpretation of this sentence, and share it with
members of the class.

From *Ceremony*   1977
Leslie Marmon Silko

He walked into the evening air, which was cool and smelled like juniper smoke from the old
man's fire. Betonie was sitting by the fire, watching the mutton ribs cook over a grill he had
salvaged from the front end of a wrecked car in the dump below. The grill was balanced
between two big sandrocks, where the hot coals were banked under the spattering meat. Tayo
looked down at the valley, at the lights of the town and the headlights and taillights strung
along Highway 66.
"They took almost everything, didn't they?"
The old man looked up from the fire. He shook his head slowly while he turned the meat
with a forked stick. "We always come back to that, don't we? It was planned that way. For all
the anger and the frustration. And for the guilt too. Indians wake up every morning of their
lives to see the land which was stolen, still there, within reach, its theft being flaunted.[1] And
the desire is strong to make things right, to take back what was stolen and to stop them from
destroying what they have taken. But you see, Tayo, we have done as much fighting as we can
with the destroyers and thieves; as much as we could do and still survive."
Tayo walked over and knelt in front of the ribs roasting over the white coals of the fire.
"Look," Betonie said, pointing east to Mount Taylor towering dark blue with the last twilight. "They only fool themselves when they think it is theirs. The deeds[2] and papers don't
mean anything. It is the people who belong to the mountain."

---

1. showed off proudly and defiantly
2. documents that transfer ownership of property

Maxine Hong Kingston   From *The Woman Warrior*

"Tis not likely that any man of a plentiful estate should voluntarily abandon a happy certainty to roam after imaginary advantages in a new world."
Robert Beverley, *History and Present State of Virginia,* 1705

"Foreign immigration, which in the past has added so much to the wealth, the development of resources, and the increase of the power to the nation—the asylum of the oppressed of all nations—should be fostered and encouraged by a liberal and just policy."
Republican National Platform, 1864

"We favor the continuance and strict enforcement of the Chinese exclusion law, and its application to the same classes of all Asiatic races."
Democratic National Platform, 1900

"Immigrant: an unenlightened person who thinks one country better than another."
Ambrose Bierce, *The Devil's Dictionary,* 1906

Maxine Hong Kingston was born in 1940 in California, where she still lives, and was educated at the University of California at Berkeley. She is the daughter of Chinese immigrants who spoke little English. Her parents, who were from the Pearl River area of China, passed on the beliefs of their native culture to their six children through storytelling. Kingston's novel and memoirs give readers a clear understanding of what it was like to be a first-generation American, torn between the ancient traditions of her native land and the modern way of life of the United States.

The Woman Warrior, which is subtitled *Memoirs of a Girlhood among Ghosts,* is a powerfully realistic portrait of Kingston's struggle to adjust to the American lifestyle while surrounded by the memories of her ancestors and the ghosts of China's past. At the same time, her account of how it felt to be a Chinese American growing up in a middle-class family in California is also somewhat humorous. Kingston imagined herself as a woman warrior, an ancient Chinese swordswoman in her mother's stories, in her battle for a chance to have a better life than her parents had had in China. As she writes in *The Woman Warrior:* "I learned to make my mind large, as the universe is large, so that there is room for paradoxes."

The Woman Warrior won the National Book Critics Circle Award for the best work of nonfiction in 1976. Other works by Kingston are *China Men* and her novel, *Tripmaster Monkey.* In this excerpt from *The Woman Warrior,* "At the Western Palace," Kingston describes how her mother, Brave Orchid, goes to the San Francisco airport to meet her sister, Moon Orchid, whom she has not seen in thirty years.

Preview

Skimming: Skim the reading to gain a general impression.
1. Read the title and first sentence of the reading.
2. Skim the reading to get an idea of its form and length.

Canton, China

Questioning: Answer the following questions and discuss your answers in class.
1. Do you know people who have immigrated to the United States?
2. Have they become Americanized or retained their traditions and culture?

Scanning: Scan to answer the following questions to get an idea of the content and style.
1. Who was helping Brave Orchid wait for Moon Orchid?
2. What did Moon Orchid look like to Brave Orchid when she arrived at the airport?

From *The Woman Warrior*   1975
Maxine Hong Kingston
                              At the Western Palace

When she was about sixty-eight years old, Brave Orchid took a day off to wait at San Francisco International Airport for the plane that was bringing her sister to the United States. She had not seen Moon Orchid for thirty years. She had begun this waiting at home, getting up a half-hour before Moon Orchid's plane took off in Hong Kong. Brave Orchid would add her will power to the forces that keep an airplane up. Her head hurt with the concentration. The plane had to be light, so no matter how tired she felt, she dared not rest her spirit on a wing but continuously and gently pushed up on the plane's belly. She had already been waiting at the airport for nine hours. She was wakeful.

Next to Brave Orchid sat Moon Orchid's only daughter, who was helping her aunt wait. Brave Orchid had made two of her own children come too because they could drive, but they had been lured away by the magazine racks and the gift shops and coffee shops. Her American children could not sit for very long. They did not understand sitting; they had wandering feet. She hoped they would get back from the pay t.v.'s or the pay toilets or wherever they were spending their money before the plane arrived. If they did not come back soon, she would go look for them. If her son thought he could hide in the men's room, he was wrong.

"Are you all right, Aunt?" asked her niece.

"No, this chair hurts me. Help me pull some chairs together so I can put my feet up."

She unbundled a blanket and spread it out to make a bed for herself. On the floor she had two shopping bags full of canned peaches, real peaches, beans wrapped in taro leaves, cookies, Thermos bottles, enough food for everybody, though only her niece would eat with her. Her bad boy and bad girl were probably sneaking hamburgers, wasting their money. She would scold them.

Many soldiers and sailors sat about, oddly calm, like little boys in cowboy uniforms. (She thought "cowboy" was what you would call a Boy Scout.) They should have been crying hysterically on their way to Vietnam. "If I see one that looks Chinese," she thought, "I'll go over and give him some advice." She sat up suddenly; she had forgotten about her own son, who was even now in Vietnam. Carefully she split her attention, beaming half of it to the ocean, into the water to keep him afloat. He was on a ship. He was in Vietnamese waters. She was sure of it. He and the other children were lying to her. They had said he was in Japan, and then they said he was in the Philippines. But when she sent him her help, she could feel that he was on a ship in Da Nang. Also she had seen the children hide the envelopes that his letters came in.

"Do you think my son is in Vietnam?" she asked her niece, who was dutifully eating.

"No. Didn't your children say he was in the Philippines?"

"Have you ever seen any of his letters with Philippine stamps on them?"

"Oh, yes. Your children showed me one."

"I wouldn't put it past them to send the letters to some Filipino they know. He puts Manila postmarks on them to fool me."

"Yes, I can imagine them doing that. But don't worry. Your son can take care of himself. All your children can take care of themselves."

"Not him. He's not like other people. Not normal at all. He sticks erasers in his ears, and the erasers are still attached to the pencil stubs. The captain will say, 'Abandon ship,' or, 'Watch out for bombs,' and he won't hear. He doesn't listen to orders. I told him to flee to Canada, but he wouldn't go."

She closed her eyes. After a short while, plane and ship under control, she looked again at the children in uniforms. Some of the blond ones looked like baby chicks, their crew cuts like the downy yellow on baby chicks. You had to feel sorry for them even though they were Army and Navy Ghosts.

Suddenly her son and daughter came running. "Come, Mother. The plane's landed early. She's here already." They hurried, folding up their mother's encampment. She was glad her children were not useless. They must have known what this trip to San Francisco was about then. "It's a good thing I made you come early," she said.

Brave Orchid pushed to the front of the crowd. She had to be in front. The passengers were separated from the people waiting for them by glass doors and walls. Immigration Ghosts were stamping papers. The travellers crowded along some conveyor belts to have their luggage searched. Brave Orchid did not see her sister anywhere. She stood watching for four hours. Her children left and came back. "Why don't you sit down?" they asked.

"The chairs are too far away," she said.

"Why don't you sit on the floor then?"

No, she would stand, as her sister was probably standing in a line she could not see from here. Her American children had no feelings and no memory.

To while away time, she and her niece talked about the Chinese passengers. These new immigrants had it easy. On Ellis Island the people were thin after forty days at sea and had no fancy luggage.

"That one looks like her," Brave Orchid would say.

"No, that's not her."

Ellis Island had been made out of wood and iron. Here everything was new plastic, a ghost trick to lure immigrants into feeling safe and spilling their secrets. Then the Alien Office could send them right back. Otherwise, why did they lock her out, not letting her help her sister answer questions and spell her name? At Ellis Island when the ghost asked Brave Orchid what year her husband had cut off his pigtail, a Chinese who was crouching on the floor motioned her not to talk. "I don't know," she had said. If it weren't for that Chinese man, she might not be here today, or her husband either. She hoped some Chinese, a janitor or a clerk, would look out for Moon Orchid. Luggage conveyors fooled immigrants into thinking the Gold Mountain was going to be easy.

Brave Orchid felt her heart jump—Moon Orchid. "There she is," she shouted. But her niece saw it was not her mother at all. And it shocked her to discover the woman her aunt was pointing out. This was a young woman, younger than herself, no older than Moon Orchid the day the sisters parted. "Moon Orchid will have changed a little, of course," Brave Orchid was saying. "She will have learned to wear western clothes." The woman wore a navy blue suit with a bunch of dark cherries at the shoulder.

"No, Aunt," said the niece. "That's not my mother."

"Perhaps not. It's been so many years. Yes, it is your mother. It must be. Let her come closer, and we can tell. Do you think she's too far away for me to tell, or is it my eyes getting bad?"

"It's too many years gone by," said the niece.

Brave Orchid turned suddenly—another Moon Orchid, this one a neat little woman with a bun. She was laughing at something the person ahead of her in line said. Moon Orchid was just like that, laughing at nothing. "I would be able to tell the difference if one of them would only come closer," Brave Orchid said with tears, which she did not wipe. Two children met the woman with the cherries, and she shook their hands. The other woman was met by a young man. They looked at each other gladly, then walked away side by side.

Up close neither one of those women looked like Moon Orchid at all. "Don't worry, Aunt," said the niece. "I'll know her."

"I'll know her, too. I knew her before you did."

The niece said nothing, although she had seen her mother only five years ago. Her aunt liked having the last word.

Finally Brave Orchid's children quit wandering and drooped on a railing. Who knew what they were thinking? At last the niece called out, "I see her! I see her! Mother! Mother!" Whenever the doors parted, she shouted, probably embarrassing the American cousins, but she didn't care. She called out, "Mama! Mama!" until the crack in the sliding doors became too small to let in her voice. "Mama!" What a strange word in an adult voice. Many people turned to see what adult was calling, "Mama!" like a child. Brave Orchid saw an old, old woman jerk her head up, her little eyes blinking confusedly, a woman whose nerves leapt toward the sound anytime she heard "Mama!" Then she relaxed to her own business again. She was a tiny, tiny lady, very thin, with little fluttering hands, and her hair was in a gray knot. She was dressed in a gray wool suit; she wore pearls around her neck and in her earlobes. Moon Orchid *would* travel with her jewels showing. Brave Orchid momentarily saw, like a larger, younger outline around this old woman, the sister she had been waiting for. The familiar dim halo faded, leaving the woman so old, so gray. So old. Brave Orchid pressed against the glass. *That* old lady? Yes, that old lady facing the ghost who stamped her papers without questioning her was her sister. Then, without noticing her family, Moon Orchid walked smiling over to the Suitcase Inspector Ghost, who took her boxes apart, pulling out puffs of tissue. From where she was,

Brave Orchid could not see what her sister had chosen to carry across the ocean. She wished her sister would look her way. Brave Orchid thought that if *she* were entering a new country, she would be at the windows. Instead Moon Orchid hovered over the unwrapping, surprised at each reappearance as if she were opening presents after a birthday party.

"Mama!" Moon Orchid's daughter kept calling. Brave Orchid said to her children, "Why don't you call your aunt too? Maybe she'll hear us if all of you call out together." But her children slunk away. Maybe that shame-face they so often wore was American politeness.

"Mama!" Moon Orchid's daughter called again, and this time her mother looked right at her. She left her bundles in a heap and came running. "Hey!" the Customs Ghost yelled at her. She went back to clear up her mess, talking inaudibly to her daughter all the while. Her daughter pointed toward Brave Orchid. And at last Moon Orchid looked at her—two old women with faces like mirrors.

Their hands reached out as if to touch the other's face, then returned to their own, the fingers checking the grooves in the forehead and along the sides of the mouth. Moon Orchid, who never understood the gravity of things, started smiling and laughing, pointing at Brave Orchid. Finally Moon Orchid gathered up her stuff, strings hanging and papers loose, and met her sister at the door, where they shook hands, oblivious to blocking the way.

"You're an old woman," said Brave Orchid.

"Aiaa. *You're* an old woman."

"But you are really old. Surely, you can't say that about me. I'm not old the way you're old."

"But *you* really are old. You're one year older than I am."

"Your hair is white and your face all wrinkled."

"You're so skinny."

"You're so fat."

"Fat women are more beautiful than skinny women."

The children pulled them out of the doorway. One of Brave Orchid's children brought the car from the parking lot, and the other heaved the luggage into the trunk. They put the two old ladies and the niece in the back seat. All the way home—across the Bay Bridge, over the Diablo hills, across the San Joaquin River to the valley, the valley moon so white at dusk—all the way home, the two sisters exclaimed every time they turned to look at each other, "Aiaa! How old!"

Brave Orchid forgot that she got sick in cars, that all vehicles but palanquins made her dizzy. "You're so old," she kept saying. "How did you get so old?"

Brave Orchid had tears in her eyes. But Moon Orchid said, "You look older than I. You *are* older than I," and again she'd laugh. "You're wearing an old mask to tease me." It surprised Brave Orchid that after thirty years she could still get annoyed at her sister's silliness.

Brave Orchid's husband was waiting under the tangerine tree. Moon Orchid recognized him as the brother-in-law in photographs, not as the young man who left on a ship. Her sister had married the ideal in masculine beauty, the thin scholar with the hollow cheeks and the long fingers. And here he was, an old man, opening the gate he had built with his own hands, his hair blowing silver in twilight. "Hello," he said like an Englishman in Hong Kong. "Hello," she said like an English telephone operator. He went to help his children unload the car, gripping the suitcase handles in his bony fingers, his bony wrists locked.

Brave Orchid's husband and children brought everything into the dining room, provisions for a lifetime move heaped all over the floor and furniture. Brave Orchid wanted to have a luck ceremony and then to put things away where they belonged, but Moon Orchid said, "I've got presents for everybody. Let me get them." She opened her boxes again. Her suitcase lids gaped like mouths; Brave Orchid had better hurry with the luck.

Glossary   From *The Woman Warrior*

beaming	sending out beams of thoughts
belly	the deep interior of an airplane
blinking	winking eyes rapidly; closing and opening eyes quickly
bun	hair worn in a roll or knot
bundles	a number of things tied or wrapped together for carrying
chicks	young chickens
conveyor belts	mechanical devices like belts for moving things
drooped	hung or bent down
earlobes	fleshy lower outer part of ear
Ellis Island	small island in upper New York Bay: former examination center for immigrants to the United States (1892–1943)
encampment	a camp or campsite
erasers	devices made of rubber for erasing pencil marks
fluttering	moving restlessly; trembling
gaped	stared with mouth open in surprise or wonder
ghosts	spirits or souls of dead persons appearing as beings
Gold Mountain	a term used by Chinese immigrants for the United States
gravity	great seriousness
gripping	holding firmly with the hands
grooves	narrow wrinkles on surface of skin
heap	a pile of things jumbled together
heaped	piled together
heaved	lifted with an effort
hollow	sunken
hysterically	wildly; uncontrolled emotionally
inaudibly	not heard; without any sound
lured	attracted, tempted
mask	covering for the face that hides the identity
oblivious	forgetful or unmindful
palanquins	covered litters used in South Asia for transportation, carried by poles on the shoulders of two or more persons
pigtail	long braid of hair hanging at back of head
provisions	stock of supplies for future needs
puffs	small pieces of material
railing	fence made of rails
slunk	moved in a quiet sneaking manner, from guilt
sneaking	moving quickly to avoid being seen or heard
spilling	revealing
stamping	imprinting
taro leaves	Asiatic plant leaves that are eaten
unbundled	unfolded
will power	strength of will, mind, or determination
wing	the main lateral section of an airplane
wrinkled	having creases in the skin caused by aging

Discussion

1. What difficulties do immigrants face in a new country?
2. How hard is it to adapt to another culture? Can you maintain your own cultural traditions and beliefs when you live in a new country?
3. Is Brave Orchid a believable character? Do you know anyone like her?
4. In what ways is Kingston's picture of Brave Orchid humorous?
5. Why do you think Kingston wrote these memoirs?
6. Do you believe in ghosts? Is a belief in ghosts a part of your culture?

Style and Language

1. Describe Kingston's style and tone in the following paragraph about Brave Orchid.

    She unbundled a blanket and spread it out to make a bed for herself. On the floor she had two shopping bags full of canned peaches, real peaches, beans wrapped in taro leaves, cookies, Thermos bottles, enough food for everybody, though only her niece would eat with her. Her bad boy and bad girl were probably sneaking hamburgers, wasting their money. She would scold them.

2. "At the Western Palace" from *The Woman Warrior* is told from the point of view of
    a. Brave Orchid (the first-person narrator).
    b. the third-person narrator (omniscient author).
    c. the third-person narrator (limited point of view).
    d. Moon Orchid (the first-person narrator).
    Explain your answer, and give quotations from the text to support your choice.

3. How does Kingston convey the personalities of Brave Orchid, Moon Orchid, and Brave Orchid's children? Underline the words and phrases that reveal their beliefs and feelings.

4. Explain the meaning of the simile in the following sentence: "And at last Moon Orchid looked at her—two old women with faces like mirrors."

Writing Assignments

1. Kingston describes some of the traditonal beliefs of the Chinese through her character Brave Orchid and contrasts them with Brave Orchid's Americanized children. Make a list of Brave Orchid's traits and a list of her children's traits, and then write an essay explaining the differences between them. Use quotations from the text to support your thesis and major points.

2. Brave Orchid uses her will power to help keep her sister's airplane in the air and her son's ship afloat in the ocean. Write an essay in which you discuss the power of traditional beliefs in the modern world. Do you share any of these beliefs?

3. Have you ever been reunited with someone whom you had not seen in a long time? What were your dominant emotions? Discuss this experience in an essay.

Group Work

In "A Song for a Barbarian Reed Pipe" from *The Woman Warrior,* Kingston writes:

> Be careful what you say. It comes true. It comes true. I had to leave home in order to see the world logically, logic the new way of seeing. I learned to think that mysteries are for explanation. I enjoy simplicity. Concrete pours out of my mouth to cover the forests with freeways and sidewalks. Give me plastics, periodical tables, t.v. dinners with vegetables no more complex than peas mixed with diced carrots. Shine floodlights into dark corners: no ghosts.

In this passage, Kingston mixes simple English statements with metaphorical expressions to explain how she changed after she left home. Working with a partner or in a small group, discuss the meaning of Kingston's words in this excerpt. Then write a paragraph explaining the inferences you can draw about the Chinese ways of seeing the world that Kingston was taught in her home by her immigrant parents.

Sandra Cisneros   **From *The House on Mango Street***

"Happy is the house that shelters a friend."
Ralph Waldo Emerson, "Friendship," *Essays,* 1841

"A comfortable house is a great source of happiness. It ranks immediately after health and a good conscience."
Sydney Smith, To Lord Murray, September 29, 1843

"I have three chairs in my house: one for solitude, two for friendship, three for society."
Henry David Thoreau, *Walden,* 1854

"A house can have integrity, just like a person."
Ayn Rand, *The Fountainhead,* 1943

"Home is where the heart is."
American saying

Sandra Cisneros, the daughter of a Mexican father and a Mexican-American mother, was born in Chicago in 1954. She is a well-known contemporary writer who has won many awards for her poetry and prose. Her short stories and novels portray the world of poverty she grew up in as one of seven children living in a working-class neighborhood in Chicago.

Cisneros's style is characterized by both stark simplicity and poetic imagery. According to the poet Gwendolyn Brooks, "Sandra Cisneros is one of the most brilliant of today's young writers. Her work is sensitive, alert, nuanceful . . . rich with music and picture."

The House on Mango Street is a series of vignettes (pictures in words) told from the point of view of Esperanza Cordero, the narrator, who is looking back at her childhood. Together, these vignettes form a short novel about the complex life of a young Latino girl. In addition to *The House on Mango Street,* Cisneros has written *Woman Hollering Creek and Other Stories, My Wicked Wicked Ways,* and *Loose Woman.*

Preview

Skimming: Skim the reading to gain a general impression.
1. Read the title and first line of each chapter.
2. Skim the chapters to get an idea of their form and length.

Questioning: Answer the following questions and discuss your answers in class.
1. Did you and your family move a lot when you were growing up?
2. Do you remember the house(s) you lived in as a child?

Scanning: Scan to answer the following questions to get an idea of the content and style.
1. "The House on Mango Street": What does the author remember most?
2. "A Smart Cookie": What does Esperanza's mother know how to do?

From *The House on Mango Street*   **1984**
Sandra Cisneros

The House on Mango Street

We didn't always live on Mango Street. Before that we lived on Loomis on the third floor, and before that we lived on Keeler. Before Keeler it was Paulina, and before that I can't remember. But what I remember most is moving a lot. Each time it seemed there'd be one more of us. By the time we got to Mango Street we were six—Mama, Papa, Carlos, Kiki, my sister Nenny and me.

The house on Mango Street is ours, and we don't have to pay rent to anybody, or share the yard with the people downstairs, or be careful not to make too much noise, and there isn't a landlord banging on the ceiling with a broom. But even so, it's not the house we'd thought we'd get.

We had to leave the flat on Loomis quick. The water pipes broke and the landlord wouldn't fix them because the house was too old. We had to leave fast. We were using the washroom next door and carrying water over in empty milk gallons. That's why Mama and Papa looked for a house, and that's why we moved into the house on Mango Street, far away, on the other side of town.

They always told us that one day we would move into a house, a real house that would be ours for always so we wouldn't have to move each year. And our house would have running water and pipes that worked. And inside it would have real stairs, not hallway stairs, but stairs inside like the houses on T.V. And we'd have a basement and at least three washrooms so when we took a bath we wouldn't have to tell everybody. Our house would be white with trees around it, a great big yard and grass growing without a fence. This was the house Papa talked about when he held a lottery ticket and this was the house Mama dreamed up in the stories she told us before we went to bed.

But the house on Mango Street is not the way they told it at all. It's small and red with tight steps in front and windows so small you'd think they were holding their breath. Bricks are crumbling in places, and the front door is so swollen you have to push hard to get in. There is no front yard, only four little elms the city planted by the curb. Out back is a small garage for the car we don't own yet and a small yard that looks smaller between the two buildings on either side. There are stairs in our house, but they're ordinary hallway stairs, and the house has only one washroom. Everybody has to share a bedroom—Mama and Papa, Carlos and Kiki, me and Nenny.

Once when we were living on Loomis, a nun from my school passed by and saw me playing out front. The laundromat downstairs had been boarded up because it had been robbed two days before and the owner had painted on the wood YES WE'RE OPEN so as not to lose business.

Where do you live? she asked.

There, I said pointing up to the third floor.

You live *there?*

There. I had to look to where she pointed—the third floor, the paint peeling, wooden bars Papa had nailed on the windows so we wouldn't fall out. You live *there?* The way she said it made me feel like nothing. *There.* I lived *there.* I nodded.

I knew then I had to have a house. A real house. One I could point to. But this isn't it. The house on Mango Street isn't it. For the time being, Mama says. Temporary, says Papa. But I know how those things go.

My Name

In English my name means hope. In Spanish it means too many letters. It means sadness, it means waiting. It is like the number nine. A muddy color. It is the Mexican records my father plays on Sunday mornings when he is shaving, songs like sobbing.

It was my great-grandmother's name and now it is mine. She was a horse woman too, born like me in the Chinese year of the horse—which is supposed to be bad luck if you're born female—but I think this is a Chinese lie because the Chinese, like the Mexicans, don't like their women strong.

My great-grandmother. I would've liked to have known her, a wild horse of a woman, so wild she wouldn't marry. Until my great-grandfather threw a sack over her head and carried her off. Just like that, as if she were a fancy chandelier. That's the way he did it.

And the story goes she never forgave him. She looked out the window her whole life, the way so many women sit their sadness on an elbow. I wonder if she made the best with what she got or was she sorry because she couldn't be all the things she wanted to be. Esperanza. I have inherited her name, but I don't want to inherit her place by the window.

At school they say my name funny as if the syllables were made out of tin and hurt the roof of your mouth. But in Spanish my name is made out of a softer something, like silver, not quite as thick as sister's name—Magdalena—which is uglier than mine. Magdalena who at least can come home and become Nenny. But I am always Esperanza.

I would like to baptize myself under a new name, a name more like the real me, the one nobody sees. Esperanza as Lisandra or Maritza or Zeze the X. Yes. Something like Zeze the X will do.

Bums in the Attic

I want a house on a hill like the ones with the gardens where Papa works. We go on Sundays, Papa's day off. I used to go. I don't anymore. You don't like to go out with us, Papa says. Getting too old? Getting too stuck-up, says Nenny. I don't tell them I am ashamed—all of us staring out the window like the hungry. I am tired of looking at what we can't have. When we win the lottery . . . Mama begins, and then I stop listening.

People who live on hills sleep so close to the stars they forget those of us who live too much on earth. They don't look down at all except to be content to live on hills. They have nothing to do with last week's garbage or fear of rats. Night comes. Nothing wakes them but the wind.

One day I'll own my own house, but I won't forget who I am or where I came from. Passing bums will ask, Can I come in? I'll offer them the attic, ask them to stay, because I know how it is to be without a house.

Some days after dinner, guests and I will sit in front of a fire. Floorboards will squeak upstairs. The attic grumble.

Rats? they'll ask.

Bums, I'll say, and I'll be happy.

Beautiful & Cruel

I am an ugly daughter. I am the one nobody comes for.

Nenny says she won't wait her whole life for a husband to come and get her, that Minerva's sister left her mother's house by having a baby, but she doesn't want to go that way either. She wants things all her own, to pick and choose. Nenny has pretty eyes and it's easy to talk that way if you are pretty.

My mother says when I get older my dusty hair will settle and my blouse will learn to stay clean, but I have decided not to grow up tame like the others who lay their necks on the threshold waiting for the ball and chain.

In the movies there is always one with red red lips who is beautiful and cruel. She is the one who drives the men crazy and laughs them all away. Her power is her own. She will not give it away.

I have begun my own quiet war. Simple. Sure. I am one who leaves the table like a man, without putting back the chair or picking up the plate.

A Smart Cookie

I could've been somebody, you know? my mother says and sighs. She has lived in this city her whole life. She can speak two languages. She can sing an opera. She knows how to fix a T.V. But she doesn't know which subway train to take to get downtown. I hold her hand very tight while we wait for the right train to arrive.

She used to draw when she had time. Now she draws with a needle and thread, little knotted rosebuds, tulips made of silk thread. Someday she would like to go to the ballet. Someday she would like to see a play. She borrows opera records from the public library and sings with velvety lungs powerful as morning glories.

Today while cooking oatmeal she is Madame Butterfly until she sighs and points the wooden spoon at me. I could've been somebody, you know? Esperanza, you go to school. Study hard. That Madame Butterfly was a fool. She stirs the oatmeal. Look at my *comadres*. She means Izaura whose husband left and Yolanda whose husband is dead. Got to take care all your own, she says shaking her head.

Then out of nowhere:

Shame is a bad thing, you know. It keeps you down. You want to know why I quit school? Because I didn't have nice clothes. No clothes, but I had brains.

Yup, she says disgusted, stirring again. I was a smart cookie then.

A House of My Own

Not a flat. Not an apartment in back. Not a man's house. Not a daddy's. A house all my own. With my porch and my pillow, my pretty purple petunias. My books and my stories. My two shoes waiting beside the bed. Nobody to shake a stick at. Nobody's garbage to pick up after.

Only a house quiet as snow, a space for myself to go, clean as paper before the poem.

Mango Says Goodbye Sometimes

I like to tell stories. I tell them inside my head. I tell them after the mailman says, Here's your mail. Here's your mail he said.

I make a story for my life, for each step my brown shoe takes. I say, "And so she trudged up the wooden stairs, her sad brown shoes taking her to the house she never liked."

I like to tell stories. I am going to tell you a story about a girl who didn't want to belong.

We didn't always live on Mango Street. Before that we lived on Loomis on the third floor, and before that we lived on Keeler. Before Keeler it was Paulina, but what I remember most is Mango Street, sad red house, the house I belong but do not belong to.

I put it down on paper and then the ghost does not ache so much. I write it down and Mango says goodbye sometimes. She does not hold me with both arms. She sets me free.

One day I will pack my bags of books and paper. One day I will say goodbye to Mango. I am too strong for her to keep me here forever. One day I will go away.

Friends and neighbors will say, What happened to that Esperanza? Where did she go with all those books and paper? Why did she march so far away?

They will not know I have gone away to come back. For the ones I left behind. For the ones who cannot out.

Glossary	From *The House on Mango Street*
baptize	to purify and name according to Christian sacrament
bums	persons with no settled residence or means of support
comadres	friends (Spanish)
lottery	a drawing in which money is distributed to the winners
Madame Butterfly	the main character in the opera *Madame Butterfly* by Giacomo Puccini
nun	a woman belonging to a religious order
smart cookie	a clever person (slang)
stuck-up	self-important, conceited
trudged	walked steadily and laboriously

Discussion

1. Would you like to write a short story about your childhood experiences?
2. Describe the kind of house in which you and your family live currently.
3. What feelings did the narrator experience when the nun from her school saw her house?
4. How does the narrator feel about her name? Explain your answer.
5. What is the theme of all these vignettes (pictures in words)?

Style and Language

1. The style of *The House on Mango Street* is simple, realistic, personal, and direct. Find examples of this writing style and read them aloud to the class.

2. The tone of *The House on Mango Street* is a mixture of sadness and happiness. In addition, Cisneros uses humor to create her picture of Esperanza's world. Identify the phrases that are humorous in tone.

3. The language in *The House on Mango Street* contains
   a. similes and metaphors.
   b. personifications.
   c. philosophical ideas.
   d. personal revelations.
   Give examples from the stories of this language.

4. In "My Name," Cisneros writes with figurative language. Identify the figures of speech and explain their meaning.

5. In "Beautiful & Cruel," Cisneros uses a metaphor in the following sentence: " . . . I have decided not to grow up tame like the others who lay their necks on the threshold waiting for the ball and chain." Explain the meaning of this figure of speech. What point is Cisneros making?

Writing Assignments

1. Write an essay about the houses you and your family have lived in since you were a young child. Attach a photograph of your current house or draw a picture of it if you can.

2. Write a vignette (picture in words) of a scene from your childhood, for example, a scene about your home, family, school, friends, or neighborhood. Model your writing style on Cisneros's style, and use first-person narration.

3. Do you like your name? Do you know what it means? Write several paragraphs explaining what your name means, why your parents gave you that name, and how you feel about it.

Group Work

Working with a partner or in a small group, reread "A House of My Own" on page 196. Discuss the style in which Cisneros wrote this vignette. Then write a short description of the kind of house you want to live in some day. Share your description with the members of your group.

Dagoberto Gilb   "Love in L.A."

"Men were born to lie, and women to believe them."
John Gay, *The Beggar's Opera,* 1728

"And after all, what is a lie? 'Tis but / The truth in masquerade."
Lord Byron, *Don Juan,* 1819–24

"Examine for a moment an ordinary mind on an ordinary day."
Virginia Woolf, "Modern Fiction," *The Common Reader,* 1925

"Mr. Gilb writes in a deft, ironic style that is all his own."
Robert Cohen, *The New York Times Book Review,* October 2, 1994

Dagoberto Gilb was born in 1950 and is a Chicano of Anglo and Mexican heritage. He grew up in the Southwest and now lives in Texas and Los Angeles. Gilb is a journeyman carpenter, a teacher, and a writer who has translated his wide variety of experiences into realistic stories about life in the United States in the late twentieth century.

Gilb has won many awards for his fiction, including a nomination for the PEN/Faulkner Award in 1993 for his book of short stories *The Magic of Blood.* His style is powerful and intense, and his content ranges from stories about poor migrant workers searching for work in the Chicano Southwest to descriptions of romantic relationships between men and women in the sunny but superficial world of California. "Love in L.A." is a story about a chance encounter between two young people on a street in Los Angeles.

Preview

Skimming: Skim the reading to gain a general impression.
1. Read the title and first sentence of the story.
2. Skim the story to get an idea of its form and length.

Questioning: Answer the following questions and discuss your answers in class.
1. Have you ever been in an automobile accident?
2. How important is it to tell the truth? What is your opinion of people who tell lies?

Scanning: Scan to answer the following questions to get an idea of the content and style.
1. What kind of car does Jake drive?
2. Where are Mariana's parents from?

Love in L.A.   1993
Dagoberto Gilb

Jake slouched in a clot of near motionless traffic, in the peculiar gray of concrete, smog, and early morning beneath the overpass of the Hollywood Freeway on Alvarado Street. He didn't really mind because he knew how much worse it could be trying to make a left onto the onramp. He certainly didn't do that every day of his life, and he'd assure anyone who'd ask that he never would either. A steady occupation had its advantages and he couldn't deny thinking about that too. He needed an FM radio in something better than this '58 Buick he drove. It would have crushed velvet interior with electric controls for the LA summer, a nice warm heater and defroster for the winter drives at the beach, a cruise control for those longer trips, mellow speakers front and rear of course, windows that hum closed, snuffing out that nasty exterior noise of freeways. The fact was that he'd probably have to change his whole style. Exotic colognes, plush, dark nightclubs, maitais and daiquiris, necklaced ladies in satin gowns, misty and sexy like in a tequila ad. Jake could imagine lots of possibilities when he let himself, but none that ended up with him pressed onto a stalled freeway.

Jake was thinking about this freedom of his so much that when he glimpsed its green light he just went ahead and stared bye bye to the steadily employed. When he turned his head the same direction his windshield faced, it was maybe one second too late. He pounced the brake pedal and steered the front wheels away from the tiny brakelights but the smack was unavoidable. Just one second sooner and it would only have been close. One second more and he'd be crawling up the Toyota's trunk. As it was, it seemed like only a harmless smack, much less solid than the one against his back bumper.

Jake considered driving past the Toyota but was afraid the traffic ahead would make it too difficult. As he pulled up against the curb a few carlengths ahead, it occurred to him that the traffic might have helped him get away too. He slammed the car door twice to make sure it was closed fully and to give himself another second more, then toured front and rear of his Buick for damage on or near the bumpers. Not an impressionable scratch even in the chrome. He perked up. Though the car's beauty was secondary to its ability to start and move, the body and paint were clean except for a few minor dings. This stood out as one of his few clearcut accomplishments over the years.

Before he spoke to the driver of the Toyota, whose looks he could see might present him with an added complication, he signaled to the driver of the car that hit him, still in his car and stopped behind the Toyota, and waved his hands and shook his head to let the man know there was no problem as far as he was concerned. The driver waved back and started his engine.

"It didn't even scratch my paint," Jake told her in that way of his. "So how you doin? Any damage to the car? I'm kinda hoping so, just so it takes a little more time and we can talk some. Or else you can give me your phone number now and I won't have to lay my regular b.s. on you to get it later."

He took her smile as a good sign and relaxed. He inhaled her scent like it was clean air and straighted out his less than new but not unhip clothes.

"You've got Florida plates. You look like you must be Cuban."

"My parents are from Venezuela."

"My name's Jake." He held out his hand.

"Mariana."

They shook hands like she'd never done it before in her life.

"I really am sorry about hitting you like that." He sounded genuine. He fondled the wide dimple near the cracked taillight. "It's amazing how easy it is to put a dent in these new cars. They're so soft they might replace waterbeds soon." Jake was confused about how to proceed with this. So much seemed so unlikely, but there was always possibility. "So maybe we should go out to breakfast somewhere and talk it over."

"I don't eat breakfast."

"Some coffee then."

"Thanks, but I really can't."

"You're not married, are you? Not that that would matter that much to me. I'm an openminded kinda guy."

She was smiling. "I have to get to work."

"That sounds boring."

"I better get your driver's license," she said.

Jake nodded, disappointed. "One little problem," he said. "I didn't bring it. I just forgot it this morning. I'm a musician," he exaggerated greatly, "and, well, I dunno, I left my wallet in the pants I was wearing last night. If you have some paper and a pen I'll give you my address and all that."

He followed her to the glove compartment side of her car.

"What if we don't report it to the insurance companies? I'll just get it fixed for you."

"I don't think my dad would let me do that."

"Your dad? It's not your car?"

"He bought it for me. And I live at home."

"Right." She was slipping away from him. He went back around to the back of her new Toyota and looked over the damage again. There was the trunk lid, the bumper, a rear panel, a taillight.

"You do have insurance?" she asked, suspicious, as she came around the back of the car.

"Oh yeah," he lied.

"I guess you better write the name of that down too."

He made up a last name and address and wrote down the name of an insurance company an old girlfriend once belonged to. He considered giving a real phone number but went against that idea and made one up.

"I act too," he lied to enhance the effect more. "Been in a couple of movies."

She smiled like a fan.

"So how about your phone number?" He was rebounding maturely.

She gave it to him.

"Mariana, you are beautiful," he said in his most sincere voice.

"Call me," she said timidly.

Jake beamed. "We'll see you, Mariana," he said holding out his hand. Her hand felt so warm and soft he felt like he'd been kissed.

Back in his car he took a moment or two to feel both proud and sad about his performance. Then he watched the rear view mirror as Mariana pulled up behind him. She was writing down the license plate numbers on his Buick, ones that he'd taken off a junk because the ones that belonged to his had expired so long ago. He turned the ignition key and revved the big engine and clicked into drive. His sense of freedom swelled as he drove into the now moving street traffic, though he couldn't stop the thought about that FM stereo radio and crushed velvet interior and the new car smell that would even make it better.

Glossary	"Love in L.A."
b.s.	nonsense; foolish, insincere, boastful talk (slang)
clot	thick, jumbled mass
daquiris	cocktails made with rum and fruit juices
dimple	small hollow on the surface
dings	small dents in the car
dunno	don't know
enhance	to make greater, to intensify
expired	ended, ceased
fan	a person enthusiastic about someone
fondled	stroked in a tender and loving way, caressed
hum	to make a low, murmuring sound
inhaled	breathed in
junk	useless, worthless car
kinda	kind of
maitais	cocktails made with rum and fruit juices
mellow	full, rich, soft
perked up	became lively, recovered his spirits
pounced	leaped on
rebounding	springing back in recovery
revved	accelerated
slouched	sat with head and shoulders drooping forward
smack	a sharp blow
smog	low-lying layer of polluted air
snuffing	putting an end to
stalled	brought to a stop

swelled	increased, expanded
tequila	strong alcoholic liquor of Mexico
unhip	not fashionable or stylish
waterbeds	heavy bags filled with water and used as beds
yeah	yes

Discussion

1. Explain the plot of "Love in L.A." What is the theme of the story?
2. Do you think this story is humorous or sad?
3. What would you have done if you were in Jake's position? In Mariana's?
4. Does Jake really want to go out with Mariana? Does Mariana want to go out with Jake?
5. Does Mariana believe what Jake tells her? Does she like him?
6. Do the events in this story justify the title "Love in L.A."? Explain your answer.
7. Which character in the story can you most identify with? Why?

Style and Language

1. Although Gilb's writing style is simple, clear, and realistic, his tone is a complex mixture of irony, humor, and sadness. Give quotations from the story that exemplify this style and tone.

2. Underline the words and phrases (not including the direct dialogue) that Gilb uses to portray his characters' personalities. Make a list of adjectives that would describe Jake and a list of those that would describe Mariana. Which character would you prefer to have as a friend? Why? Which character will be more successful in life?

3. Listen while two members of the class read aloud some of the dialogue from "Love in L.A." How realistic is the conversation between Jake and Mariana? What does the dialogue reveal about the relationship between them?

4. Although Gilb does not use much figurative language, there are four similes in "Love in L.A." Underline the similes, and explain how they enhance the meaning of the story.

5. Reread the concluding paragraph and explain its meaning. How effective is this paragraph in bringing the story to an end? What is your reaction to the conclusion?

6. "Love in L.A." is told from the point of view of
   a. Jake, the first-person narrator.
   b. the third-person narrator (omniscient author).
   c. the third-person narrator (limited to Mariana's perspective).
   d. the third-person narrator (limited to Jake's perspective).
   How does this point of view affect the telling of the story?

Writing Assignments

1. Write an essay in which you analyze Gilb's portrayal of Jake in "Love in L.A." Is he a realistic character? Is he immoral or just clever? What motivates his behavior? What are his dominant emotions? How does his personality differ from Mariana's?

2. In an essay, compare and contrast Hamlin Garland's "A Day's Pleasure" (chapter 1, page 9) and Gilb's "Love in L.A." You may use the following thesis: Although both "A Day's Pleasure" and "Love in L.A." are realistic short stories, they differ greatly in regard to plot, setting, characters, and theme.

3. Imagine that three months have passed since the events in "Love in L.A." Jake can't forget Mariana, so he has decided to call Mariana in order to try to see her. Although Mariana is angry at first, she becomes friendly as they continue to talk. Write the dialogue of their telephone conversation.

Group Work

Working with a partner or in a small group, read the following proverbs and sayings about love, and discuss the meanings. Then write a short sequel (follow-up story) to "Love in L.A." with one of these proverbs as the theme of your story. Use the same setting, point of view and characters that are in "Love in L.A." Include realistic dialogue in your story.

"Follow love, and it will flee thee;
Flee and it will follow thee."
Old English rhyme

"Seek love, and it will shun you;
Haste away, and 'twill outrun you."
Old English rhyme

"Blue eyes say 'Love me or I die';
Black eyes say 'Love me or I kill thee.' "
Spanish proverb

"If love be timid, it is not true."
Spanish proverb

"Love tells us many things that are not so."
Ukrainian proverb

"Love unrequited is like a question without an answer."
Italian proverb

"To love a woman who scorns you is to lick honey from a thorn."
Welsh proverb

"Love 'em and leave 'em."
American saying, 1910

Chapter Synthesis

Write a synthesis on the subject of cultural diversity in the United States in the late twentieth century. Use Momaday's *The Way to Rainy Mountain,* Kingston's *The Woman Warrior,* Cisneros's *The House on Mango Street*, and Gilb's "Love in L.A." Thesis: Although people in the United States may share certain common values and beliefs, the United States is primarily a land of cultural diversity, not unity.

Appendixes

Appendix A

Glossary of Literary Terms

Most of the definitions are based on those in *Webster's New World Dictionary,* second college ed., (New York: Simon and Schuster, 1986).

allegory: A story in which people, things, and events have a hidden or symbolic meaning behind the literal meaning; allegories are often used for teaching moral and religious principles and use personification to give abstract qualities a human shape. For example, in "The Canterbury Pilgrims" by Nathaniel Hawthorne, the characters Josiah and Miriam symbolize idealism, hope, and love.

alliteration: Repetition of an initial sound or stressed syllable, usually a consonant or consonant cluster, in two or more words of a phrase or line of poetry (e.g., *sad song*).

allusion: A reference to a famous person, place, event, or artistic work that many readers are familiar with, such as the Greek epic poet Homer.

ambiguity: A double or multiple meaning; openness to different interpretations, which is a central concept in the interpretation of poetry and may lead to an enrichment of meaning.

American Renaissance: The period before the Civil War when American literature flourished in the works of Emerson, Thoreau, Hawthorne, Melville, and Whitman.

analogy: A form of comparison in which an unfamiliar idea or thing is compared to a familiar one that is similar in some way; similarity in some respects between things otherwise unlike.

antagonist: A character in a story or novel who opposes the protagonist.

autobiography: The story of one's own life, written or dictated by oneself.

ballad: A folk song or poem meant for singing that tells a popular story in short stanzas and simple words, with repetition or refrain; the story is often a tragic tale from legend or history. Ballads began in an oral tradition. "Annabel Lee" by Edgar Allan Poe and "Ballad of the Landlord" by Langston Hughes are examples of modern ballads.

biography: An account of a person's life, written by another, and considered as a branch of literature.

blank verse: Unrhymed verse, usually having five iambic feet per line (iambic pentameter); blank verse became the standard meter for English dramatic and longer narrative poetry.

character: A person in a novel, short story, or play; a character may be either simple and unchanging or complex, undergoing growth and development throughout the literary work, depending on the author's characterization.

closed couplet: Two lines of metrical rhymed verse in which the grammar and meaning come to a conclusion or strong pause at the end of the second line.

comedy: A drama, novel, or narrative having a nontragic or comic theme and tone, humorous treatment of characters and situation, and a happy ending; the purpose of comedy is to amuse the audience. Comedy began as a dramatic form with the Greek playwright Aristophanes in the fifth century B.C. and includes satire, romantic comedy, and comedy of manners.

conflict: The opposition between characters, groups, or individuals and larger forces (nature, society). Conflict may also be internal, within a character. It is the essence of plot.

connotation: What is suggested in addition to the simple, explicit meaning; the psychological or emotional overtones of a word or term.

content: The essential meaning or substance of a work of literature, as distinguished from its form; all that is contained in a literary work.

couplet: Two successive lines of poetry, usually of the same length, that rhyme; couplets were first used in English by Chaucer in *The Canterbury Tales.*

denotation: The exact, explicit, literal meaning of a word or term as stated in the dictionary.

determinism: The doctrine that everything, especially one's choice of action, is determined by a sequence of causes independent of one's free will; writers in the naturalist and realistic movements sometimes were influenced by a belief in determinism, for example, Theodore Dreiser, who wrote the novel *Sister Carrie.*

dialect: The form or variety of a spoken language peculiar to a nation, region, community, social group, or occupational group; dialects differ in pronunciation, grammar, and vocabulary.

dialogue: The passages of talk in a play, novel, short story, or poem; a written work in the form of a conversation.

didactic: Used or intended for teaching or moral instruction. Most ancient literature is didactic, as well as much European literature from the Middle Ages, whose purpose was often to teach religious doctrine. Allegories and satires tend to be didactic.

drama: A literary composition (play) that tells a story, usually of human conflict, using dialogue and action and performed by actors.

dramatic monologue: A type of poem in which an imaginary or historical character reveals his or her thoughts and personality by speaking to someone (e.g., T. S. Eliot's "The Love Song of J. Alfred Prufrock").

elegy: A formal lyric poem of lament and praise for the dead; any poem in a mournful, reflective tone. The elegiac stanza is a quatrain of iambic pentameters with a rhyme scheme of abab. Written after Abraham Lincoln's death, Walt Whitman's "O Captain! My Captain!" is a famous modern elegy.

epic: A long narrative poem in a dignified style about the deeds of a traditional or historical hero, such as Virgil's *Aeneid* and Homer's *Iliad* and *Odyssey*; epics include literary epics (Milton's *Paradise Lost*), folk epics (*Beowulf*), and any long poem having the structure and style of an epic, such as Dante's *Divine Comedy.*

epistolary novel: A novel written in the form of a series of letters from the characters, especially popular in English and French novels of the eighteenth century. A modern example is John Barth's *Letters.*

essay: A short, literary composition in prose, analytical or interpretive in nature and dealing with its subject from a personal point of view or in a limited way. The French author Montaigne wrote the first modern essays in his *Essais* (1580). In 1597, Francis Bacon wrote the first English essays. Ralph Waldo Emerson, the nineteenth-century American Transcendentalist, is a well-known essayist.

fiction: A literary work whose content is produced by the imagination and is not based on fact; the category of literature comprising novels, short stories, and plays.

figurative language: Based on or making use of figures of speech; metaphorical or symbolic.

figure of speech: An expression, such as a metaphor or simile, in which a nonliteral and intensive sense of a word or words is used to create a forceful, dramatic, or illuminating image. Such language is often used in poetry and includes metaphor, simile, personification, hyperbole, image, symbol, and irony.

first-person narrative: A method of storytelling in which the narrator tells the events of the story using the first-person pronoun I. The narrator may be either a major character in the story or a witness to the action, for example, Mark Twain's Huckleberry Finn.

foot (plural: feet): A metrical (rhythmic) unit consisting of stressed or unstressed syllables in traditional poetry; the most common feet in English poetry are iambic and trochaic. The number of feet in a line of poetry determines the description of its length: three feet = trimeter; four feet = tetrameter; five feet = pentameter. Emily Dickinson wrote her poetry in iambic trimeter and tetrameter.

foreshadowing: A literary technique in which an author gives a clue about what will happen later in the story, often for the purpose of building suspense.

form: The design or structure of a work of literature; the style or manner of presenting ideas in a literary composition. Form can refer to a literary genre (short story, novel) and is distinguished from the content of a work.

free verse: Poetry that does not follow a regular meter or stanzaic pattern and has either an irregular rhyme or no rhyme (from the French *vers libre*). Free verse is the most common form of twentieth-century poetry and began in the nineteenth century with Walt Whitman.

genre: A French word used to describe a type or category of literary work, such as poetry, prose, novel, or satire.

Gothic novel: A tale of terror, suspense, and the supernatural, such as Mary Shelley's *Frankenstein* and Daphne du Maurier's *Rebecca*.

heroic couplet: A verse unit consisting of two rhymed lines in iambic pentameter. It was established by Chaucer and was a popular form of English verse during the late seventeenth and eighteenth century.

hyperbole: A figure of speech using extravagant exaggeration for emphasis.

iambic pentameter: A line of poetry consisting of five metric feet, each foot containing a short or unstressed syllable followed by a long or stressed syllable. Perhaps introduced by Chaucer, it is the most common type of metrical verse in English. The lines can be either rhymed or unrhymed (blank verse).

image: A vivid description, representation, or figure of speech that appeals to the senses and emotions or evokes a mental picture by reference to concrete objects or actions.

imagery: The use of vivid descriptions or figures of speech in writing to produce mental pictures; a metaphoric representation in literary works that appeals to the senses and emotions or evokes a mental picture by using concrete objects or actions.

impressionism: A term taken from late-nineteenth-century French painting to describe a writing style that is highly descriptive and personal.

irony: The use of words to convey the opposite of their literal meaning; a difference between what is said and what is meant. Irony is found in many types of literature, particularly in satire.

journal: A personal record of occurrences, reflections, and experiences kept on a regular basis; a diary (e.g., Thoreau's *Journals*).

literal: In accord with the exact or primary meaning of a word or words; avoiding exaggeration or metaphor or any figurative sense.

literature: Imaginative or creative writing in prose or verse, especially of recognized artistic value; writing that has claim to consideration on the ground of beauty of form or emotional effect *(Oxford English Dictionary)*.

lyric: Relating to a category of poetry that has the quality of music in its sound pattern and is generally characterized by subjectivity and sensuality of expression. Lyric poetry is the most popular type of verse and is often written on the subjects of love and sadness. The word is derived from the Greek lyre, a musical instrument used to accompany the ode and elegy.

metaphor: A figure of speech in which a thing, idea, or action is referred to by a word that describes another thing, idea, or action in order to suggest a common quality shared by the two. Metaphors are commonly used in poetry to create emphasis, variety, or new ideas and are implicit comparisons (e.g., "a wild horse of a woman" [Cisneros]).

meter: The measured rhythm characteristic of verse; a specified rhythmic pattern of verse, determined by the number and kinds of metrical units (feet) in a typical line. Dimeter = two feet; trimeter = three; tetrameter = four; pentameter = five; hexameter = six; heptameter = seven. The most common meter is iambic meter, in which an unstressed syllable is followed by a stressed syllable.

modern age: The current period of literary activity, often dated from the end of the nineteenth century (1890).

modernism: A term applied to experimental forms of early twentieth-century literature, such as symbolism, imagism, and surrealism, which rejected nineteenth-century conventions of realism and chronological development in fiction.

monologue: A long speech made by one person; a literary composition in the form of a dramatic soliloquy.

myth: A traditional story from ancient times often dealing with supernatural beings, heroes, or ancestors; a serious story that sets forth ideas of a culture about the structure of the universe and the place of human beings.

mythology: A collection of myths about the origin and history of a people and their gods, ancestors, and heroes.

narration: The act or process of giving an account of something or telling a story such as in a novel or short story (also called *narrative*).

narrative poetry: Poetry characterized by the telling of a story; it includes ballads, epics, and romances. A modern example is Edwin Arlington Robinson's "Richard Cory."

narrator: The person who gives an account of something or tells a story; a novel or short story may have three types of narrators or points of view: first-person narrators are witnesses or participants in the story; third-person narrators are outside the story; an omniscient author is a third-person narrator with knowledge of the characters' thoughts and of all the events in the story.

naturalism: A movement in nineteenth-century literature whose members stressed realistic or factual representation of life and truth to nature. The naturalists saw human beings as victims of their environment and of the irrational forces of nature. Émile Zola was the leader of the naturalist movement in France. Theodore Dreiser's *Sister Carrie* was a famous American novel of naturalism.

Neo-Classic Age: American writing of the eighteenth century. Writers like Benjamin Franklin and Thomas Jefferson focused on science and politics.

nonfiction: Literary works other than fiction; writing based on facts rather than the imagination.

novel: A fictional prose narrative of considerable length, usually having a plot that is developed by the actions, speech, and thoughts of the characters. Cervantes's *Don Quixote de la Mancha* (1605) is considered the first novel. Daniel Defoe's *Robinson Crusoe* (1719) and *Moll Flanders* (1722) are the first English novels. The first well-known American novelist is James Fenimore Cooper (*The Last of the Mohicans* [1826]). In the eighteenth and nineteenth centuries, the novel became a dominant literary form. The novel as a genre has no standard structure, style, or subject, but it is generally characterized by realism in the portrayal of human nature and characters who undergo change and growth.

novella: A short prose fiction tale, longer than a short story and shorter than a novel (from the Italian *novella,* which means new or novelty). The novella was first established in Germany in the late eighteenth century. Henry James wrote many novellas.

ode: A lengthy lyrical poem, usually in rhyme, addressed to a praised person or quality and characterized by a formal poetic style and tone. An example of a modern ode is Allen Tate's "Ode to the Confederate Dead."

onomatopoeia: A figure of speech often found in poetry in which words sound like the sounds they refer to (e.g., *buzz, cuckoo, crash*).

oxymoron: A figure of speech that combines two contradictory terms in a paradox, such as "heavy lightness" (Shakespeare).

paradox: A statement that is contradictory or opposed to common sense and yet is perhaps true. Paradox is often found in poetry, for example, in Walt Whitman's poem "Facing West from California's Shores": "I, a child, very old."

pathetic fallacy: A convention in poetry by which natural phenomena are described as if they were human. It was very popular during the nineteenth-century Romantic movement in England in the poetry of Wordsworth and Shelley.

Petrarchan sonnet: A sonnet form developed by the Italian writer Petrarch (1304–74); it contains an octave (eight lines) in abbaabba rhyme scheme and a sestet (six lines) in cdccdc or cdecde rhyme scheme. The subject, which is usually a description of the pains of love and the beauty of the loved one, is a presentation of the conventions of courtly love. The Petrarchan sonnet is also called the Italian sonnet.

personification: A figure of speech in which a thing, quality, idea, or animal is represented as a person, (e.g., "saddest city lane" [Frost]).

plot: The plan of action of a play, novel, short story, or poem, often showing a process of change and growth in the characters and a conflict that is resolved. Aristotle (fourth century B.C.) first discussed plot in his *Poetics*. He described plot as the major element in a play and said a plot must have a beginning, middle, and end, and should form a coherent whole.

poem: An arrangement of words written or spoken, usually with a rhythmic pattern (meter), sometimes rhymed, expressing experiences, ideas, or emotions in a style more concentrated, imaginative, and powerful than that of ordinary speech or prose.

poetry: Poems, poetical works; the poetic qualities of rhythm (meter), rhyme, concentrated expression, and feelings.

point of view: The viewpoint from which a story is narrated. First-person narration is restricted to one person's point of view (the "I"); third-person narration may be omniscient (knowing all of the thoughts and action) or may be limited to one character's point of view; multiple point of view reveals the story from more than one person's perspective.

prose: The ordinary form of written or spoken language, without rhyme or meter; speech or writing that is not poetry.

protagonist: The central character in a drama, story, or novel, around whom the action centers (hero or heroine).

Puritan Age: American writing of the seventeenth century. The earliest American writers, who came from England and settled in the South and New England, wrote historical prose and religious sermons.

quatrain: A stanza or poem of four lines, usually rhyming abab, abba, or abcb.

refrain: A line, group of lines, or part of a line repeated at certain intervals in a poem, usually at the end of a stanza (e.g., Walt Whitman's "O Captain! My Captain!").

realism: The portrayal in literature of people and things as it is thought they really are, without idealizing or romanticizing them; an attempt to present life as it actually is through detailed and accurate descriptions. Realism began in England with Daniel Defoe's novels in the eighteenth century and became dominant in the nineteenth-century French novel and drama. In American literature, realism began with Mark Twain and Henry James.

regionalism: The use in literature of a particular region of a country as the setting of stories or plays in order to depict its influence on the lives of the characters. Regionalism was a major characteristic of American prose writers in the nineteenth century, such as Mark Twain, Sarah Orne Jewett, and Kate Chopin. It is also known as local-color literature.

rhyme: A piece of verse or poem in which there is a regular repetition of similar sounds, especially at the ends of lines; correspondence of end sounds in lines of verse or in words. Usually the rhyme is in the last stressed vowel in the line and the following sounds (tree/sea) (mother/brother). In eye rhyme, the sounds are different but the spellings are the same (above/move). In half-rhyme (slant rhyme), the vowel sounds are different (give/love). Rhyme can also be found in the line (internal rhyme). Rhyme has characterized American poetry since the seventeenth century, but much modern poetry is unrhymed (free verse and blank verse).

Romantic Age: American writing of the nineteenth century. The writers focused on emotions rather than reason, freedom of the human spirit, and intuition.

Romanticism: A belief in the power of the individual, the beauty of nature, and the correspondence between God and nature, as presented in the writings of the American and English Romantic poets of the nineteenth century; the spirit, attitudes, and style of the Romantic movement.

satire: A literary work (poetry or prose) in which human vices, failings, and stupidities are made fun of and criticized through the use of sarcasm and irony; satire may be direct or indirect, gentle or harsh in tone.

setting: The time, place, environment, and surrounding circumstances of an event, story, or play.

Shakespearean sonnet: A sonnet composed of three quatrains, usually with a rhyme scheme abab cdcd efef, and a final couplet with the rhyme gg; the final couplet acts as a conclusion (or "turn") to the poem. It is also called the English or Elizabethan sonnet.

short story: A kind of story shorter than the novel or novella, usually developing a single central theme and limited in scope and number of characters. The fables, folktales, and tales of earlier ages preceded the short story, which became a major literary form in literature of the nineteenth and twentieth centuries, particularly in the United States.

simile: A figure of speech in which one thing is compared to another dissimilar thing by the use of *like* or *as* (e.g., "songs like sobbing" [Cisneros]); similes are very common in both poetry and prose. They differ from metaphors in being more explicit. An epic simile, used in narrative poems like Homer's *Iliad* and *Odyssey,* is an elaborate description.

sonnet: A poem normally of fourteen lines, often in rhymed iambic pentameter, expressing a single theme or idea; there are two types of sonnets, Italian (Petrarchan) and English (Shakespearean). The Italian is the most common pattern. The sonnet began in Italy in the fourteenth century and was a form of love poetry, but it grew to include the subjects of religion, politics, and philosophy.

stanza: A group of lines of verse forming one of the sections of a poem or song; it is usually made up of four or more lines and typically has a regular pattern in the number of lines and the arrangement of meter and rhyme. The four-line quatrain is the most common form and is used in ballads. Stanzas are separated by spaces when poems are printed.

story: A narrative or tale about a series of events, true or fictional; a literary composition in prose fiction or poetry, shorter than a novel.

stream-of-consciousness: A narrative technique in which the thoughts of the characters of a novel or short story are recorded as a continuous series of occurrences, without logical or chronological order. Laurence Sterne first used this method in *Tristram Shandy* (1758), and Virginia Woolf and James Joyce expanded it in the twentieth century.

structure: The form or pattern of design of a literary work, apart from its content.

style: Specific manner of expression in language, which is typical of an author, literary period, or genre; the way of using words to express thoughts. Style is determined by sentence structure, word choice, imagery, and rhythm of language.

symbol: Something that stands for or suggests something else, especially an object or emblem used to represent an abstract idea; a symbol is a type of image that has further meaning. For example, a rose symbolizes beauty and love; a lion symbolizes bravery.

symbolism: The representation of abstract ideas by use of symbols; it is the name of a literary movement in nineteenth- and early-twentieth-century poetry in which poets used symbols to convey their meaning indirectly. Symbolism is also found in novels such as Melville's *Moby Dick* and Hawthorne's *The Scarlet Letter*.

theme: A recurring unifying subject or idea in a literary work; it may be stated directly but more often is revealed indirectly through the actions and statements of the characters.

third-person narrative: A method of storytelling in which the narrator stands outside the story and refers to the characters as "he," "she," or "they." Third-person narrators may be omniscient (all-knowing) or limited in their knowledge. It is the most widely used point of view in novels.

tone: A manner of writing that shows the intellectual and emotional attitude on the part of the writer toward the audience and the subject. Tone results from word choice, phrasing, and sentence structure. Tone creates the mood or atmosphere in a work of literature, e.g., subjective, objective, serious, humorous, positive, negative, ironic, satirical, balanced, or melancholy.

tragedy: A serious play or novel dealing with the problems of a central character, usually heading to an unhappy ending. Ancient tragedies centered on the power of fate and a tragic flaw in the character (e.g., *Hamlet, Macbeth*). Modern tragedies emphasize psychological and social/family conflicts.

tragicomedy: A play that is a mixture of tragedy and comedy, such as Shakespeare's *The Winter's Tale* and *Troilus and Cressida*.

Transcendentalism: A spiritual and intellectual movement of the mid-nineteenth century that emphasized romantic individualism and independence. It began with Ralph Waldo Emerson's publication of *Nature* in 1836.

verse: A sequence of words arranged metrically in accord with a design; a single line of poetry or a stanza. Verse is often used as a term for poetry in general as distinct from prose and indicates the use of rhythm and meter.

vignette: A brief, descriptive composition in prose such as a sketch, essay, or short story (e.g., the stories in *The House on Mango Street* [Cisneros]).

Appendix B

Writing a Critical Analysis

Literature can be divided into four categories or genres: poetry, narrative, drama, and nonfiction prose. To help in preparing a critical analysis of the reading selections in the text, I have developed two outlines, one for poetry and the other for prose fiction and nonfiction.

Poetry Analysis Outline

I. Form
   A. Structure (sonnet, lyric, ballad, ode, narrative, epic, dramatic monologue)
   B. Rhyme scheme
   C. Rhythm (meter)

II. Content
   A. Theme
   B. Major ideas
   C. Conclusion

III. Style
   A. Language
   B. Tone
   C. Figures of speech

Prose Analysis Outline

I. Form
   A. Genre (narrative, drama, nonfiction prose)
   B. Structure (short story, novella, novel, satire, biography, autobiography, essay)

II. Content
   A. Theme or thesis
   B. Plot or action
   C. Characters
   D. Setting
   E. Point of view

III. Style
   A. Language
   B. Tone
   C. Figures of speech

Example of a Critical Analysis

I. Introduction
    A. Purpose (author, title, date)
    The purpose of this essay is to analyze American Transcendentalist Ralph Waldo Emerson's essay "Self-Reliance," which he wrote in 1841.

    B. Background and main idea
    Emerson was one of the greatest writers and thinkers of his time. He originally became a minister but left his church and began to give lectures throughout the United States and Europe. He lectured for almost forty years on philosophy, religion, and politics. In "Self-Reliance," Emerson stresses the idea that a good society is based on strong individuals who are nonconformists and trust themselves.

II. Summary
    A. Form and content
    "Self-Reliance" is written in the form of a philosophical essay. It is highly personal and loosely structured but contains an introductory section, a discussion of major points, and a conclusion. Emerson's main idea is stated in his well-known quotation: "Whoso would be a man, must be a noncomformist." He supports this idea with the following major points: We must trust and rely on ourselves, rather than envying or imitating others, and remain true to our ideals and beliefs. This self-reliance must be found in all aspects of life: religion, education, art, and ways of living. He tells the reader: "Insist on yourself. Never imitate. . . . Where is the master who could have taught Shakespeare?"

    B. Style
    Emerson writes in a beautiful and simple style. His sentences are not complex or too difficult to understand. His meaning is conveyed clearly and directly in a balanced yet authoritative tone. For instance, this essay contains many statements that have become famous quotations because of their conciseness and clarity: "An institution is the lengthened shadow of one man"; "to be great is to be misunderstood"; "a foolish consistency is the hobgoblin of little minds."

III. Critique
    A. Critical analysis
    "Self-Reliance," although rather long and informal, is an interesting philosophical discussion of the value of being an independent, individualistic person. Emerson writes in a strong and dramatic tone that is enjoyable to read. Some of the vocabulary is unfamiliar, and several of Emerson's philosophical ideas are too abstract to grasp in one reading. But, in general, Emerson's language is understandable because he uses specific examples to support his major points and writes in an energetic, conversational manner. This can be seen when he contrasts the "reading, writing, thinking American" with the "naked New Zealander" to prove that "society never advances . . . the civilized man has built a coach but has lost the use of his feet."

B. Personal response

I found this essay challenging but worthwhile reading. It offers suggestions about how to find contentment and personal satisfaction by living according to your own ideals, even if these ideals do not conform to those of society. This essay made me think about how I am living my life and whether I have become a conformist.

IV. Conclusion

"Self-Reliance" has had an effect on how I want to live my life—with integrity, independence, and the courage to be unique. I will remember this essay and many of Emerson's statements, especially: "Nothing can bring you peace but yourself."

Writing an Essay

An essay is an analytical or interpretative composition that deals with its subject in a limited way. It may be completely objective or contain the writer's opinion. Writing an essay can be done efficiently if the writer takes a systematic approach to the writing process by using the POWER method. The following are the five steps in the POWER method:

1. Plan
2. Outline
3. Write
4. Edit
5. Rewrite

I. Plan
   A. Determine the purpose of the essay, the audience, and the type of information to be included.
   B. Collect and evaluate the information needed.
   C. Develop a tentative thesis (controlling idea).
   D. Choose a method of organization (deductive or inductive).

II. Outline
   A. Write a one-sentence thesis or controlling idea for the essay.
   B. Write an outline of three or four major points, minor points, and supporting data.
   C. Arrange the major points and minor points in logical order.
   D. Write a topic sentence for each major point.

III. Write
   A. Write the introduction to the essay, including the thesis (controlling idea).
   B. Write the body of the essay, following your outline and making each major point a separate paragraph.
   C. Add supporting data (facts, examples, details, quotations) to support the major points.
   D. Write the conclusion to the essay by restating or paraphrasing your thesis and adding concluding data (summary, prediction, or solution).

IV.   Edit
      A. Check for accurate and coherent content.
      B. Check for logical and clear organization.
      C. Be certain that the style is appropriate to the content.
      D. Delete any unnecessary information or add missing information.

V.   Rewrite
      A. Write the essay again with the editorial changes.
      B. Proofread the essay for errors in grammar, punctuation, or spelling.
      C. Check the format for correct title, headings, spacing, and margins.
      D. Make all necessary corrections for the final copy.

Examples of Essays

Chapter 1: Writing Assignment 3, page 4

"On the Eve" and "Acquainted with the Night"

Robert Frost and Denise Levertov are twentieth-century poets who express their emotional reactions to everyday experiences with simplicity and clarity. In "Acquainted with the Night," Frost explains how he often takes long walks at night and therefore has become "acquainted with the night." In "On the Eve" Levertov describes a walk she once took with a friend in the early evening. Although "On the Eve" and "Acquainted with the Night" are both informal and conversational in style, they differ in their form and content.

The styles of "On the Eve" and "Acquainted with the Night" are similar. Each poet uses informal language in a personal and conversational tone. Frost speaks directly to the reader, revealing how accustomed he is to going on long walks in the evening: "I have walked out in rain—and back in rain." Levertov also speaks directly to the reader, remembering a walk she once took with a friend during sunset: "We walked / the short grass / the dry ground of the hill." In addition to writing in conversational English, both poets use personifications to clarify their meaning. Levertov says: "The moon / tuned its whiteness a tone higher." Frost writes about "the saddest city streets" and a clock that "proclaimed the time was neither wrong nor right."

While the styles of these poems are alike, the form of "On the Eve" differs greatly from the form of "Acquainted with the Night." Levertov's eleven-line poem is in free verse, with no regular rhythm or rhyme (although lines 1 and 2 rhyme: "white" and "daylight"). "Acquainted with the Night," on the other hand, is in the form of a sonnet, fourteen lines with iambic pentameter rhythm (five beats in every line). The poem is also in the form of an Italian terza rima, which links each three-line tercet with the following three lines through the rhyme scheme: aba bcb cdc ded aa. Thus, Frost has used a traditional and complicated form, while Levertov has combined her poem's informal style with a simple modern structure.

The content of these poems may seem similar since they are both about walking in the evening, but, in fact, the content is quite different. Frost describes his frequent solitary walks in a city, even in the rain, while Levertov's poem portrays one walk on a grassy hill with a friend. Also, Frost's poem has a restless, melancholy quality that evokes his mental state, but in "On the Eve," the atmosphere of the poem is one of calm and quiet beauty: "The moon was white / in the stillness. Daylight / changed without moving." The last major difference in the content is the general air of mystery in "Acquainted with the Night." We wonder if quarrels or disagreements cause Frost to go out walking late at night: he hears "an interrupted cry / . . . But not to call me back or say good-bye." Nor will he give the reason for his evening walks: "And dropped my eyes, unwilling to explain." Levertov's poem has less mystery. It is a clear description of two friends walking in the evening as the moon rises: "We talked / of change in our lives."

In conclusion, "On the Eve" and "Acquainted with the Night" are similar in certain stylistic aspects but are much different in their form and content. Both Levertov and Frost use a natural and conversational style without difficult words or complex grammatical structures. However, "Acquainted with the Night" is a sonnet, and "On the Eve" is written in free verse. Moreover, Frost's poem presents a man who often walks alone at night, appearing to find comfort in his solitude, while Levertov's poem is a brief picture of two friends enjoying an evening walk in the moonlight.

Chapter 2: Writing Assignment 2, page 41

"The Cask of Amontillado" (Poe)

"The Cask of Amontillado" was written by Edgar Allan Poe in 1846. Poe was a romantic writer who lived a tragic life and died at an early age. Even though he only became famous after his death, Poe is considered the father of the modern short story. "The Cask of Amontillado" is a story of revenge and terror. Montresor, the narrator of the story, tells the reader how he got revenge on his so-called friend Fortunato. The terrifying atmosphere in "The Cask of Amontillado" results from the frightening setting, the suspenseful plot, and the first-person narration by Montresor.

The frightening setting helps to build a terrifying atmosphere in the story. The most important events in the story take place in a crypt inside Montresor's palazzo, which he made sure would be empty when he came home: "There were no attendants at home." During the whole time Montresor and Fortunato are inside the palazzo, Montresor talks about the vaults, bones, and chemicals that are surrounding them: "Nitre?"; "These vaults are extensive."; "the foulness of the air"; "The bones had been thrown down." By using all these elements, Poe creates a setting that indicates that something dreadful is about to happen.

The suspenseful plot makes the atmosphere of the story even more terrifying by keeping the reader in the dark about Montresor's plans for revenge on Fortunato. By doing this, the author increases the tension, and the reader becomes more and more anxious to know what is going to happen. For example: "I laid the second tier, and the third, and the fourth; and then I heard the furious vibrations of the chain." Also, when readers think they know what is going to happen next, Poe surprises them with something else: "I had completed the eighth, the ninth and the eleventh; there remained but a single stone to be fitted and plastered in. I struggled with its weight; I placed it partially in its destined position. But now there came from out the niche a low laugh. . . ."

Lastly, the first-person narration by Montresor intensifies the terrifying atmosphere in "The Cask of Amontillado." Montresor reveals many of his feelings throughout the story, and we can see that his intentions are not good from the start: "I vowed revenge"; "I must not only punish but punish with impunity"; "I hesitated, I trembled." If the narration were in the third-person, the impact of Montresor's evil intentions and abnormal feelings might not be so clear.

These techniques, the frightening setting, the suspenseful plot, and the first-person narration by Montresor, create a terrifying atmosphere and help prepare readers for the ending of the story.

The scene in the vaults and crypt of Montresor's palazzo hints at death, and Montresor's step-by-step narration indicates he is planning some type of punishment for Fortunato. However, most readers are shocked by Poe's horrifying conclusion in which Montresor leaves Fortunato tied in chains to the wall to slowly die. This is what makes Poe's story a true tale of terror.

Eliane Nishiguchi

Appendix D

Writing a Synthesis

A synthesis is an essay that is developed from two or more sources from which the writer selects information to support a thesis. A synthesis may be organized according to various organizational patterns: argument, comparison-contrast, cause-effect, definition, description, example, or process. Writing a synthesis requires that the writer find relationships among the several reading selections being analyzed. The following is a suggested sequence for the process of writing a synthesis:

1. Read
2. Underline
3. Outline
4. Write
5. Edit
6. Rewrite

I. Read
   A. Read the selections carefully.
   B. Think about the authors' themes and main ideas.
   C. Develop a tentative thesis (controlling idea) that can be supported by all the readings.

II. Underline
   A. Read the selections again, underlining the sentences that relate to your thesis.
   B. Underline any other major points or key terms that support your thesis.

III. Outline
   A. Write a one-sentence thesis that is the foundation for the synthesis.
   B. Write an outline of three or four major points, minor points, and supporting data.
   C. Arrange the major points and minor points in logical order.
   D. Write a topic sentence for each major point.

IV. Write
   A. Write an introduction, including sources (authors and titles) and thesis.
   B. Write the body of your synthesis, following your outline and making each major point a separate paragraph.
   C. Use brief quotations or paraphrased passages from the readings to support the thesis.
   D. Write the conclusion to your synthesis by restating or paraphrasing your thesis and summarizing your synthesis.

V. Edit
  A. Check for accurate and coherent content.
  B. Check for logical and clear organization.
  C. Be certain that the style is appropriate to the content.
  D. List your sources (authors and titles) at the end of your synthesis under the heading *References*.

VI. Rewrite
  A. Write the synthesis again with the editorial changes.
  B. Proofread the essay for errors in grammar, punctuation, or spelling.
  C. Check the format for correct title, headings, spacing, and margins.
  D. Make all necessary corrections for the final copy.

Example of a Synthesis

Chapter 3: Chapter Synthesis, page 110

The Theme of Freedom in Nineteenth-Century American Literature

In the nineteenth century, America was showing rapid growth in science, technology, population, and wealth. Many people in the United States had optimistic views on their country until the Civil War, a tragic war partly caused by the conflict over slavery. In the literature of that time, the question of slavery was often discussed, and the desire for freedom was an important issue. Although the search for freedom was a common theme in nineteenth-century American prose, freedom had a different meaning for each author, as we can see in Henry Thoreau's *Walden,* Harriet Jacobs's *Incidents in the Life of a Slave Girl,* Harriet Beecher Stowe's "Sojourner Truth: The Libyan Sibyl," and W. E. B. Du Bois's *The Souls of Black Folk.*

Thoreau wanted to escape from society by living a free and independent life in the woods at Walden Pond. In *Walden,* Thoreau explains how he created a self-sufficient existence. The woods were home for him, but he visited the village for information: "The village appeared to me a great news room." He loved coming home in darkness and described finding the way in the darkest night: "my feet felt the path which my eyes could not see, . . . and I have thought that perhaps my body would find its way home if its master should forsake it." His body was used to living in the natural world. He said that getting lost in the dark woods was a learning experience because he believed that "not till we are completely lost, or turned round . . . do we appreciate the vastness and strangeness of Nature." Thoreau was an idealist who loved the simple life of nature. In fact, he sought and found his freedom in nature.

Incidents in the Life of a Slave Girl is a slave narrative that tells how the author, Harriet Jacobs, escaped from slavery into freedom. Jacobs was a slave who ran away from her master, Mr. Flint, in the middle of the night. She went to the house of the friend who was to conceal her. Because of "the law against harboring fugitives," she needed to go to the free states to be truly free. After hiding in a garret for nearly seven years, she finally succeeded in crossing into the free states. Harriet Jacobs was able to find her freedom in the free states.

"Sojourner Truth: The Libyan Sibyl," by Harriet Beecher Stowe, is about a slave who later became a traveling preacher and worked for women's rights and the abolition of slavery. In "Sojourner Truth," Stowe, the famous author, writes about a visit from Sojourner, who preaches in front of Stowe and her friends. When Stowe's father asks Sojourner if she preaches from the Bible, she answers: "No, honey, can't preach from de bible,—can't read a letter. . . . When I preaches, I has just one text to preach from, an' I always preaches from this one. *My* text is, 'When I found Jesus.' " Then, Sojourner tells how she became religious when she suddenly saw God and felt love in her soul. She cried out loud: "Lord, Lord, I can love *even de white folks!*" Sojourner realized that being against slavery did not mean hatred of whites. Stowe describes Sojourner Truth as a woman who found real freedom in her religion.

In *The Souls of Black Folk,* W. E. B. Du Bois reveals the racial prejudice that blocked freedom for blacks living in a village in Tennessee. For two summers he lived in the village, which he called "the little world," teaching the children in a log hut. Du Bois had already experienced discrimination against black people, which he described as the "Veil." For example, when he went to the commissioner's house with a white teacher, the commissioner offered them dinner. Du Bois writes: "but even then fell the awful shadow of the Veil, for they ate first, then I—alone." The whole village was poor because of "the Veil that hung between us and Opportunity." There was "a common hardship in poverty, poor land, and low wages." Although children were eager to go to school, some parents kept them at home to work on their farms. Du Bois, however, tried to teach the children the importance of learning and to enlighten the parents about how children needed education, as Du Bois believed the way to freedom lay in self-help and education.

All of these authors present the search for freedom, but freedom has a unique meaning in each selection. Henry Thoreau discovered his freedom in nature, Harriet Jacobs in the free states, Sojourner Truth in religion, and W. E. B. Du Bois in education. Thus, searching for freedom was a common theme for many nineteenth-century American writers.

References

Du Bois, W. E. B. *The Souls of Black Folk.*

Jacobs, Harriet. *Incidents in the Life of a Slave Girl.*

Stowe, Harriet Beecher. "Sojourner Truth: The Libyan Sibyl."

Thoreau, Henry. *Walden.*

Yukari Komuro

Appendix E

Outline Worksheet

General topic: _____

General method of organization (deductive or inductive): _____

I. Paragraph 1: Introduction
Controlling idea of the communication (thesis): _____

_____

II. Paragraph 2: Body
A. Major point (aspect of controlling idea): _____

B. Topic sentence: _____

C. Types of supporting data: _____

III. Paragraph 3: Body
A. Major point (aspect of controlling idea): _____

B. Topic sentence: _____

C. Types of supporting data: _____

IV. Paragraph 4: Body
A. Major point (aspect of controlling idea): _____

B. Topic sentence: _____

C. Types of supporting data: _____

V. Paragraph 5: Conclusion
A. Major point (restatement of controlling idea): _____

_____

B. Topic sentence: _____

C. Types of concluding data: _____

Writing a Poem

Although there are many ways in which you can create a poem, sensitivity to and love of language are essential. For those who find it difficult to write poetry or who have never tried to do so, I would like to offer the following three techniques. Try each technique to determine which works best for you, or perhaps you will develop your own method.

Technique 1

1. Close your eyes.
2. Relax and think about the subject you want to write about (for example, an emotion, an experience, a person).
3. Open your eyes and write down any words, phrases, or sentences that came into your mind while your eyes were closed.
4. Keep writing for about fifteen minutes without worrying about being logical or correct.
5. When you have finished, read aloud what you have written, and revise if you want to.

Technique 2

1. Read a poem by an author that you like.
2. Write down several words or phrases from that poem that are meaningful to you.
3. Brainstorm (free associate) by writing down any words, phrases, or sentences that come into your mind after thinking about those words or phrases from the poem.
4. Write for fifteen minutes using your brainstorming ideas as a focus for your poem.
5. When you have finished, read aloud what you have written, and revise if you want to.

Technique 3

1. Think about the subject you want to write about (an emotion, an experience, a person).
2. Begin by speaking out loud to yourself about the subject.
3. Write down what you have said aloud.
4. Continue to speak out loud and write down your spoken words.
5. When you have finished, read aloud what you have written, and revise if you want to.

Index